D0803569

Jean Anouilh

Published by Hill and Wang

Jean Anouilh

(FIVE PLAYS)

VOLUME II

A MERMAID DRAMABOOK

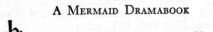 HILL AND WANG – NEW YORK

Manufactured in the United States of America
by the Colonial Press Inc., Clinton, Mass.

11   12   13   14   15   16

CHRONOLOGY OF PLAYS BY JEAN ANOUILH

Taken from *Jean Anouilh* by Edward Owen Marsh. The dates following the titles indicate the year written.

  *Published in DRAMABOOKS, *Jean Anouilh* Volume I
 **Published in DRAMABOOKS, *Jean Anouilh* Volume II
***Published in DRAMABOOKS, *Jean Anouilh* Volume III

CONTENTS

Jean Anouilh

RESTLESS HEART

Translated by

LUCIENNE HILL

Restless Heart by Jean Anouilh, translated by Lucienne Hill.
Copyright © 1959 by Jean Anouilh and Lucienne Hill.

*All applications for permission to perform this play, whether by
amateurs or professionals, must be made to Dr. Jan van Loewen,
Ltd., International Copyright Agency, 81-83 Shaftesbury Avenue,
London, W.1. No performance may take place unless a license
has first been obtained.*

CHARACTERS
(*In order of appearance*)

THÉRÈSE TARDE
MONSIEUR TARDE } Orchestra at
MADAME TARDE } the Café
GOSTA } Lebonze
JEANNETTE
MONSIEUR LEBONZE
WAITER
FLORENT FRANCE
HARTMANN
MADAME BAZIN
MARIE FRANCE
FITTER
HER ASSISTANT
HEAD HOUSEMAID
SCULLERY MAID
CUSTOMERS AT THE CAFÉ LEBONZE

ACT ONE

The interior of a café in a seaside resort. The greater part of the stage is taken up by the bandstand. Service door, left, through which the waiters come and go, with their loaded trays. Two tables, both unoccupied, one of them reserved. The rest of the café is not seen. The orchestra consists of GOSTA, *pianist,* TARDE, *double bass,* MME. TARDE, *cellist,* THÉRÈSE *and* JEANNETTE, *violins. When the curtain goes up, the orchestra is just finishing a very spirited piece. The waiter is by the bandstand, listening. A customer calls him and he dashes forward, dusting a table as he passes.*

WAITER. Yes, sir!

The musicians lay down their instruments. A little half-hearted applause.

Jeannette [glancing at the unoccupied table beside the platform]. He's late today.

Thérèse [laying down her violin]. He said he might be. He's meeting his manager on the ten-thirty train.

Jeannette. Aren't you afraid he might not come again, sometimes?

Thérèse. Some evenings I'm afraid, yes.

Jeannette. I've had men promise to marry me too, you know. Getting to that altar rail though, that's the thing.

Thérèse. I'm so happy as we are, that even if we didn't get as far as that. . . .

Jeannette. Now, now, careful! Don't you ever give him the idea that you're resigned to only being his mistress! And another thing. When you go out with him, watch your manners. In your position a girl can never be too ladylike.

THÉRÈSE *bursts out laughing.*

[*Imperturbably.*] As far as the rest goes, leave it alone. Don't harp on it, it only irritates them. But the trimmings now, you want to talk about *those*—your trousseau, the loose covers. . . .

3

Thérèse [*still laughing*]. Just think how I should bore him if I did!

Jeannette. There's no way round it, my child. Ask any girl who's been through it. Take fat Louisa now. She had a good dodge when she managed to land her gasworks engineer. She used to pat the heads of kids in the street and sigh that she'd do anything to have one of her own. Him with his worship of children, he'd blubber into his mustache. That's the way *she* hooked him. It didn't commit her to anything. After they were married, she refused to have any.

Thérèse [*laughing*]. Jeannette, you're wasting your time. If he wants to marry me, good! If he doesn't. . . .

TARDE *goes round with the music sheets.*

Tarde. Come along, look lively! It's gone midnight. Time for the finale. [*He hangs up a card bearing the figure 12, and writes the title of the number on a slate.*]

Gosta [*looking at the clock and going to* THÉRÈSE]. It's midnight, Thérèse.

Thérèse [*blankly*]. Yes. . . .

Gosta [*giving her something*]. There. Don't let anybody see.

Thérèse. What is it?

Gosta. Open it.

Thérèse [*unwrapping the parcel*]. A bottle of scent? But —why?

Gosta. You're twenty years old tonight, Thérèse. Nobody but me remembered.

Thérèse. My birthday—today? But. . . .

Gosta [*with a smile*]. Tomorrow really, but it's midnight.

Thérèse. Oh, Gosta, it's sweet of you! Gosta. . . . There's something I've been meaning to tell you. . . .

Tarde. Gosta, what have you done with your music? I can't find it anywhere. Hurry. M. Lebonze has just come in. [*He hustles him away.*]

Jeannette. What did he give you?

Thérèse. A bottle of scent. It's sweet of him . . . I haven't dared to tell him yet. I still think I ought to tell him myself. . . .

Jeannette. But your father said he would do it!

Thérèse. He'll do it so clumsily.

Jeannette. Well, you can't expect everyone to know how

he feels! He hasn't told a soul that he's in love with you, you know!

Thérèse. No, poor thing.

Jeannette. What does your mother say about it?

Thérèse. Oh, you know my mother. She'd go to any lengths to keep him. I daren't turn round. Are they talking to him?

Jeannette [*glancing round*]. No. They're putting their heads together. Gosta's at the back. He's looking for his music.

Thérèse. I can't face it. [*Calling.*] Father, I'm going out for a minute. [*She beckons to him.*] Are you going to tell him?

Tarde. It's my duty! Don't stay out too long. The boss is in the house. [*He goes back to his wife as* THÉRÈSE *slips out.*] Do you think he suspects something? There's a nasty glint in his eye.

Mme. Tarde. No. But we must tell him before M. Florent calls for Thérèse. You never know, he might turn ugly.

Tarde. What—here, in public?

Mme. Tarde. Yes.

Tarde. I never heard of such a thing!

Mme. Tarde. Suppose we waited till we've played the finale?

Tarde. No. I'd rather tell him straight out and then give the signal to strike up. It's the march from Tannhäuser. He can work it off on the piano. Right. Here goes. [*He takes a step toward* GOSTA, *but turns back again.*] Was he in a good mood at suppertime?

Mme. Tarde. Not very.

Tarde. Oh. [*Squaring his shoulders.*] Dammit, I really don't see why we should be scared to tell him! Who's the master here?

Mme. Tarde. I couldn't say, I'm sure.

Tarde. What do you mean, you couldn't say? Who is your husband, who's the leader of this orchestra, who's Thérèse's father, tell me that?

Mme. Tarde. You are. In theory.

Tarde. What do you mean in theory? I shall be firm!

Mme. Tarde. Please yourself. But if he blacks your eye don't say I didn't warn you.

Tarde. Blacks my eye! Blacks my——! Good grief,

woman, let's be logical about this! Do we have to consult him before we give our girl in marriage? What business is it of his anyway?

Mme. Tarde. None at all. But that may not stop him knocking you down.

Tarde. Knocking me down! Knocking me——! He doesn't know when to stop, that chap! I've been closing my eyes for thirteen years to his fun and games with you. What more does he want?

Mme. Tarde. You know as well as I·do how fond he is of the child.

Tarde. Keeping it in the family, eh? I'm within my rights! I shall put my foot down!

Mme. Tarde. I daresay, but you know his temper. Just take care, that's all.

Gosta [*coming downstage with his music*]. I've found it. Shall we start?

Tarde [*sighing*]. Yes, off we go. [*Going to* Mme. Tarde.] How many drinks has he had?

Mme. Tarde. One.

Tarde. Good. [*He walks resolutely over to* Gosta.] Now then, have you found that music yet?

Gosta. Yes.

Tarde [*clears his throat, then begins nervously to lay the music sheets on to the stands*]. Did you read about that Sicilian fellow in the papers?

Gosta. Yes.

Tarde. Shot twelve! Terrible business. [Mme. Tarde *gives him a nudge.*] Oh, yes! That reminds me. You've heard about Thérèse, have you?

Gosta [*looking up*]. Thérèse? No, what about her?

Tarde [*to* Mme. Tarde]. Didn't you tell him?

Mme. Tarde. No.

Tarde. But gracious me, he should have been told! You tell him! I'll fetch Thérèse. I see M. Lebonze getting impatient over there.

Mme. Tarde [*catching hold of his arm*]. Oh, no, you don't!

Gosta *has risen, anxiously.*

Gosta [*going to them*]. What was it you wanted to tell me about Thérèse?

Tarde. Well now—um, it's like this. . . .

Mme. Tarde. Oh, it's nothing very serious, you know!

Gosta [*looking at them*]. You're going to lie to me, the pair of you. [*To* MME. TARDE.] Your mouth is all crooked like when you know you've got a clout coming.

Mme. Tarde. What are you raving about?

Tarde [*laughing on the wrong side of his face*]. He's mad! Absolutely mad! A clout coming! I ask you! Why, the very idea!

Gosta. Well, what about Thérèse? What do you want with her?

Tarde [*inanely*]. Me? Why, nothing—nothing at all! [*Solemnly.*] Ah, yes, I was forgetting. The best, that's what I want for my little girl. You know the famous M. France —the composer—the one who gave a recital last month at the Casino?

Gosta. Yes. What about him?

Mme. Tarde. That dark gentleman who's been here several times and who spoke to Thérèse? That's him.

Gosta. Does she know him?

Tarde. Yes. You know how quickly young people get together in these seaside towns.

Mme. Tarde. He's very nice you know, Gosta. . . .

Tarde. Besides, there's no getting away from it, he's a genius! The undisputed king of his profession!

Gosta. What are you trying to tell me? I don't like that look on your faces. We'd got to Florent France. Go on from there.

Tarde [*backing*]. Fine musician.

Gosta. I know that.

Tarde. It's men of that caliber who've made our country what it is!

Gosta [*seizing his tie*]. Will you talk, damn you!

Tarde [*backing*]. Now, now—not on the bandstand, Gosta!

Mme. Tarde [*hanging onto* GOSTA's *arm*]. It's the child's happiness, Gosta! It's her future that matters! He's going to marry her, don't you see! He's going to marry her! It's too good to be true!

Gosta [*shaking her off without letting go of* TARDE]. I might have known it! Take your hands off me, you! You've been trying long enough to sell her off to somebody! How much are you making on the deal, eh? Answer me! [*He shakes him.*]

Tarde. Gosta, you're mad! On the bandstand! Suppose M. Lebonze came along!

Gosta. I'd tell him what a slimy rat you are and tan the hide off you in front of him!

Tarde [struggling to keep upright]. But this is insane! After all, who's the master here?

Mme. Tarde. She's in love this time, Gosta, I swear she is!

Gosta. She's a baby! You've dazzled her with the thought of the money she might have—money she doesn't even want! Because she's worth a hundred of you put together! And it's you, you greasy old ruin, who——

Tarde [as GOSTA shakes him]. Who's the master here?

JEANNETTE *has run to the cloakroom door.*

Jeannette. Thérèse! Thérèse! Quick!

Gosta [holding TARDE at arm's length]. You scum! I'd like to squash you under my shoe, like the piece of dirt you are! That's right, try and look dignified. Straighten your tie, go on!

Tarde [whimpering]. Godstrewth, who's the master here?

THÉRÈSE *has come running in.*

Thérèse. Gosta! Let him alone! You don't know what you're talking about. Nobody drove me to it! I love him!

GOSTA *has released* TARDE. *He looks at her.*

Gosta. Why didn't you tell me?

Thérèse. I didn't tell you because. . . . *[She stops short, in embarrassment.]* I don't know why I didn't tell you.

M. LEBONZE *comes bustling in with his napkin under his arm.*

M. Lebonze. When are we going to have that finale, this evening or next week?

Tarde. Very sorry, Monsieur Lebonze, I'm sure! Right away! Gosta, to your stool! *[Yelping.]* Come along! Come along! Business before pleasure!

Gosta [pale, his fists clenched]. Will you shut your mouth?

Tarde [faltering under the other's gaze]. Business before pleasure—I mean . . . that's all I said.

Thérèse [gently]. Go to the piano, Gosta, please. I'll explain everything later.

GOSTA *turns on his heel and goes to the piano.*

M. Lebonze. My word, but you're acting as if you owned the place, the pack of you!

Tarde. We're all set, Monsieur Lebonze! Ready everybody? One, two, three!

The music strikes up.

M. Lebonze. And about time! Now don't let me hear another word out of any of you about anything! Otherwise there'll be trouble!

He stalks majestically away, pushing a chair into position and flicking a table with his napkin as he goes. The following lines are rapidly exchanged during the music.

Mme. Tarde. You fool! I knew you'd make a mess of it!

Tarde. He didn't make a mess of me, though! [*He heaves at his little joke, then says sternly.*] If he starts again, he'll be sorry. I shall be ruthless!

Music.

Mme. Tarde [*sighing*]. Let's hope he doesn't leave me! You don't think he'll leave me, do you?

Tarde. Now look here! I've closed my eyes to your fancy man for thirteen years, but if he's tired of thumbing his nose at me, you don't imagine I'm going to go running after him, do you?

Mme. Tarde. You're a coward!

Tarde. You said so before.

Mme. Tarde. I despise you, do you hear me? I despise you!

Tarde. You'd do better to play in tune. Meet you at the next rest!

Mme. Tarde. Coward! Coward!

Tarde. When do we get those sharps then, tomorrow?

Mme. Tarde. Cuckold! Daft old cuckold!

Tarde. Whose fault's that? [*Suddenly beaming.*] Look out. Here he comes!

FLORENT *comes in with* HARTMANN. TARDE *bows over his double bass.*

Tarde. Maestro!

MME. TARDE *simpers.* THÉRÈSE *gives a little smile but does not move.* HARTMANN *and* FLORENT *sit down, facing the orchestra.*

Florent. Well, Hartmann?

Hartmann. Well.

Florent. What do you think of her?

Hartmann. Not the dark one?

Florent [*with a little laugh*]. No, of course not.

A *pause.*

Hartmann. Is that the father, the old fellow with the double bass? He's unbelievable!

Florent. The mother is the cellist.

Hartmann [*studying them with a smile*]. Florent, you're an extraordinary fellow! You seriously intend to marry that little thing in spite of those two characters? She didn't insist on it, I presume?

Florent. She is my mistress.

Hartmann. You're in love with her, then?

Florent [*laughing*]. That seems a good enough explanation.

Hartmann [*puts on his thick tortoise-shell glasses and carefully scrutinizes* THÉRÈSE]. She's very pretty, of course, but . . . I've always been a sort of father confessor to you, Florent. Are you sure it isn't a mistake?

Florent. Sure? I who am never sure of anything, I feel for the first time absolutely certain. I can't tell you how wonderful it is!

Hartmann. What about your work?

Florent. It's just as well you came to fetch me. For the last month I've done nothing, needless to say.

Hartmann. Oh, yes, you have. You've lost a lot of money. I've already paid six hundred thousand francs in compensation money.

Florent. Suppose I told you that I haven't touched my piano once?

Hartmann. The devil you haven't! [*Looking at* THÉRÈSE *again.*] She *is* very pretty.

Florent [*softly*]. I love her, Hartmann.

Hartmann. I'm beginning to believe you do. [*He listens to the music a moment, and pulls a face.*] I'll tell you one thing. She's a terrible violinist.

Florent [*smiling*]. I know. But I don't care. I'm not taking her away for her to play the fiddle. I'm taking her away so I'll be happy, all my life, with her.

Hartmann. Is that true?

Florent. Those are the very words I say to myself each morning when I wake. Is it true? And I answer myself very quickly: Yes, it's true.

Hartmann [*smiling*]. And is it?

Florent. I couldn't lie to myself every morning.

A *pause.*

Hartmann [*with a sigh*]. Lord, but she plays badly.

Florent. She plays badly, Hartmann, but she loves me well.

Hartmann. Does she tell you so?

Florent. Never. But when we're alone, she rubs her head against me like a little fawn. She looks at me, deep down into my eyes. With me, she says, there's no need to be an especially good diver—you reach the bottom in not time at all. Is she right, Hartmann?

Hartmann [*after looking at* THÉRÈSE *for a while*]. How lucky for you that the girl you love should be as open and straightforward as yourself, Florent.

Florent. Why?

Hartmann. No reason. You are a charming man, Florent, and I'm sure you'll make her very happy.

Florent. Hartmann, you're hiding something! I feel you're about to tell me that I'm a monster without knowing it!

Hartmann [*smiling*]. Maybe.

Florent [*lightly*]. Have I some hidden vice? Speak now, for tomorrow is my wedding day!

Hartmann. A kind of vice, yes.

Florent. It's name?

Hartmann. It has several. Brilliance, intelligence, effortlessness—luck too.

Florent [*laughing*]. Why, that sounds perfectly charming to me!

Hartmann. It is. But I trembled to think you might fall in love with a suspicious, demanding, tormented sort of girl. How fortunate that she should be a child of light like you! [M. *and* MME. TARDE *throw ingratiating nods and smiles to* FLORENT *as they play.*] The parents are superb! The rest of the band aren't so bad either! What has it done to her, I wonder, rubbing shoulders with them all?

Florent. Nothing can soil her. She is immune. It could have made her lewd and cheap. It has merely decked her

in strength and candor, in a sort of virility. Do you know
that she refuses to take a penny from me? She makes her
own clothes and uses cheap face powder and she won't
even let me buy her a present!

Hartmann. But if you marry her, she'll let you feed and
clothe her, surely?

Florent [*smiling*]. I hope so. I'm none too sure. Yesterday, for the first time, she accepted some money to buy
herself some suitcases. But I had to bully her into it. She
would have come away quite happily with her two dresses
in a cardboard box. That must appeal to you, I'm sure!

Hartmann [*looking at him with a good-natured grin
now*]. Well now, I'll forgive her for her wrong notes.
[*Sighing.*] To think you'll have made a success of everything, Florent, even falling in love.

Florent. I'm lucky.

Hartmann. Almost too lucky.

Florent. You can never be too lucky.

Hartmann. You can—sometimes.

The number is over. THÉRÈSE *comes quickly down the
platform and runs to* FLORENT, *who rises and goes to meet
her.*

Thérèse. How late you were today!

Florent. Hullo, my little wild thing.

Thérèse [*indicating the café and laughing*]. Did you hear
that pathetic applause? Look, they're all slinking out! They
don't do that when *you* play, do they?

Florent [*laughing with her*]. They're philistines. Music
is wasted on them. [*Taking her by the shoulders.*] Quick.
Now for my questionnaire. Have you thought about me
today?

Thérèse. Every minute.

Florent. Are you sure you haven't told anyone that you
love me?

Thérèse. Yes, I have. I told my friend.

Florent. Thérèse! And you never say it to me!

Thérèse [*in his ear*]. I never want to say it to you. But
if I didn't say it to other people now and then I think it
would choke me.

Florent. And no afterthoughts?

Thérèse. My thoughts are all before you. In my eyes—
and on my lips. [*She lifts her face up to him to be kissed.*]

Florent [*murmuring*]. In front of everyone?

Thérèse. Who are *they*? [*He leans toward her. She pushes him gently away with a glance at* GOSTA.] No, not yet.

Florent. Why not?

Thérèse. I'll tell you later.

GOSTA *has come down off the rostrum. He picks up his hat, crosses them and goes out without a glance in their direction.* FLORENT *takes* THÉRÈSE'S *arm as she stands looking after* GOSTA *and guides her over to* HARTMANN.

Florent. Thérèse, this is Hartmann. He's only my friend really, but when we meet businessmen, he pretends to be my manager, because he talks bigger than I do.

Thérèse. How sternly he's looking at me! Perhaps he isn't going to like me?

Florent. Yes, he will. I'm sure he will. Well, Hartmann, what's the verdict?

Hartmann. Nine out of ten. She's passed with honors.

Florent. You look thoughtful. Was I lying?

Hartmann [*taking* THÉRÈSE'S *hand*]. Florent, you never lie. Thérèse is perfect. Thérèse is the one girl on earth who deserved you. But those eyes are very bright, that little forehead is very wise. She will need a lot of loving.

Thérèse [*withdrawing her hand*]. Why do you say that?

Florent. He thinks I'm a monster. He thinks I'm incapable of making anybody happy.

Thérèse. Then he can't know you very well.

Florent. He does. He's known me for years. That's what's so serious.

Thérèse. Not the way I know you. [*To* HARTMANN.] I've looked at him asleep beside me; I've listened to him talking in his dreams as he turns over. Well, even in his nighttime kingdom, I am sure of him.

Hartmann. And are you sure of yourself?

Thérèse [*like a child answering a question*]. Yes, sir.

Hartmann. Do you believe that he will never hurt you?

Thérèse. He is the soul of kindness.

Hartmann. And doesn't it frighten you to meet the soul of kindness, the soul of intelligence and joy? You're a brave girl.

Florent. Hartmann is a silly old woman. Promise me you'll never listen to him, Thérèse.

M. *and* MME. TARDE, *who with much winking and nudging, have stayed up on the rostrum all this time, putting away their instruments, venture forward, obsequiously rubbing their hands.*

Mme. Tarde. Good evening, Monsieur Florent! So it's tomorrow morning that you plan to take my little girl away, is it?

Florent. Yes, madame.

Tarde. Doesn't it just show you! Life's a funny thing. I'm only a poor man, maestro, and yet I'm giving you a treasure!

Mme. Tarde. A precious treasure that it breaks our hearts to part with, believe you me!

M. LEBONZE *comes in, shouting over his shoulder.*

M. Lebonze. Certainly, sir, certainly, certainly! Anything you care to name! [*Sotto voce to* TARDE.] The customer over in the corner has just ordered two more bottles— one for the band. Don't pack up yet. I'll go and ask him what he wants you to play. [*He goes out again.*]

Jeannette [*sitting down again crossly*]. This is another two in the morning lark!

Tarde [*taking out his music, highly excited*]. Yes, but champagne!

Jeannette. Oh, we all know that old dodge! They'll charge him for vintage and give us moussec!

M. LEBONZE *reappears.*

M. Lebonze. Change of plan. You can all go except Gosta. He doesn't want the band now, he just wants the piano. He wants to hear the "Moonlight Rhapsody" on the piano. He's crying. He says it'll remind him of his wife.

Tarde. Well now, er—the thing is, Gosta. . . . We had a slight tiff. I think he's gone.

M. Lebonze. Have you finished making a fool of me? I said nobody was to move from here! [*To the* WAITER.] You there! Go and fetch him back. He must have gone up to his room.

Waiter. Very good, Monsieur Lebonze. But do you think you could calm the customer down? He says if we don't play the "Moonlight Rhapsody" at once, he'll get it played elsewhere. He says he's tired of waiting.

M. Lebonze [*going out, apoplectic*]. Give me strength!

If Gosta isn't here in one minute, I swear I'll throw you all out, bag and baggage! [*He storms out.*]

Tarde [*sinking into a chair*]. It's the finish of us! I'm ashamed, maestro, that you should see such lack of discipline in this orchestra. We meet with acclaim everywhere we go! But he's a brute of a man! A fiendish temper to him—always flaring up over nothing!

The WAITER *comes back at the same time as* LEBONZE.

M. Lebonze. Well?

Waiter. His door's locked. He doesn't answer.

Thérèse [*to* FLORENT]. I'm the only one who can persuade him. I shan't be long. Come with me, Jeannette. [*The girls go out.*]

M. Lebonze. Right: I'm not going on my knees to any third-rate piano thumper! Take my car and fetch me the pianist from the Royal. [*To* TARDE.] As for you, you can pack your traps and clear out. I'm getting another band tomorrow.

Tarde. Monsieur Lebonze, Monsieur Lebonze, I've a wife and child to support!

M. Lebonze. That's your worry!

Florent [*stepping forward*]. Look, I think I could solve the problem. I'll play the piece if you like.

M. Lebonze [*grunting*]. Yes, but can you play?

Florent. A little. [*To* TARDE.] Do you have the music of the "Moonlight Rhapsody"?

M. Lebonze [*grumbling*]. H'm! Calls himself a pianist and can't play the "Moonlight Rhapsody" by heart! All right then, do your worst. It's you or nothing. [*To* TARDE.] But I'm warning you, if the customer isn't satisfied, you can start packing! [*He goes out.*]

Tarde. Oh, maestro, I don't know how to thank you! Condescending—in this establishment—in my orchestra . . . !

Mme. Tarde [*who has gone to fetch the music*]. Here's the music, Monsieur Florent. Oh, they don't make many like you and that's a fact!

HARTMANN *goes up on the platform with* FLORENT.

Hartmann [*over his shoulder to* TARDE *as he goes*]. Normally it's two hundred thousand francs, old chap.

Tarde [*weak at the knees*]. Two hundred thousand francs! On my bandstand!

THÉRÈSE *comes back with* JEANNETTE.

Thérèse. He isn't in his room. The doorman says he saw him go toward the beach. Why, who's that playing?

Tarde [*drawing himself up to his full height*]. Maestro Florent France! In my orchestra!

Thérèse. Father, are you out of your mind! You let him——

Tarde. He insisted. And do you know how much this is costing me?—at least how much it could cost me. Two hundred thousand francs!

Thérèse. Oh, I'm so ashamed.

Tarde. What?

Thérèse. For that drunken sot—in this cheap saloon! You shouldn't have let him!

Tarde. Don't be silly. I'm going to see if M. Lebonze is pleased. [*He trots out, rubbing his hands.*]

THÉRÈSE *watches* FLORENT *playing for a moment or two.*

Thérèse [*murmuring*]. Florent. . . . It's odd to see him playing up there. . . . [*A pause. She goes on dreamily.*] Come to think of it, I should have liked it if he'd been a member of the band and I'd grown to love him as we worked together. . . .

Jeannette [*putting her violin into its case*]. You're joking, I hope?

Thérèse. No. Oh, I know I'll learn to forget about his money if I try. But it isn't always very easy.

Jeannette [*with a short laugh*]. You're making me cry.

Thérèse. If he were poor and unhappy, it's funny but I feel he would belong to me more. . . . It would be rather as if he were a little boy again. I could hold him close to me, and stroke his hair and say, "There, don't be sad, I'm here, I'll help you."

Jeannette [*tucking her violin under her arm*]. You'll find all the unhappy men you want, I shouldn't worry. Meanwhile, make the most of this one now you've got him. [*Giving* THÉRÈSE *a kiss.*] Good-by, Thérèse. I hope I'll see you tomorrow morning before you go. But in case I shouldn't, here's a tip. Get him to buy you diamonds, dear, all the diamonds you can. They're still the easiest things to sell.

Thérèse. What do you mean?

Jeannette [*going out*]. Nothing, nothing. Good luck, anyway. [*She goes.*]

Mme. Tarde. What was she talking about? Be careful of her, she's no good. And don't go out with her and Florent whatever you do. She'd pinch him soon as look at you.

Thérèse [shrugging]. You're talking nonsense.

Mme. Tarde. Ah, my child, you don't know the male sex! When a woman who knows what's what offers herself to a man. . . . [*Eyeing* FLORENT.] Especially a lovely lad like him. What a nice gesture, offering to play like that! Oh, you're going to be so happy, and cosseted and spoiled! [*She sighs.*] That's the kind of man I should have liked. Gosta has been a big disappointment to me, by and large. With you gone, who's to say that he won't leave me? Ah well, your happiness comes first! [*With another deep sigh, she comes nearer to* THÉRÈSE *and says impulsively.*] Give me a kiss! This may be the last time we're alone together. You are my little girl, after all. The eve of a wedding, that's when a mother feels these things.

Thérèse [freeing herself slightly]. In the first place, there isn't any wedding yet. And, you know as well as I do that we've never been exactly loving.

Mme. Tarde. That's what I mean! This evening it's all come to a head! It's welling up inside me! My girl, my little girl!

Thérèse [pushing her away]. No. No theatricals, please.

Mme. Tarde. Oh, you are a hard little bitch! But blood's thicker than water, I don't care what you say. Besides, a mother has her duty. On a night like this, there's a certain little talk we ought to have with the bride-to-be! [*Putting on a suitable expression.*] Be sweet and docile, dear. Just lie back. Don't be afraid.

Thérèse. Don't be absurd. I'm not a little girl, and well you know it.

Mme. Tarde [frantic]. Shush! You didn't tell him so, I hope?

Thérèse. Of course I did.

Mme. Tarde [furious]. You fool! Suppose he threw you over?

Thérèse [smiling]. At last. That sounds more like you.

Mme. Tarde. You don't know your luck! I don't mind telling you I never thought he'd marry you. Oh, let me kiss you!

Thérèse. Not again! What is all this leading up to?

Mme. Tarde. With his connections, you must see to it

he does the very best for you. Don't give up your art. This time next year, you must be a star!

Thérèse [*softly*]. I think he thinks I play badly.

Mme. Tarde. Never mind, never mind! He'll coach you! Either way, don't you give him a moment's peace until he's started you on your career. Make your hay while the sun shines, my girl. Take it from me, it doesn't shine long.

Thérèse [*trying to break away*]. Please! Leave me alone now, will you?

Mme. Tarde [*catching her*]. No, no, wait, wait! Gracious me, you *are* jumpy! Listen a minute. . . . You know how difficult things are just now. And I needn't tell you how mean your father is with his money. You might see your way to doing a little something for me—on the quiet, of course——

Thérèse [*shaking slightly*]. What do you mean?

Mme. Tarde. Oh, nothing, bless me—nothing at all! I waited till tonight because there was no point in bothering you before. And anyway, I had to come to terms regarding the commission. Well, now, it's like this. I went to see Vinteuil—you know, the big jewelers on the Avenue de la Plage. Very high-class establishment; branch in London, two in Paris. To cut a long story short, I told him everything.

Thérèse. What? What did you tell him?

Mme. Tarde. Well, I told him you were getting married —to a very rich man!

Thérèse. But you shouldn't have! I told you you weren't to tell anybody!

Mme. Tarde. Now be sensible, what difference does it make? People will have to know sometime. So, anyway, as I was saying. He'll be buying you a ring, obviously. Now, what would it cost you to say, "I've seen just what I want in Vinteuil's window"? Wait, wait . . . ! There's a square-cut diamond, platinum setting; a beauty—— No, wait! Let me finish, do! Vinteuil wants eight hundred thousand for it. I told him that if you were to say you'd set your heart on it, he could certainly ask nine hundred. If your fiancé argues about the price, of course he'll come down. But he's promised me the difference.

Thérèse [*recoiling*]. Oh, you make me sick!

Mme. Tarde [*changing her tone*]. Make you sick? Make you sick do I? Oh, stop acting the dainty miss. You were never that particular before. What can a hundred thousand more or less mean to him with his millions? And for me, it's a windfall!

Thérèse. And did you think I would agree to deceive him?

Mme. Tarde. But I tell you he'd never know!

Thérèse. Even if he never knew! Especially if he never knew! [*She buries her head in her hands.*] What do you take me for, all of you?

TARDE *hustles in, very excited.*

Tarde. I've got a stupendous proposition to make to you! Old Pa Lebonze can't contain himself at the thought of who he's got strumming away there on his old piano!

Mme. Tarde [*with a conspiratorial look at* THÉRÈSE]. Think it over, Thérèse. Remember all I sacrificed for you. But mind, it's between ourselves, eh? [*She goes out.*]

Tarde [*anxiously*]. What was she saying to you? You want to watch out for her. She isn't a bad old girl, as they go—but she has a small mind. Listen, chick. Something Pa Lebonze said gave me a brilliant idea. All you have to do is postpone your going away for a couple of days. That won't kill you, will it? Now don't interrupt till you've heard what I've got to say. Well, now. . . . You know we're giving a benefit performance at the end of the season. Right. To mark the occasion of your leaving us, M. Lebonze has agreed to bring it forward a week. You follow me?

Thérèse. Yes, Father.

Tarde [*on unsure ground*]. That's my girlie! Well now. This is a proposition that might bring us both in quite a bit of money. (I'd see you got your fair share, that goes without saying.) Right. Now then. The idea came to me in a flash when I saw your fiancé at the piano up there. Now, I ask you, couldn't you, on the occasion of this farewell concert—you could say it brought back memories, that you'd love to see him up on that platform where you'd been working for so long. . . . It's perfectly natural —you're such a sentimental little thing! (Just like me, soft as putty.) Couldn't you, I say, persuade him—on an honorary basis of course—to come and play one or two little pieces with us? As one of the family! It would be so nice!

Thérèse [*stammering*]. You too, you too. . . .

Tarde. What do you mean, me too? Don't tell me your mother had the same idea?

Thérèse. Do you think he's a machine for making money for you? Can't you forget that wretched money for one second?

Tarde. We'd like to, but it's mighty difficult. Oh, come on, don't be such a little prig. You're as mercenary as I am.

Thérèse. That's not true! You tried to teach me to be, but I'm not with *him!*

Tarde. Oh, be quiet! You prefer your mother's little scheme because you think you'll make more out of it. How much is she offering you?

Thérèse. Go away!

Tarde. Not before we've come to terms.

Thérèse [*on the verge of tears*]. Oh, leave me alone! Please, please, leave me alone!

Tarde [*lumbering after her*]. How much did your Ma offer you? I'll give you seventy-five per cent. There! You can't call me mean, now can you?

THÉRÈSE *runs up on to the bandstand, interrupts FLO-PENT's playing and throws herself into his arms.*

Thérèse. Florent! Florent! Take me away from here!

Florent. Thérèse, what's the matter?

Thérèse [*clinging to him*]. Let's go, please, please! Let's go quickly so I shan't see them any more!

The WAITER *comes in, pushing* GOSTA *in front of him.*

Waiter. Here he is. I'll give you three guesses where I found him. On the beach, at the end of the jetty!

M. LEBONZE *comes running in.*

M. Lebonze [*bawling*]. So you've shown up at last! All right, all right! Don't give me any excuses! I'll deal with you in the morning! [*To* FLORENT.] My dear sir, I can't thank you enough. I may not be much of an expert, but I know talent when I see it. Did Thérèse mention the little proposition we——

Thérèse [*quickly*]. Yes—yes, I did.

M. Lebonze. Think it over. It might do us both a bit of good. [*Holding out his hand.*] Now, if you'll excuse me . . . in the catering trade, morning's at six, as they say. I'm

off to bed. [*To the* WAITER *as he goes out.*] You! Look
sharp and stack your chairs! And switch off those center
lights while you're about it. No point in burning money.

*He goes. The end of the Act is played in softer lighting
among the chairs which the* WAITER *stacks round the
bandstand, in readiness for the sweepers.*

Thérèse [*gently to* GOSTA, *who is staring at her, motionless*]. Gosta, you're fond of me, aren't you? I'm happy
tonight. I should like everybody to be happy too. This is
Monsieur Florent France—you know, the composer.
Florent, this is Gosta, an old friend of mine, whom I'm
very fond of.

Florent. Then I'm very happy to know him. [*He holds
out his hand.* GOSTA *does not take it.*] Won't you shake
hands with me?

Gosta [*roughly*]. What do you want with her? [*He
advances on* FLORENT.]

Mme. Tarde [*screaming*]. Gosta!

Gosta. What do you want with her? [*He seizes* FLO-
RENT *by the lapels.*]

Florent [*freeing himself and pushing him away*]. Are you
out of your mind? Who are you?

Gosta. Nothing! That's what I am! Nothing! Nothing
but a poor wretch who watched her grow up and who
wouldn't want to see her turn into a whore!

Mme. Tarde [*screeching*]. Gosta! Gosta darling!

Thérèse [*quietly*]. Oh, Gosta, how could you? He's rich,
I know, but that isn't my fault.

Gosta. No, of course it isn't your fault! Still, it's a funny
thing isn't it? You never fell in love with mortal man
before, yet he's the one you love!

Thérèse. But I can't help it if I love him!

Gosta. Of course not! That's your instinct! And there
you were, sniffing after money with your dirty little snout,
just like all the others!

Thérèse [*in a small, broken voice*]. Oh, you're vile! Go
away!

Gosta. All right, all right, we'll clear the floor for you,
don't worry! We're none of us good enough for you now!
Oh, God, I never thought it of you! I never thought you'd
be like all the rest!

Thérèse [*in a murmur*]. It's too silly. . . .

Mme. Tarde [*to* GOSTA]. Hush now, darling, be quiet.

You know what happens when you get excited. You'll have an upset stomach for a week.

Thérèse. Take him away, Mother. Gosta, go away, please go away. You're not yourself.

Gosta [*as the* Tardes *try to drag him away*]. That's right, I'm mad! That's the easiest way round it, isn't it? I'm mad. . . .

Mme. Tarde. There, there, my poor old dear! Don't take on so! [*She kisses him.*] It hurts, I know, I know. . . . Come along now, lovey. [*They manage to drag him out.*]

Florent. But—who is this man?

TARDE *comes back.*

Tarde. In my capacity as conductor of this orchestra, may I apologize for any——

Thérèse. Go away.

Tarde [*hastily*]. Right! You make my excuses for me! [*He scuttles out.*]

Thérèse [*quickly, without looking at* Florent]. He's one of our musicians. He's known me since I was a little girl. He's a simple, violent man. He thought they'd driven me into it. He thought I was giving myself to you for your money.

Florent. But your mother . . . ?

Thérèse. Yes. That's another thing I hoped I shouldn't have to tell you yet. She called him darling. He's her lover—has been for a long time.

Florent. Thérèse, I'm very sorry.

Thérèse [*quickly*]. No, don't!

MME. TARDE *comes in simpering.*

Mme. Tarde. Back I come, disturbing the lovebirds again! He's quietened down now. I came back for my bag. I've some tablets that will help him sleep. Ah, men, men! You're all the same, dear maestro, demons every one of you! There's a song I used to sing, when I was Thérèse's age—in my early cabaret days, you know. [*Singing, with gestures, while continuing to hunt for her bag.*]

Someone's lost her ocarino
Poor Nana
Nana's lost her nono
With his ocarino
Nono's lost his nana with his ocarino.

Where *did* I put that bag? In the cloakroom, maybe. . . .

[*She goes out.* THÉRÈSE *stands frozen.*]

Florent. I can't wait to take you away from here, Thérèse.

Thérèse [*tonelessly*]. Yes.

Florent. You'll like it in my house.

Thérèse. Yes, I'm sure I will. . . .

Florent. My sister is innocent and sweet like you. You'll be great friends. And my aunt is the most enchanting old lady in the world.

The song is heard next door. Then MME. TARDE *crosses the stage, and goes out again with an arch little smile and a nodded good night, singing as she goes.* THÉRÈSE *runs to the open door, pushes it to and leans against it.*

Thérèse. Get out. Get out. If I could only shut her out of my sight. She's ugly, isn't she? Ugly and crude and vulgar when she sings those dirty songs! And that lover of hers. . . .

Florent. I know, darling, but what does it matter? We'll wipe out all that.

Thérèse. Do you think you can?

Florent [*firmly*]. Yes, my darling.

Thérèse [*with a sudden cry*]. Oh, don't be so proud of your strength, so certain of yourself! [*A pause.*] Forgive me, Florent. But if you knew how horrible she is! And my father too. If I told you all the things I know, the things I've seen!

Florent [*taking her in his arms*]. Thérèse, you're trembling! Yet you've let me see them quite happily for the last month? You weren't ashamed before.

Thérèse. Until just now—it's funny—I didn't know. That's another thing they have just taught me.

Florent. Taught you? What have they taught you?

Thérèse. What I am. What you are.

Florent [*kneels beside her and clasps her knees*]. Oh, my foolish darling! But I'm only your lover! And you are more of a miracle, I promise you, than money and expensive education. Did nobody ever tell you that you were the wealthy one?

Thérèse. How sweet and clever you are. . . . Earlier on, yes, I thought I was somebody despite your money. I said so to the girl who plays in the orchestra with me. She laughed her head off. I see what she meant now.

Florent. My sweet silly! How could a girl as free and

proud as you be affected, for one second, by a mere matter of money?

Thérèse [*shaking her head with a sad little smile*]. Not only money. No, Florent. A while ago, you could have comforted me, I'm sure. Now, your very way of doing it, so sensitive, so right, wounds me a little.

Florent. You mystify me, darling.

Thérèse. Yes, it's funny, I hardly understand myself any more. Just now, when poor Gosta wanted to fight you, I knew you were the stronger of the two. I ought to have been proud of you. I almost hated you for being stronger in that way too. For being the strongest, always.

Florent [*smiling*]. Sweet nitwit. Now you're blaming me because I'm strong! I'll pick a quarrel with that waiter, shall I—and have him lay me flat so that you'll love me?

Thérèse [*trembling slightly*]. You're quite right to laugh at me. I *am* being silly, aren't I, Florent? I do deserve you, I am like you, aren't I? Aren't I? Florent, tell me I'm not like them?

Florent. No, Thérèse, I swear you're not.

Thérèse. But they do make you ashamed though, don't they?

Florent. Not the slightest bit. They make me laugh.

Thérèse. What's wrong with me, then, tell me? Why do I feel like this? I'm not happy in the way I was.

Florent [*holding her*]. My love, my little love. Why, everything hurts you! [*They kiss.*]

Enter the TARDES.

Tarde. Delicious pair!

Mme. Tarde [*beaming*]. It takes me back to my giddy young days!

FLORENT *breaks away from* THÉRÈSE *in slight embarrassment.*

Tarde. Kiss her, my boy, go ahead and kiss her! She's all yours!

Mme. Tarde. Don't mind us, dear maestro. We're all artistes here. I'm as hot-blooded as they come myself!

Thérèse [*with a sharp cry*]. Mother!

Tarde. Her happiness! That's all we've ever thought about—our little girl's happiness! We're not like other parents. [*With a glance at* MME. TARDE.] Yes, well . . .

hrrm. The only thing that bothers us, I'm bound to say, is Thérèse leaving at such short notice. From the professional point of view. . . .

Florent. But you can find a violinist to take her place, surely?

Tarde. Oh, of course, of course, but that isn't the point, I'm afraid. She was very popular here, you know, and. . . . The fact of the matter is, M. Lebonze has given us notice to quit the day that Thérèse leaves. Financially speaking, it's a disaster.

Florent [*taking out his wallet*]. But I must compensate you for that, of course! It's the least I can do. After all, if it hadn't been for me——

THÉRÈSE *leaps forward.*

Thérèse. No!

Tarde. What do you mean, no? Why ever not, girlie?

Mme. Tarde. Come now, Thérèse, your fiancé says himself that it's the least he can do!

Thérèse. No! Not that eternal money again! You've done me enough harm already, you've made me lose enough happiness as it is, today! You're not to touch his money! And I won't have you going into ecstasies because he's good enough to want to marry me! I'm beautiful, I'm young, I love him—that's worth his riches and his fame! I won't hear another word about that money! [*To* FLO-RENT.] You gave me some to buy myself some luggage yesterday. I don't even want that! [*She runs to fetch her bag.*]

Tarde [*wildly*]. Don't listen to her! Don't listen to her!

MME. TARDE *follows after her, whimpering.*

Mme. Tarde. Thérèse! Thérèse, baby, be reasonable!

Thérèse. There! There! There! Take it! [*She throws the notes at* FLORENT'*s feet. The* TARDES *make to dash forward.*] Stay where you are! Don't you dare move, either of you!

Tarde. But you're crazy! He *gave* it to you, stupid!

Thérèse. Yes, I'm crazy! [*She looks at* FLORENT, *panting.*] There!

Florent [*bursts out laughing*]. My darling! What a wonderful girl you are! But what does money matter? We'll never mention the dirty word again! We won't even have

any if you'd rather. We can manage perfectly well without.
[*He pulls his money out of his pockets.*]

Thérèse [*murmuring*]. How simple it all is for you. I'm cold with shame and you're playing a pretty little game.

Florent [*laughing as he throws away all the money he has on him*]. Away it goes! There! All gone! So much for money! From now on we won't even know what the word means!

Tarde [*incoherently*]. Oh, but you're too kind! Oh, it's too much! [*To his wife.*] Lock the doors!

Florent [*throwing down his last coin*]. There, my darling. Now will you let me kiss you? I haven't a single cent left on me.

THÉRÈSE *stands passively as he kisses her. She looks at the* TARDES *who are quivering with thwarted greed.*

Thérèse. Look at them both! It gives them a pain to see those bank notes on the floor. How gracefully you threw them down, Florent. People like us don't have that talent. Just look at their faces, will you? [*A pause. She cries suddenly.*] I was a fool to start this. It hurts me too, despite myself, to see that money on the floor. I've pricked my finger too often with my needle, I've stayed too long bent over my sewing for my paltry wage! I wanted to act proud, but I was lying. [*She drops to her knees.*] Down on my knees! I must go down on my knees and pick it up so I'll not act a lie! I belong to the same breed.

Florent. Thérèse! Don't! [*He lifts her to her feet. She stands stiffly, with tightly shut eyes and clenched teeth.*] My mad darling!

Tarde [*exploding*]. That's right! Mad, that's what she is, mad! You see to her! We'll pick it all up for you—and give it you back. . . . You can trust us!

The TARDES *scramble forward.* HARTMANN, *who has watched the whole scene without moving, comes over to* FLORENT, *who is holding* THÉRÈSE, *in tears, in his arms.*

Hartmann [*quietly*]. You will have to tread very carefully, Florent.

The other two are still busily picking up the money as the Curtain falls.

ACT TWO

A paneled room lined with books, large french windows looking out on to the grounds. Family portraits on the walls. It is afternoon. Thérèse *stands watching* Tarde *who is trying all the armchairs in the room in turn.*

Tarde. I wish I could remember which chair it was I fell asleep in last night. It was sensational. Not that they aren't all pretty good. Must be worth quite a bit, a chair like that. [*He starts all over again.*] No. I've tried that one. Come to think of it, that particular sensation of well-being was more likely due to the dinner. Marvelous, that stuffed grouse we had last night. The trout this lunchtime wasn't so dusty either. [*He helps himself to a cigar and sniffs it.*] Man of taste, your fiancé. [*On second thought, he takes another and puts it in his pocket.*]

Thérèse. You'll leave one or two, won't you?

Tarde. What do you take me for? I'm a gay old dog but I know my manners. [*Settling himself comfortably.*] Aren't you going to sit down? That little one over by the fireplace is quite cozy. [*A pause.*] You'd pay about five hundred francs for a cigar this size. That's the equivalent of twenty whiffs! If Lady Tarde could see me now! You've written to her, I hope?

Thérèse. Have you?

Tarde [*with a nonchalant wave of his cigar*]. That's different. She's your mother. I've been so booked up lately, what with my morning constitutional and my afternoon nap. . . . We're having chicken Milanese tonight.

Thérèse. How do you know?

Tarde. I asked the cook. [*Dreamily.*] Chicken Milanese . . . have you any idea what that is? [*No answer. He turns round.*] Can't you answer me? You're not very nice to your old father. On our own, fair enough. I'm used to it. But it must look jolly odd to strangers. After all, I can't think what you've got against me. I'm a neat dresser. I know how to behave. I've plenty of small talk. You just try and think, out of the fathers of the girls you know, which one could wear a dinner jacket with my ease and smoke a five hundred franc cigar? [*Pause.*] Naturally, you won't say. You love making me feel small. But I defy you to mention *one*. [*Another pause. He stares absorbedly at a small cabinet beside him. He begins to look worried.*] What's happened to your young man today? He doesn't leave us after lunch as a rule.

Thérèse. I don't know. He's talking with Hartmann.

Tarde [*very worried now*]. I say, if they're working, he won't be back for quite some time. Maybe you could serve the drinks yourself? After all, you're the young lady of the house, eh, girlie?

Thérèse. No.

Tarde [*rising*]. It isn't quite the thing for me to help myself, I suppose. Still, we *are* in the country. . . .

Thérèse [*catching his arm*]. I forbid you to touch that cupboard!

Tarde. Well! Bless me, why ever not?

Thérèse. I'm tired of seeing you ferret about in all the cupboards in this house.

Tarde. I hope you aren't calling your father a thief!

Thérèse. I wouldn't put it past you to help yourself to the odd ornament.

Tarde. Oh, you are unfair to me! Can't you understand that I merely take an artistic interest in the objets d'art of this mansion! [*A pause. He sits down, suddenly deflated.*] You shouldn't have brought me here, Thérèse. Your old father has felt the kiss of luxury and gracious living. You know, I never should have consecrated my life to that thankless muse of music. I was meant for better things. Because your mother, don't forget, was a woman of the people—"was"—hark at me! I feel so good here that I keep imagining she's dead. Your mother, I should say, *is* a woman of the people, but my parents gave me the best middle-class blood. And willy-nilly, under the old Bohemian, the solid burgher stock will out. [*He has risen as he speaks, and tried without success to open the cocktail cabinet. He now takes out a penknife and tries to pick the lock.*]

Thérèse. Which is it—the solid burgher or the old Bohemian, who's busy tinkering with the cocktail cabinet?

TARDE *shuts his penknife, peeved, and goes back to his chair, picking up another cigar on his way, which he puts in his pocket.*

Tarde. What's got into you? You've been on edge all morning. I can't think why you insisted on bringing me here if all you wanted was to make my life a misery. And do you know why, even? I'm going to surprise you, girlie. You don't. [THÉRÈSE, *tired of this, leans her head against the window pane.*] Oh, of course, your father's a silly old fool, we all know that! But then, would you mind explaining something to the old fool, which he can't quite grasp? You're ashamed of me, aren't you? Right. Since this morning, as a matter of fact, you haven't missed a chance of rubbing it in. Don't tinker with the cocktail cabinet, don't ferret about, don't smoke all the cigars. Your fingernails are dirty, there's dandruff on your collar—and so on and so on. (Dandruff, I may say, is common to all artists—it's an occupational disease.) So you're ashamed of me. Right. You've always gone on at me about my nails and my dandruff. You've a nasty nature, nothing new in that. But now, this is where it all becomes peculiar. How many days have we been here, girlie? [*She says nothing.*] I'll tell you. Six. One, two, three, four, five, six. So there were five days —the first five of our stay here—when you weren't ashamed of me. Now you may say you're not obliged to feel ashamed of me every day of the week. Well, I'll tell you something, girlie, in all honesty. If there was one time—which Heaven forbid!—when my conduct might have given you cause to blush, it was during the first two or three days of our stay here. Yes, I won't deny it, the first day I lost my head. Those magnificent dinners, those unlimited cigars, the brandy that used to come round, regular as clockwork, after every meal. [*He heaves a sigh and eyes the drinks cupboard again.*] Dinnertime that first evening, I'll admit it, I behaved disgracefully. I had five helpings of chocolate mousse. I dropped an anchovy into my wineglass. I burped. I may say it didn't matter a scrap. Each time, I came out with just the right little witticism to turn the merriment on to my side. Still, that day—you see your old father admits it, very humbly—that day, I might—conceivably— taken all in all—I might, I repeat, have given you cause to feel ashamed of me.

Thérèse. You needn't go round and round the point. You did.

Tarde. Ah, I did! I did—did I? And how did you behave at table that first evening, pray? You roared with laughter every time I put my foot in it. It was you who pressed me to that fifth helping of chocolate mousse. Not content with that, you deliberately misled me as to the function of that little bowl of warm water we were presented with after the pudding. If your young man hadn't intervened, you'd have stood by and watched me drink it, you wicked girl! And when I let out that unfortunate little noise, your fiancé, who knows how to behave, looked the other way. Not you. You laughed out loud, you applauded, very ostentatiously, and you shouted "Good luck, Father!" Do you deny that you cried "Good luck, Father"?

Thérèse [*wearily*]. Yes, I did.

Tarde. Do you deny that after we'd retired to the lounge, you played on the understandable weakness of an old man who never tasted the good things of life and made me smoke four cigars; you filled my brandy glass seven times so I'd get drunk and make an exhibition of myself. Which I did, naturally. When I've had a drop in, I'm apt to break into song. But even so, there are songs and songs. Left to myself I might have warbled "La Madelon." But no. You insisted on a rendering of "Fifi the Fan Dancer" with gestures. And you laughed like an inebriated barmaid. Why, I blush for you when I think of it. Do you deny your behavior that first evening?

Thérèse. No, Father.

Tarde. You will therefore admit that it is in complete contradiction to the way you're criticizing me today over nothing at all?

Thérèse. Yes, Father.

Tarde. Can you tell me, in that case, the meaning of this sudden change of attitude?

Thérèse. That's for you to find out, isn't it?

The MAID *comes in with the coffee.*

Maid. M. Florent begs Mademoiselle to excuse him for a moment longer. He said not to wait for coffee.

Tarde [*calling out as she goes*]. I say. Miss—ma'am! Is the drinks cupboard locked?

Maid. No, sir. It's never locked. [*She opens it.*]

Tarde [*to* THÉRÈSE]. I told you! [*With a gracious smile.*] Very many thanks, ma'am.

Maid. Thank you, sir.

Tarde. You're welcome, ma'am. [*The* MAID *goes out.* TARDE *walks purposefully to the cocktail cabinet.*] Mine's a brandy. What about you, girlie?

Thérèse. No, nothing.

Tarde. I'll give you a little armagnac. [*He fills a second glass.*] Flush with the brim, the way you like it! [*He drinks, sinking comfortably into his chair.*] You know, girlie, I've a confession to make. I've been thinking things over. I was wrong to want your young man to play in that shoddy joint of old man Lebonze's, for a paltry hundred or so profit. [*He empties his glass and sets it down.*] There, I'm making a clean breast of it. I'm even wondering whether I won't give him back a part of what he lent me.

Thérèse. You must be out of your mind!

Tarde. No, no. I'm quite sane. [*He pours himself another drink.*] Yes, I'm not sure that I won't give him back part of the money. [*He takes a swallow.*] Mind you, I haven't the slightest doubt that he meant it as a gift. [*A swallow.*] I'm even wondering whether a gesture of that sort wouldn't be the tiniest bit rude. . . . [*The glass is empty.*] A touch more armagnac? [*She does not answer. He pours himself another drink and settles back in his chair.*] In short, there's a lot to be said for and against. However, I'm wondering if I shouldn't make at least a symbolic gesture—a few hundred francs, a thousand maybe. [*He drinks dreamily.*] If it's a symbolic gesture, you might say that five hundred francs would meet the case. [*A pause.*] Four hundred, come to that. [*He takes another swallow.*] On the other hand, I wouldn't for the world have anybody think me mean. . . .

Thérèse. You want to make a symbolic gesture—you of all people? You—afraid of looking mean?

Tarde. Well, there we are.

Thérèse. Who would have thought it? Who would have guessed that deep down all you wanted was respectability!

Tarde. I've always been respectable. It was your mother who rubbed off on me.

Thérèse. Yes, there you are, you, who've had egg on your waistcoat for sixty years, wearing a neat white collar every day! [*She starts forward.*] Where did you pick up that tie? It isn't yours.

Tarde. I did not "pick it up"! Your fiancé gave it to me.

Thérèse. Did you ask him for it?

Tarde [*genuinely indignant*]. What do you take me for? He was wearing it. I merely said it was very smart and pointed out that it had the same purple thread in it as my country suit. Which is perfectly true, you can check up. So then—I don't know what came over him—he burst out laughing, took it off his neck and gave it me. The dear, impulsive fellow . . . ! [*He pulls out a little pocket mirror and arranges his tie, humming gaily.*] Pom . . . pom . . . pom . . . You'd pay a good two thousand francs for a tie like this. [*He tucks away his mirror and continues to smoke nobly.*]

Thérèse [*smiling despite herself*]. How happy you are here!

Tarde. So much so that I daren't even admit it to my-self.

Thérèse. Why not?

Tarde [*humbly*]. I'm afraid you'll send me away. [*He touches wood.*]

Thérèse. And I, would you say I was happy?

Tarde. Oh, you're such a funny girl. It's so hard to tell with you. Aren't you?

Thérèse. Do you think, if I'd come here with the idea of being happy, I'd have insisted on bringing you with me, Father?

Tarde. Why shouldn't you like the joys of family life, just like any other girl, lass?

Thérèse. Don't talk like a fool. You aren't one. Doesn't it strike you as odd that I should bring you here? Don't you ever ask yourself questions, at night, after your last glass of brandy, in your handsome quilted bed?

Tarde. Oh, you know me, I'm not very inquisitive. You want me, here I am. Besides, I fall asleep so soon after my dinner.

Thérèse. Doesn't it seem strange to you that I should encourage you to be vulgar, obscene?

Tarde. Now, now—let's not exaggerate. I wasn't obscene.

Thérèse. Yes, Father, you were. And I wanted to scream —I dug my nails into the palms of my hands so as not to cry.

Tarde. But you should have told me, girlie! You know me. Once I get going, I don't realize——

Thérèse [*her eyes closed*]. No. I wanted you to go even further. I'd have liked you to prance about in your under-wear to make us laugh—to go on drinking until you were sick in front of everybody.

Tarde [*appalled at the very thought*]. Thérèse, you're frightening me! [*Going to her.*] Thérèse, look at me!

Thérèse. Well?

Tarde. What would your young man have said if I'd been sick all over his carpets?

Thérèse. You would have disgusted him so much, and so would I too, probably, that he'd have thrown us both down the front steps.

Tarde. But this is dreadful! You tried to wreck your future marriage—on purpose? But why? Dammit, I am your father, I insist on knowing why! I feel I'm going mad! I've got to understand why!

Thérèse [kindly]. That would really be beyond you, Father.

Tarde [dropping into a chair]. I've given birth to a monster! A monster of pride!

Thérèse. Would you call me especially proud?

Tarde. On your mother's side, they're as spineless as jellyfish. But with the Tarde family, pride is unconquerable! And it's me you take after, girlie.

Thérèse. It would be lucky, Father, if it were only pride.

Tarde. I ask you, what is it, if it isn't pride? Why else should you feel so strongly about a man that you don't love?

Thérèse. But who said I didn't love him?

Tarde. If you did, do you think you'd amuse yourself getting your father drunk so that he'd be disgusted?

Thérèse. It's true though, Father.

Tarde. Oh, no, no, no! I simply won't believe it! I've been in love, too, lass—not your mother—later . . . (you're a big girl now, I can tell you these things). She was a harpist we had in the orchestra for a time. A tall, slender creature she was, and real style with it. Lovely girl. Well, I swear to you nothing so farfetched would ever have entered my head. And yet, in some ways, I'm more passionate than you.

Thérèse [her eyes closed]. And it wouldn't have entered your head to be purposely nasty, purposely coarse? To cling tooth and nail to your right to rebel?

Tarde. Rebel? Good grief, girl, explain yourself! What are you rebelling against? Come along now, girlie, calm down and tell me all about it.

Thérèse. Against him and all that's like him here.

Tarde. All that's like him? What pray?

Thérèse. His house, that looks so bright and welcoming the first day the better to show you that you don't belong in it. Father, I run when I have to cross the drawing room alone! Every chair reproaches me for wanting to install myself here! And all those old ladies in their great gilt frames!

Tarde. Pretty handsome some of them are too, I must say.

Thérèse. And his books! Look, those rows of books that made him what he is, that know him better than I'll ever know him! His books that I don't know at all and can't defend myself against!

Tarde. Well, bless me, it's simple enough! Read them, girlie!

Thérèse [*pitifully*]. I've tried. But they don't speak to me the way they speak to him. He'd have to explain to me, and I don't want that. Oh, but I won't have them think they frighten me! [*She tumbles the books out onto the floor.*] There, that's for the one that makes him melancholy! There, that's for the one that makes him dream! There! There! There! That's for all the ones that make him laugh and not me!

Tarde [*picking them up after her*]. Thérèse, girlie! Thérèse, you're mad! You'll spoil them! Thérèse, stop it now! [*The books are falling faster than he can pick them up. He struggles with an armful of them. THÉRÈSE snatches them out of his hands, and throws them down again.*]

Thérèse. You're not to pick them up! I want him to find them on the floor when he comes in!

Tarde [*drops the last book he was holding and flops into a chair, discouraged*]. Your behavior leaves me speechless, my child. I fail to see how a few harmless books. . . .

Thérèse. Everything here is for him, and against me! [*Pointing at a picture.*] Look, his mother. She's dead and gone, couldn't she have stayed in her frame up there and let me be? But even the dead are in league with him! I know they are!

Tarde. Oh, well of course, if you're going to start invoking the dead . . . !

Thérèse. Have they told you about his mother yet?

Tarde. Delightful woman, I believe, sweet, distinguished, every inch a lady.

Thérèse [*with a dry laugh*]. And can you see me up in a frame like that, all sweetness and distinction? Tell me, Father, can you?

Tarde. Ah, now wait a minute! In the first place, you can't deny that none of your friends are half as ladylike as you. And as for sweetness—well, I wouldn't call you any less sweet than the next girl, really. . . .

Thérèse. Wouldn't you? Do you remember how sweet I was the day you wanted me to be "nice" to old father Lebonze?

Tarde [*rising outraged*]. This is a fine time to rake all that up! Oh, you've really surpassed yourself, you have! Talk about tact! [*He storms up and down the room, furious.*] Anyway, we're artists! Artists can be as eccentric as they like in any company, you ask anybody!

Thérèse. Artists! Why I do believe you really mean that! Have you ever listened to your efforts on the double bass? Have you heard me play the violin? And then have you listened to him play, even with one finger—without its breaking your heart?

Tarde. Ah, now I won't have that. You're a very nice little performer, chick. And as for me, you mustn't forget that I won the bronze medal at the Arcachon Academy of Music. There are quite a few folk we could hold a candle to, you know.

Thérèse [*with a little, hopeless smile*]. Well, we'd better hurry up and find them, hadn't we, and hold our candle to them. Because, with the rest of the world. . . . [*She stops in front of the mother's portrait.*] She can smile away there, in her fine frame. It must be good to come into a house as a real bride, without shame, without defiance—to be clear and gentle—and have people love you. . . .

FLORENT *comes hurrying in, followed by* HARTMANN.

Florent. Darling, do forgive me. Have you had coffee?

Tarde. Oh, yes, thanks very much. And we had a message to say M. Florent said to have the brandy without him. So naturally, we started to have it. . . .

Florent. Good. My dear Monsieur Tarde, you asked if I could lend you a morning coat.

THÉRÈSE *looks up.*

Tarde [*ill at ease*]. Yes, chick. You see, your fiancé told me he had two. So I thought—a wedding only lasts one day after all. Silly to go to all that expense. And a morning coat doesn't need to fit all that well.

Florent. The coat is on your bed. Would you like to go up and try it on?

Tarde. Why, certainly, certainly, my dear son-in-law to be—and thank you, thank you, thank you. [*Everybody is waiting for him to go. He sits down timidly.*] As soon as we've had the liqueurs, I shall be only too delighted to—er. . . .

Florent [*going to the cocktail cabinet*]. What will you have?

Tarde. I was just comparing cognac and armagnac before you came in and I'm bound to say I was in two minds about which I——

Florent. Here's the cognac, and here's the armagnac. [*He puts them into his arms.*] Which is your glass?

Tarde. Oh, any one will do, I'm not fussy.

Florent. There you are. Do you think you could go up to your room right away and have your brandy without us?

Tarde [*rising with dignity*]. And what, may I ask, am I to understand by that?

Florent [*smiling*]. Why, just what I said.

Tarde. This is a sort of dismissal, unless I'm much mistaken?

Florent. In a way, but not for long. And with two full bottles to keep you company.

Tarde [*with a very noble gesture*]. No need to labor the point. I quite understand. [*He takes a step.*] I'm not obliged to stay in my room though, am I? If I get tired of waiting, is it all right to go for a walk?

Florent [*seeing him to the door*]. Of course.

Tarde. In that case—since you were so civil about the suit, would it be agreeable if I asked for the loan of a walking stick? I feel very odd walking without a cane and —in all the rush, I forgot to bring mine.

Florent. You'll find several in the hall. Take whichever one you like. [*He pushes him.*]

Tarde. Well then, if you don't mind, I'll take the one with the gold and ivory knob. That's the one I like the feel of best—that is to say, the—er—look of.

Florent. It's yours. I'll get it for you. [*He goes out.*]

Tarde [*dashing after him and shouting*]. Please don't trouble! Please don't trouble! [FLORENT *has already gone. His voice drops.*] Please don't trouble. . . . Oh, it's too silly, he really shouldn't have troubled. [*He calls timidly through the half-open door.*] Don't bother to look . . . there's no rush. . . .

FLORENT *comes back with another cane.*

Florent. Odd. I could have sworn I'd seen it there yesterday. Would you like this one instead?

Tarde [*waffling*]. I was meaning to tell you . . . I thought you'd say yes . . . it's up in my room. . . .

Florent [*laughing as he pushes him out*]. Splendid! Off you go!

TARDE *goes out.*

Thérèse. What's the matter? Why did you send him away?

Florent. Thérèse, I received an anonymous letter this morning. Do you recognize the style? [*Reading the letter.*] "I take up my pen because there is something important you ought to know about the party to whom you are proposing to give your name."

Thérèse. Well?

Florent. The letter was brought by the waiter from the Station Café, where the sender was waiting to see me. I need hardly tell you that I treated the whole thing as a joke. But I didn't want to give anyone a chance to pester you, so I sent Hartmann along. He found your friend from the orchestra and for reasons best known to himself he's brought her back here. Do you want to see her, or shall I send her away?

Thérèse. I want to see her.

Florent. Very well. I'll fetch her. [*He goes out.*]

HARTMANN *goes to* THÉRÈSE.

Hartmann. I'm afraid I've been rather indiscreet. I met your friend and instead of sending her away as Florent had said, I bought her a drink and asked her one or two questions. [THÉRÈSE *looks at him.*] She didn't say much, but I got the impression that the anonymous letter wasn't her idea. She was sent for by—a certain person. [*He looks at* THÉRÈSE *with a smile, then takes her suddenly by the shoulders.*] My child, are you sure you aren't doing something silly?

Thérèse [*freeing herself*]. I don't know what you mean.

Hartmann. Thérèse my dear, look me in the eye. I'm

not sure what evil genie it is you're grappling with. I can
vaguely guess. No, don't shrug like that. One day you
may realize that I'm the only person in this house who
can talk to you like this. [THÉRÈSE *has broken away from
him. He catches her, takes her by the arms and says gently,
but firmly.*] You love Florent. That is something solid,
something real. Why not forget all this tedious nonsense?

Thérèse. It isn't tedious nonsense.

Hartmann. Yes it is. Listen to me. In this house, every
time you feel pain when you haven't cut your finger—
every time you cry when nothing has hurt you, that will
be a piece of tedious nonsense. You forget you are in the
house of happiness where pain and sorrow have no place.
The owner has held the door open for you. Don't hesitate.
Make haste and come in.

Thérèse. I won't listen to you and your fine talk. What
business is it of yours anyway? Why can't you leave me
in peace?

Hartmann. I'm an old egoist, Thérèse, and I've let a
good few people cut their own throats in my time. But
it looks as though I must care for you a great deal. This
time it seems to me too silly to let you run away from
happiness.

Thérèse [*tearing herself away*]. Happiness! Anyone would
think happiness was the only thing on earth! Yes, I do
want to run away from it! I won't let it swallow me whole!
I have a right to go on suffering and crying with the pain
of it. Extraordinary, isn't it? You can't understand that,
can you?

Hartmann [*quietly*]. How do you know, Thérèse?

FLORENT *comes in with* JEANNETTE.

Florent. Thérèse, here is your friend. We'll leave you
together.

Thérèse. No. Don't go. [*The girls look intensely at
each other.*] Well? Say what you have to say. Go on then,
talk. You sent an anonymous letter. You've something to
say, say it. [JEANNETTE *says nothing.*] You're ashamed to
talk in front of me, is that it? All right, I'll go.

Florent [*restraining her*]. No, Thérèse. I won't listen to
a word unless you're here.

Thérèse. But can't you see she's afraid? She won't talk
if I'm here.

Florent. Then she won't talk at all.

Thérèse. Yes! I want her to tell you what she's come to say. Go on, you, talk! What's the matter, have you lost your tongue?

Jeannette. Talk—talk—what do you mean, talk? What do you want me to do—say what you told me to say or say what you told me not to say?

Florent. What?

Jeannette. I've changed my mind. Get someone else to do your dirty work. I'm going. [*She turns to* FLORENT.] Can somebody drive me back to the station?

Thérèse. Oh, no, you don't! You came here to say something, my girl, and say it you will!

Jeannette. Thérèse, you're mad! Let me go!

Florent. I think we ought to let her leave, Thérèse.

Thérèse. No, I want her to speak. I want her to say the dirty thing she's brought with her. Look at her, with her flashy clothes and her cheap jewelry. She doesn't even need to say anything. She's brought her wretched little bit of filth in here, along with her cheap scent and the fag end in the corner of her mouth! Come on, Jeannette, come on, my old girl friend, talk! Talk, can't you? [*She shakes her.*] For God's sake, what are you waiting for? That's what you came for, isn't it? You're scared!

Jeannette. No, but if you want to know, it makes me sick. I don't want to look like what I'm not. [*She turns abruptly to* FLORENT.] I don't say I wasn't envious of her luck, as who wouldn't be? But as for coming and throwing muck all over everything, that's not my way. It was she wrote and asked me to come.

Thérèse. Fool! Fool!

Jeannette. I was to get my train fare and an extra ten thousand francs.

A *pause.* FLORENT *turns to* THÉRÈSE.

Florent. Why did you send for this girl? What did you want her to tell me? [THÉRÈSE *says nothing. He turns to* JEANNETTE *and takes her by the arm.*] What was it you had to say to me?

Jeannette [*freeing herself*]. All right! There's no need to break my arm! I'll tell you and glad to, since you're that keen to know. She wrote and asked me to come and tell you she had been Gosta's mistress.

Florent. Gosta. . . .

Jeannette. Yes, her mother's lover. Sorry it isn't more exciting!

Florent [*to* THÉRÈSE]. But this is insane! Why did you want to make me believe that?

Thérèse. Did you hear? Did you hear? Sorry it isn't more exciting, she says! There's no point now that you know I sent for her. But I made her say it just the same so that you would hear those words ringing in here, so that your mother should hear them in her gold frame— and your old gardener whom I loathe and your prim old housemaids and your books too, your foul, foul books!

Jeannette [*picking one up*]. Talking of books, you've quite an overflow, haven't you?

FLORENT *sees all the books on the floor, and looks at* THÉRÈSE.

Thérèse. I threw them on the floor.

Florent. Why?

Thérèse. No reason.

Florent [*taking her by the shoulders*]. Thérèse, I want you to tell me why.

Thérèse. Go on, dig your great hands into me, I shan't tell you why! I wanted you to know what I'd have tried to make you believe if that fool hadn't made such a mess of it. I want you to know that I threw your books about, that I brought my father here and let you give him money and got him drunk and made him sing his dirty songs— on purpose! But why I did those things, why I hate you all, that I'll never tell you, because you hadn't the wit to find out for yourself!

Florent [*stunned*]. But . . . Thérèse, I can't believe it . . . only an hour ago we were so happy!

Thérèse. You were happy, not me.

Florent. You're trembling!

Thérèse. Yes, I'm trembling. I'm trembling at being the only one here who can't smile, the only one who's poor and dirty and ashamed! [*She flings herself down on the settee. He looks at her helplessly, not daring to go near her.*]

Hartmann [*taking* JEANNETTE *aside*]. Come with me, I told the taxi to wait.

Jeannette. No. I'm not leaving without talking to Thérèse in private. I don't mind coming on a four-hour train journey and being made to look a damn fool at the end of it, but I don't intend to be out of pocket into the bargain.

Hartmann. I have full authority to settle that side of the matter.

Jeannette. Have you? That's different. [*Turning to her.*] Good-by, Thérèse—and act sensible, girl, I should. You've got yourself a good place here, keep it. [*To* HARTMANN *as she goes out.*] If I were in her shoes . . . !

Hartmann. Ah, but then you aren't.

They go out. THÉRÈSE *is on the sofa, her head buried in the cushions.* FLORENT *stands beside her.*

Florent [*murmuring*]. You were unhappy, my darling, and I never guessed. My little silly, trying to make me believe she was her mother's lover's mistress! What a complicated thing to think of! Her mother's lover's mistress! It seems to me that if I had been a little goose who was set on pretending to be as black as pitch, I still think I should have thought of something less farfetched.

She lifts her head, looks at him, opens her mouth to speak, then drops wearily back again.

[*Sitting beside her.*] Do you think I'm going to let a single sorrow live in you? [*He raises her and holds her facing him. She turns her head away.*] Don't I look stronger than all the heartache in the world? Look into my eyes. [*She has not moved. He shakes her, tries to see her face.*] Now, what was it you said about my house? You feel poor in it, do you? You feel alone? My foul books. Why foul? It's by reading these books that I learned to wait for you and love you ever since I was nineteen years old. When you get to know them, you'll love them too. [*He picks them up.*] Come, let's tidy the place up a bit. All this bad feeling because you don't know each other very well. I'll introduce you. Give me your hand. [*He tries to lift her to her feet, but she clings to the settee.*] Won't you stand up? It's not very polite to shake hands sitting down. Still, I'm sure the house will excuse you. These old country places are very easygoing. [*He begins, half laughing, half moved, as if he were talking to a child, while he sits stroking her hair.*] Well now, you trees, and old paneled walls, and armchairs, I must ask you to excuse this young lady, who is a tiny bit sad still because she hasn't learned how to make friends with you. You're a bit pleased with yourselves, anyway,

all of you. You should have taken more care not to frighten
her. You chairs over there, you should have told her you
weren't as fearsome as all that, in spite of your grand airs,
and anyway, you've none of you any style to boast of. You,
grandfathers and great uncles, why did you look so superior? You none of you set the world on fire when you were
in it. And as for you, Mother, I'm surprised at you. She
was unhappy, and you never said a word to her! Why
couldn't you sing her the lullaby you used to sing to me
when I was small and couldn't sleep?

Suddenly THÉRÈSE *begins to sing, in a voice harsh with
tears, her face hidden in the sofa cushions.*

  Thérèse. Someone's lost her ocarino
            Poor Nana
            Nana's lost her nono
            With his ocarino
            Nono's lost his nana with his ocarino.
[*She stops, choked by a sob.*]
  Florent. What were you singing?
  Thérèse [*her head in her arms*]. That's the song *my*
mother used to sing to me!
  Florent. Thérèse! [*He lifts her forcibly to her feet. Her
face is bathed in tears. She reels slightly—he shakes her,
and cries, frightened.*] Thérèse, look at me! Thérèse, you're
crying. I thought this was only a little girl's tantrum, like
the other day, because they all thought you were marrying
me for my money. Thérèse, it isn't only that, is it?
  Thérèse [*softly*]. Listen. You will have to let me go. [*He
is about to speak, but she stops him with a gesture.*] You
see, I'm not shouting. I'm not making a scene. You are
going to have to let me go.
  Florent. Thérèse, you're mad!
  Thérèse [*backing away as if she were afraid of him*].
Don't touch me.
  Florent. I want to take you in my arms. I must hold you
close to me, now, and make you well again.
  Thérèse. No. Everything hurts too much now. You don't
know how it feels, you'll never know. It seethes and swells
and bursts inside. . . . You must let me go away, without
scenes, without tears, while I still can. Please. I'm asking
you. Because if I stayed a little longer, I'd go mad. . . .
  Florent. At least tell me when it was I hurt you, if you
don't want me to go mad too.

Thérèse [*with a helpless gesture, like a little girl*]. I can't.

Florent. You must. I won't let you leave this room until you do.

Thérèse [*shaking her head*]. No, please. Let me go. [*She looks squarely at him and adds in a hard voice.*] If you love me.

Florent [*calm and sure of himself*]. I shan't let you go because I love you and because you love me, I know you do. I don't know what pride or evil spite it is that's twisting your face at this moment. But I do know that they are only weeds growing inside you and not the real you at all. Struggle as you may, I'll pull those weeds out one by one.

Thérèse [*crying out suddenly*]. For pity's sake, can't you be quiet! I'm ashamed, I'm ashamed of being like this, but I always will be. Can't you leave me alone, all of you! [*She sinks into an armchair, trembling.*]

Florent. I'm going to hurt you. Forgive me, darling, but I must save you from yourself. Something is driving you away just now from this house and from me. But I know that something just as strong is keeping you here too. You're weeping and you're trembling because those two forces are at war in you. So don't think I'm going to stand by and do nothing. I told you once that I liked fighting. Look at me and speak if you dare. After that I may let you go. [*He forces her head up. She looks at him, panting.*] Look at me. You can feel, can't you, that I'm stronger than you and all the pain in you?

Her head is pressed back against the chair. Fearfully she looks into those clear eyes, which are searching her own. She is about to yield when her father comes in. He is wearing morning dress and a silk hat.

Tarde. I know you said not to come in, but I couldn't resist it. What do you think of your father now, eh, girlie?

Florent [*striding over to him*]. Will you get out of here?

THÉRÈSE *runs to her father and clings to his arm.*

Thérèse. No, Father! Stay here! I need you!

Florent. Thérèse, let go of him.

Thérèse. No, I shan't, I shan't! Oh I'm so glad you came down, Father! I'm saved now! You're here! You're here!

Florent [*shaking his other arm*]. Will you clear out!

Thérèse. Father, stay where you are!

Tarde. Well, but girlie, I'm beginning to wonder if I'm not rather "de trop."

Florent. Yes, you certainly are! Get out!

Thérèse. No. Father! I need you! [*She puts her arms round him.*] Father, dear little Father! Oh I'm glad, glad that you're so scruffy and ridiculous, and vulgar!

Tarde. Hey, hey, hey, girlie! I know you're joking, but even so, I'm your father, don't you forget that!

Thérèse [*with a sort of horrible joy*]. Oh, I'm not forgetting it! I'm your daughter, all right! I'm the daughter of the little gent with the black nails and the dandruff on his collar; the little gent who talks so grand, but who tried to sell me, here there and everywhere, as soon as I was of an age for men to fancy me!

Tarde [*with dignity*]. What are you talking about? I simply do not understand. [*To* FLORENT.] She doesn't know what she's saying.

Thérèse. Oh, no, I'm not forgetting you're my father! I'm not forgetting any of the sordid secrets that tie me to you more surely than if I loved you! Oh, we make a good pair, Father! We don't need to blush for each other, we're the same breed, aren't we, you and I?

Tarde. Of course, child, of course. [*To* FLORENT.] I don't know what's got into her, I don't really.

Thérèse [*to* FLORENT]. Have you nothing to say now? You can feel, can't you, that I'm a long way away now, that I'm clinging to him! Oh, you'd pulled me over to your side, you know, with that great strength of yours. But I've escaped you. You'll never reach me now.

Florent. No, Thérèse, you're struggling to get away but you haven't escaped me.

Thérèse. Yes, now that I've lost all hope I have escaped you, Florent. I'm in a country now where you've never set foot, and you would never know the way to follow me and bring me back. Because you don't know what it's like to feel the ground give way under you. You don't know what it's like to fight for air and flounder in the mud and sink. You know nothing about anything that's human, Florent. [*She looks at him.*] You never had a real pain—a hurt that's as shameful as an oozing, secret wound. You never hated anyone, one can tell from your eyes—even those who've done you harm.

Florent. No, Thérèse. But I can teach you how not to hate either, I know I can.

Thérèse. How sure of yourself you are.

Florent. Yes. And I'm sure I can make you happy too.

Thérèse. How strong you are.

Florent. Yes.

Thérèse. You've never been ashamed or poor. I've gone miles out of my way so as not to go up some steps because I had holes in my stockings. I've run dirty errands for people and I was a big girl and I smiled and said thank you for the tip and bit back my shame at it. Did you never run errands, Florent—did you never break the bottle of wine and linger in the dark hallway, not daring to go up the stairs again?

Tarde. Must you relate all that silly rubbish!

Thérèse. Yes, Father, I must.

Florent. No, I've never been poor, Thérèse, but that isn't my fault.

Thérèse. Nothing is your fault! You've never been ill, either, I'm sure. I've had ringworm and scabies and nits —all the diseases of the poor. The teacher used to part my hair with a ruler when she'd noticed it.

Tarde [*outraged*]. Nits, I ask you!

Florent [*shaking his head*]. I'll fight, Thérèse, and I'll be stronger than everything that poverty did to you.

Thérèse [*with a mirthless laugh*]. Did you hear that. He'll fight! You fight blithely against other people's suffering because you don't know that it drops on you like a cloak that sticks to your skin. If you'd ever been weak or cowardly, you would take infinite precautions before you touched that bleeding cloak. You must take great care not to hurt the feelings of the poor. [*She takes her father's hand.*] Come, Father. Put on your topper and let's go. [*Turning to face* FLORENT.] Let us pass, please.

Florent [*barring the way*]. No, Thérèse.

Thérèse [*shivering as she looks into his eyes*]. "She is adorable." I heard you saying that to Hartmann. You didn't expect this, did you? This hatred that plows up my face, this shrill voice, these squalid details. I must be as hideous as poverty just now. You're as white as a sheet. The conquered are frightening, aren't they?

Florent. Why do you use such silly words? You aren't conquered. And the last thing I could ever be is a conqueror.

Thérèse. You are a rich man. That's worse. A conqueror who never fought a battle.

Florent. But you can't go on forever blaming me for my money! What do you expect me to do with it?

Thérèse. Oh, nothing, Florent. You could throw it all to the winds, laughing, the way you did the other day, but my pain wouldn't vanish with it. You aren't only rich in money, you see, you're rich in the house where you grew up, rich in your life's deep peace and the age-old tranquillity of your forefathers. You are rich in your joy of living, that never had to attack or to defend itself, and in your talent too. You see, there really are too many things to be thrown overboard. And you mustn't think that you're a monster. You've tortured me, but you're kind, you know, and it isn't your fault, because you know nothing. [*She looks at him for a second, then suddenly anger floods her. She advances on him.*] You know nothing! That's what hurts the most! It's your privilege to know nothing! Oh, I feel heavy tonight with all the pain that must have seared the hearts of the poor when they found out that rich people knew nothing, and that there was no hope that one day they'd find out. But tonight, you will know, you'll know about me if nothing else! Go on, Father, you tell him, if you have the courage! Tell him all the shabby little details he can never have known and which have given me this sorry knowledge, I who am younger than he. . . . Go on, tell him! Tell him about when I was eleven, and that dear old gentleman who was so kind——

Tarde. She's mad! He was a friend of the family! She doesn't know what she's saying!

Thérèse. Tell him about all the times when Mother came home drunk and sick and I had to undress her and put her to bed!

Tarde. Stop it, for mercy's sake!

Thérèse. And he wanted me to love his mother, did I tell you? He wanted me to shed tears over this gracious lady here, with her lullabies and her rose garden. But that's not all! Tell him some more, so we'll make a really graceful exit. Tell him it wasn't so farfetched what I wanted Jeannette to tell him about this afternoon. Tell him that Mother nagged me often enough to give in to Gosta so she wouldn't lose him!

Tarde [*sincerely*]. Oh, no, that I should never have stood for!

Thérèse. Tell him that at fourteen I had a lover!

Tarde. I forbid you to say any more! Don't listen to her!

Thérèse [*pushing past him*]. I had a lover at fourteen, do you hear? A boy I didn't even know! He took me and I let him have his way, without love—and not from viciousness either, from a sort of apathy, a resignation you could never understand. I only saw him once. I became pregnant. When I found out, he'd been gone a long time. I got rid of it myself, alone in my room.

Tarde. Girlie!

Thérèse. All alone. And I lay bleeding on the floor . . .

Tarde. I forbid you. . . .

Thérèse. . . . and bit everything in sight so that I shouldn't scream! There. I never told it to a living soul. And now it's out. Now I'll never have the courage to look you in the face again. [*She flings herself down exhausted, and hides her head in her arms.*]

Tarde [*exploding, sincerely outraged*]. This time you've gone too far! I'm an old scoundrel and life hasn't always been too easy. And I've often let myself sink lower than you'd believe. But to talk about it, for all the world to hear, to be proud of it almost, never—never, do you hear me?—never would your father have done that!

A pause.

Florent [*in a strange voice*]. What do you want me to do, Thérèse?

Thérèse. Let me go without looking at me, if you still love me a little. [*She gets up and goes to the door without looking round.*] Come, Father.

Tarde [*as he goes*]. I must ask you once again to excuse this outburst, which offends and humiliates me and for which I am not responsible. After all, speaking man to man—one does a lot of things, but to shout them from the rooftops!—no, there I draw the line! [*He bows and goes out after* THÉRÈSE.]

HARTMANN *comes hurrying in.*

Hartmann. What happened? I've just met her running up to her room!

Florent [*quietly*]. She's lost.

Hartmann. You must do something, Florent!

Florent. I don't know what to do. I feel so **helpless,** Hartmann.

Hartmann. You, helpless? What in the world can she have said to you?

Florent. I don't understand her. She blames me for never having been poor, for not knowing how to hate or be unhappy. She's ashamed of her father and she brings him here on purpose! She's ashamed of her past life and she sends for that girl to tell this dirty lie!

Hartmann. Do you remember what I told you the night I met her? I said how lucky you were that she wasn't a hard, demanding, tormented sort of girl.

Florent. Why, do you think I haven't enough love in me to give a girl like that?

Hartmann. You are like all very rich folk, Florent, who never have enough small change to give to beggars. You said once that one can never be too lucky. You've just had proof that one can. You are like the kings of old. You have been given, in profusion, and for nothing, what the rest of us have to pay very dearly for. So resign yourself, like royalty, to being a little bit of an outsider on this earth.

Florent. But I love her, Hartmann.

Hartmann. That's where you broke the rules. Kings must never love anything but their delight.

Florent. It isn't only that. We don't understand her, Hartmann. That can't be the only thing that has hurt her so much.

Hartmann [*quietly*]. Yes, Florent, it is. You can believe me. I who really know her.

FLORENT *looks up and meets his eye. Instinctively, he steps back.*

Florent. What are you trying to say to me?

Hartmann. When I met you I was an old man trying, with fumbling fingers, to wrest harmonies out of unresponding matter—a man lost in the hopeless quest for those celestial voices which you had already found, unaided, on the day you were born. [*A pause. He smiles.*] I didn't weep, I didn't scream in protest—I wasn't your sweetheart. But it had something of the same effect on me. I hated you.

Florent [*haltingly*]. But what have you all got against me? I can't help it.

Hartmann [*picking up his unlit pipe*]. No. You can't help it. And now I'm only an old businessman who knows the exact measure of his musical potentialities and who is very fond of you. [*He knocks out his pipe to hide his emotion.*] It's funny, I never thought I should ever tell you that. But at least let it help you not to leave her upstairs, packing her shabby little suitcase, and sinking, deeper and deeper, all alone.

Florent. I'm afraid of seeing her look at me the way she did just now. In five minutes I know it will be too late. But what am I to do? Tell me. Tell me what to do. . . . [HARTMANN *looks away evasively.* FLORENT *turns to him, his face ravaged with grief, and murmurs.*] Oh, God, help me.

Hartmann. That may be the answer. To suffer and need help, if you know how to learn. [*He has moved to the doorway. He bumps into* THÉRÈSE, *who is wearing her outdoor clothes.*]

Thérèse [*in a small, level voice. She goes to* FLORENT]. Good-by, Florent. [*She holds out her hand.*] I didn't want to slink away like a coward. I can still look you in the face, you see. Don't keep too sad a memory of me.

Florent [*mutters, without moving*]. Good-by, Thérèse. Forgive me. I didn't know. . . .

A pause. She looks at him.

Thérèse [*quietly*]. Why, you're crying. [*He does not answer.*] You know how to cry, then?

Florent [*mechanically wiping his cheek*]. Am I? I'm sorry.

THÉRÈSE *looks at him for a little while.*

Thérèse. So you aren't always sure of yourself, sure of the happiness you spread, sure that all the policemen in heaven and on earth are on your side?

Florent. I feel as ignorant and helpless as a father whose child is dying of an unknown illness. You're in pain, and it's my love that hurts you. You're in pain, and my love can't make you well again. You talked of sufferings that I could never know. Can you imagine this one?

Thérèse [*gently*]. If only you could try, just once, to be like everybody else—cowardly, petty, selfish, mean. Just once—couldn't you?

Florent. I can't.

Thérèse. If you could try, instead of succeeding always, in everything you do, to carve out your niche painfully like other people, making a mess of it, and starting again

—with sweat and pain and shame. If you could try, I might perhaps be set free?

Florent. I can't. It isn't easy, you know, to unlearn how to be happy. Before, I did feel sometimes that I was more privileged than other men, that I should never have to pay for anything with a tear or a cry. It suited me. Tonight, I've come to see that suffering too is a privilege that isn't given to all.

Thérèse [*weeping for joy*]. Oh, my dearest, you're unsure too! You're ashamed, you're unhappy. Why, then you aren't one of the truly rich! [*She picks a tear from* FLORENT's *face.*] There. Look at it, all shining on my finger tip. What do I care about anything else now that you've paid me with a tear. Oh, why didn't you cry out and tell me you were weeping so I should feel less lonely!

Florent. I was afraid you wouldn't understand.

Thérèse. Honestly? So you need to be understood—you need to be helped, then, too? And I was going away like a fool, without knowing it! [*She throws herself into his arms.*] Oh, need me, need me, if only for your meals and for your walks, the way a child does, if you don't need me like a man! Need me so that I shan't suffer too much!

Florent. I need you.

Thérèse. That was another thing that hurt. You have so many things around you that watch over you and clothe you and keep you warm.

Florent. I need you, Thérèse.

Thérèse. More than all your other joys?

Florent. More than all my other joys.

Thérèse [*smiling*]. Then call them back quickly! They don't scare me now! [*Hiding her head on his breast.*] I lied, you know—I love you. I love you as you are. Don't try to be like other people. I don't care any more about not having friends or a family, or a home. Ask your sister and your aunt to come here. I know I shall love them. I'm clear, I'm crystal clear too and rich! You are my home and my family and the air I breathe and the sun that keeps me warm.

TARDE *comes in, carrying his overcoat and his two decrepit suitcases.*

Tarde. As God is my judge, I never wanted this. It broke my heart to shut these two bags.

Thérèse. Father! I'm happy! I'm happy, happy, happy, Father!

Tarde. Good God! After a shindy like that I'd like to know how you can manage to be happy!

Thérèse. I'm happy because you're going away, Father, with your two battered suitcases—and because I'm free of you at last!

Tarde. Going away? Where to?

Thérèse. Anywhere you like, Father! The farther away the better!

Tarde [*pitifully*]. But I'll come back for the wedding, won't I?

Thérèse [*ringingly*]. No, Father!

Tarde. But I say, girlie—your old dad . . . !

Thérèse [*pitiless*]. No, Father.

Tarde. Well. . . . You'll be staying, will you?

Thérèse. Yes, I'm staying! And I'm strong and I'm proud and I'm young and I have all my life ahead of me in which to be happy!

She is in FLORENT'S *arms, transfigured.* TARDE *has pathetically picked up his two suitcases.*

Curtain.

ACT THREE

Same set. Evening, but it is still fairly light outside. The sound of the piano is heard from time to time. THÉRÈSE *is standing in the middle of the room, being fitted for her wedding dress. The two workgirls are on their knees beside her.* MME. BAZIN, *Florent's aunt, a sweet old lady in lace and ribbons and brooches, is sitting knitting on the veranda upstage.*

HARTMANN *is sitting in a far corner of the room, smoking his pipe. Outside, on the terrace behind* MME. BAZIN, *three servants, among them the little* SCULLERY MAID, *are staring wide-eyed at* THÉRÈSE.

MME. BAZIN [*to the servants*]. Now, be off with you. You've seen enough for one evening. You can gaze your fill on the day of the wedding.

Head Housemaid [*to the* SCULLERY MAID *who is still standing entranced*]. Come along, you! Don't stand there, gawping! You shouldn't be here in the first place. You know you're not allowed into the master's garden. Now then, back to your kitchen and look sharp about it. [*To* MME. BAZIN.] I do apologize, madame. She followed me in without my noticing.

Mme. Bazin. I can't understand it. She always knew her place before.

Maid. Madame is right. I don't know what's got into her lately. She's always nosing about where she shouldn't. I'm very sorry, madame, I'll see it doesn't occur again. [*She goes.*]

Mme. Bazin. The evenings are drawing in already.

A pause.

Fitter [*to the girls*]. Spread the train right out. [*To* THÉRÈSE.] We can see the whole effect so much better down here than in your room, mademoiselle. Now, we must hurry if we don't want to miss the express.

Marie [*yawning*]. You've been at it for hours! I wanted to teach you to play tennis. I do think it's eccentric of you not to play.

Thérèse. Yes.

Marie. If only there were a river anywhere near. I'm simply dying to get on to the water again. I haven't done any rowing since I left England in May.

Another pause.

Fitter. Give me those pins.

Marie. Have you ever been to England?

Thérèse. No.

Marie. I've just spent three years there. I went to an absolutely marvelous school. You can't imagine how different it is! What a shame your parents didn't send you there. There's nothing like it for teaching a girl about life.

Thérèse [*gently*]. There are one or two other ways, you know.

Marie. Oh, of course. But in France we're so strictly brought up, we're dumbbells until the day we get married. There is one way, of course, if your parents aren't too old-fashioned—and that's to go out to work. But that's easier said than done.

Fitter. Mademoiselle is unfortunately right. Another fifty girls were dismissed this season from M. Lapérouse's.

Marie. Oh, it isn't that so much. With a little influence one can always get some sort of job. I meant family objections. There are still some parents who look on work as degrading for a girl. I can't think why! I think working is absolutely marvelous, don't you?

Thérèse [*with a faint smile*]. It depends. One should always work at something one likes very much, like Florent.

Marie. Oh, no, artists don't count! I meant proper work. A well-paid job in a bank, say, or an insurance company.

Mme. Bazin. Well, all my life I've never stopped working—knitting, tapestry, crochet work or whatever it happened to be—and I must say, I've thrived on it. It's funny, but I'm not happy unless I'm doing something. Now, I pay two gardeners, but do you know, I often cut my own flowers of a morning.

Marie. The main thing about working, though, is that it gives a girl complete independence.

Thérèse. You do a lot of clock watching, you know, in an office or a workroom.

Fitter. Mademoiselle is so right! M. Lapérouse has quite a novel way of solving that problem. He's had all the clocks in the establishment removed and none of the girls is allowed to wear a watch.

Thérèse [*lifting the chin of the little workgirl kneeling at her feet*]. Tell her that one doesn't have fun every day of the week at Lapérouse's

Fitter. Oh, I can assure you, all our girls are very contented with their lot, mademoiselle—very contented indeed!

Thérèse [*smiling gently at the little workgirl*]. I'm sure they are.

Mme. Bazin. When I was a girl, seamstresses used to work sixteen hours a day. They were worse off than they are now, of course, but on the other hand, one felt much more inclined to give them things. Many's the dress I've given to the women who used to come and work at home, and very good, wearable dresses they were too. Nowadays, it wouldn't occur to one. The working classes are better off than we are these days.

Marie. Darling Thérèse! You really are terribly old-fashioned! I suppose you think a young lady's place is in the home! Didn't it ever bore you, sitting at home all day?

Thérèse [*smiling*]. Oh, mine was rather an unusual home, you know.

Mme. Bazin. You're quite right, Thérèse. Stand up to her. Marie's nothing but a little socialist!

Marie. Of course I am! I think every girl should go out to work. It's good for the soul. One must move with the times, Aunt Caroline!

Mme. Bazin. That's what we used to say in my day too. But that was mostly so Mamma would let us ride a bicycle.

Marie. But those days are over! The upper classes aren't the salt of the earth now. All men were created equal, and man's lot is to earn his bread by the sweat of his brow!

Fitter. I'm inclined to agree. The modern girl should earn her own living. Unfortunately, far too few of them have given the matter sufficient thought.

Thérèse [*to the girl*]. I hope you gave the matter sufficient thought before you went to work at M. Lapérouse's?

Fitter [*with a polite little laugh*]. Mademoiselle will have her little joke. . . . Besides, I quite see that in your case our little controversy doesn't apply. A married lady has a house to run, social engagements to fulfill. But in Mademoiselle France's circumstances, I do definitely think a young lady should have a job. As a matter of fact, M. Lapérouse has made a special study of outfits exclusively for the working girl. He is bringing out two models this season, one of sea-green broadcloth trimmed with mink, called "Forty Hour Week," and the other, rather more formal in heavy midnight blue faille, worn with just the one, utterly simple diamond clip, which he has christened "Miss Trade Unionist."

Mme. Bazin. Odd how the language changes. In my day trade unionists were people who blew up railway trains.

Fitter. Because of course, it *is* quite a problem. The young lady who goes out to work in the afternoon simply hasn't time to change for the odd cocktail party or informal dinner. The problem was to create a model which would be equally suitable for office, restaurant, cinema— or, at a pinch, one of the smaller theaters. I'm sure M. Lapérouse would be delighted to send someone along with the two models, should you proceed with your plans.

Marie. Thank you. But I don't aim to start work before

next season. During the summer months, with invitations literally flooding in, it really can't be managed. In October, if he has anything interesting, I'll be glad to have a look at it.

Fitter. I'll tell M. Lapérouse. Leontine—take that thread out, will you? [*To* Thérèse.] Would you like a rest, mademoiselle?

Thérèse. No.

Fitter. We've nearly finished, one has to be so careful of the hem, it is so very tricky. [*To* Marie.] I do hope your decision doesn't mean that you will give up the idea of that delicious little skiing outfit I was telling you about.

Marie. Oh, I shall still take a month's holiday in January. I don't believe in being too rigid.

Fitter. I'm so glad! It would break my heart to see anybody else wear it! It might have been designed for you!

Marie. Another advantage of having a job is that I can pay for it myself. There won't be any recriminations over what I spend this time. I shall pay my hotel bills and buy my clothes out of my own money.

Fitter. That is the working girl's great strength.

Marie. Of course! Shopgirls and typists envy us but they don't know their luck. Think of the freedom your own money gives you, money you've actually earned yourself! If they only knew the cheese paring that goes on in the best French families!

Thérèse [*to the girl*]. You see, I bet you never guessed how lucky you were.

Marie. But it's obvious! Look, I know a girl who's been working as a secretary in a bank for the last year. I've never been allowed to have my own car. She's just bought herself a little two-seater!

Thérèse. And she's a secretary? She must have a wonderful job.

Marie. Well, to tell the truth, her father is paying half.

Thérèse. Ah, I see.

Marie. She and a girl friend are going on a motor tour through Italy and Greece.

Thérèse. But what about the bank? Will she have a long enough holiday?

Marie. Of course. It's her uncle's bank.

Thérèse. Ah, that's all right, then.

Mme. Bazin. I don't care what you say, dear, I just don't see the fun of working for other people. I simply don't understand how any self-respecting person can take orders from strangers. I've been my own mistress all my life and very proud of it I am too!

Fitter. There. If you could bear to wait five minutes, mademoiselle, we must just put the finishing touches to the little jacket. Then you can see the whole effect. Come along, you two. We must hurry if we want to catch that train.

She makes for the door, followed by her two girls. THÉRÈSE *runs after the little workgirl and takes hold of her arm.*

Thérèse. Wait a minute. . . . [*To the* FITTER.] Do you mind? I should like a word with this child.

Fitter. Certainly, mademoiselle. Leontine, join us in the linen room, will you? [*She goes.*]

Thérèse [*drawing the girl into a corner*]. Leontine—that is your name, isn't it?

Girl. Yes.

Thérèse. How old are you?

Girl. Fourteen. I'm small for my age. There are five of us at home. I'm the smallest.

Thérèse. I'm making you work late tonight, for my dress.

Girl. It won't be the first time, don't you worry. This time it's rather fun, coming out into the country.

Thérèse. Listen, Leontine—I only wanted to say . . . I know it isn't true what they were saying. It's tiring, having to work, and it's dull and it goes on day in day out. So . . . I don't quite know how to say this—I expect you'll think it's silly. That dress costs so much, and I'll only wear it once. A whole year of your wages at Lapérouse. Listen . . . [*She leans over and whispers.*] Leontine, forgive me for the dress. [*She pushes her out.*] Run along now, quick. And don't look at me like that! It's nothing to laugh at. . . .

The girl runs out. MME. BAZIN *peers at her over her spectacles.*

Mme. Bazin. It's frightening, how thin those little things are. But there, what can you expect? I've seen them in Paris, lunching off coffee and a roll. They would rather buy a lipstick than a good thick steak. Most foolish. I'm old now and I have to watch my diet, but when I was young, I couldn't for the life of me have gone without red meat.

THÉRÈSE *turns abruptly as if to say something. She meets* HARTMANN'S *eye, as he sits smiling behind his pipe. She stops and smiles too.*

[*Gathering up her things*]. There. That's done. It takes me weeks to make these woollies. I was never a very good knitter. I keep dropping stitches, oh dear! But the poor are so grateful when they know that one has knitted them oneself! [*To* MARIE.] All this talk about earning your own pocket money! You know perfectly well that if you would knit for my slum comforts fund I would give you three thousand francs for each woolly. [MARIE *shrugs. This is evidently an old argument.*] Ah, these modern girls don't bother their heads about charity the way we old ones do. We were brought up to worry a great deal about the poor. But they? All they think of is clothes and motor cars. [*She gets up.*] I'm going to look at those new rose trees before it gets quite dark. I don't trust that gardener of Florent's. They need constant attention. You'll call me in when they bring the jacket, Thérèse, won't you? [*To* MARIE.] Will you keep me company, child?

Marie [*rising*]. If you like, aunt.

Mme. Bazin [*leaning on her shoulder as she goes out*]. Those poor wretches are always so short of winter woollies. If you'd agree to join my knitting party, I'd have given you as much as four thousand francs a garment. You'll never earn as much as that in a bank.

They go.

Hartmann [*smiling*]. H'm. I think we came very near to a little righteous intervention then, eh?

Thérèse [*smiling too*]. I don't mind for myself any more. Only I was ashamed, because of that little girl. I'm a fool.

Hartmann. You're never a fool, Thérèse.

A pause. They listen. FLORENT *is heard playing next door.*

Thérèse [*murmuring, with a smile full of tenderness*]. How well he plays. . . . He's happy, isn't he? I *am* trying.

Hartmann. Yes, he's happy.

Thérèse. I want to believe in him, Hartmann. I want to believe in them. I want to understand. Before, I never even tried. I used to say, I'm too young. I'll understand when I'm old. I wanted to rebel with all my might. Now. . . .

Hartmann. Now?

Thérèse [*smiling*]. I'm trying. [*A pause.*] But why are they so charming, so open, and yet so heartless without knowing it? I try, often, to chat with Marie. We're the same age. It's funny, we have nothing to say to each other. M. Bazin gives me little talks about life, sometimes. I feel like an old woman beside her. I'm the one who's chary of teaching her too much.

Hartmann [*taking her hand*]. How calmly you say that now.

Thérèse [*smiling*]. I've stormed so much. . . . Oh, those six days, those six horrible days! Sometimes, it was as if a great horse were rearing up inside me. [*A pause. She says dreamily.*] He's run away. He's a long, long way off now. I mustn't be sorry he's gone. He was an evil beast.

Hartmann. Don't say that, Thérèse. He was a good horse, noble and black and proud. Letting him go was the price you paid for your happiness. That damned happiness he fought so shy of, do you remember? I'm sure it has begun to wrap itself around you, hasn't it—that damned happiness?

Thérèse. It's true. I need their warmth now that they've taken away my own. But what a strange game it is, that happiness of theirs.

Hartmann. You must learn to play your part in it, Thérèse.

Thérèse. I am learning. Already I feel bathed in ease and sweetness. I feel less hard. Less pure too. I can feel quietude making its steady inroads in me day by day. I don't seek into the heart of things any more. I understand, I explain, I make few demands . . . I'm growing less vulnerable too, I'm sure. Soon, all the little tongues of pain in me will have slithered away like lizards under stones, and I'll have nothing but small birdlike sorrows, just like them.

Hartmann. Soon? Aren't they all gone yet?

Thérèse [*still smiling*]. Hush! Listen. . . . How easy everything is when he plays. Every note sets something back into its ideal place. Oh, it's a wonderful feat of organization, that happiness of theirs! Evil becomes a wicked angel you grapple gaily with for practice and which you always crush. Poverty, a chance to prove your goodness by being charitable. Work a pleasant pastime for the leisurely. And love . . . this smooth delight, without fears, or doubts, or heartache. Listen to the way he plays, Hartmann, without asking himself anything, ever. I am only one joy among his other joys. As soon as he thought he'd shut me up inside his happiness—having shed his little tear—he never felt another pang of doubt about any mortal thing. He is as sure of me as he is of everything. [*She adds in a murmur.*] I who am so unsure.

Hartmann. He loves you, Thérèse.

Thérèse. I want to believe it, Hartmann, I do, I do! But that tear he shed for my sake—oh, I wish I could have kept it in a little box. It dried and now I've nothing.

Hartmann. You have your anxiety and your love. . . . That's the best part.

Thérèse. Hartmann, he doesn't even need my love, he's much too rich. . . . [*She stiffens suddenly.*] Oh, but I'm not tamed yet! There are still some things that I refuse to understand!

She stops short. The little SCULLERY MAID *is creeping along the terrace, gazing hungrily at* THÉRÈSE. *One can feel that she is afraid of being caught in the forbidden stretch of garden. As* THÉRÈSE *turns round she runs away, stammering in her confusion.*

Maid. Oh, I'm sorry, mademoiselle. I was just going through—— [*She vanishes.*]

Hartmann. Have you never noticed what she does? Every night she braves that forbidden stretch of garden—for you. She runs the risk of a scolding or dismissal, but she's shut up all day in the kitchen, and if only for a few seconds every night, she wants to see you, to draw her sustenance from you. You are her idol, Thérèse.

Thérèse. Me? But that's absurd!

Hartmann. She must think you so beautiful, and clean and scented. She doesn't have you one single minute to herself, yet she doesn't rebel against her lot.

Thérèse. But, Hartmann. . . .

Hartmann. And who knows, maybe she has a dog tied up in the yard, which waits for her each night, and thrives on a brief glimpse of her, and which she doesn't even notice.

A pause. FLORENT *is heard playing.*

Thérèse [*quietly*]. It's good of you to help me, Hartmann. But how one has to scrape away the remnants of one's pride to love like this.

Hartmann. Take life as it comes. You'll see, little by

little, a strange thing will work a change inside you. You'll
grow to think in the way they do, quite naturally. I was
a human being pitted against the world myself once. But
the serene days glided over me, one after the other. You'll
see, soon you won't feel any pain at all. Soon, you'll ask
nothing more from them but a warm corner in their joy.

A pause.

Thérèse. But that's a little bit like being dead.

Hartmann. A little.

Thérèse. I love him, I don't mind being a dead thing
beside him. But what about you, Hartmann? He told me
you had money of your own, that you don't need to be his
manager.

Hartmann [*quietly*]. I love the god that dwells in his
hands.

A pause. FLORENT *is still playing.* THÉRÈSE *is curled up in
a deep armchair. Suddenly she says in a small voice:*

Thérèse. The important thing is never to think that
there are others who live and fight and die. I shall stay
here all my life and when I go out it will always be with
them, in their handsome trains and airplanes and their
fine hotels with their silky-smooth headwaiters—won't I,
Hartmann?

Hartmann. Yes, Thérèse.

Thérèse. My eyes will only rest where theirs do, on
flowers, and precious stones and kindly faces. And I'll become translucent and serene too, just like them—and not
know anything any more. [*She repeats it, like a wonder-
struck child.*] To know nothing. . . . That must be good,
Hartmann, to know nothing any more.

Hartmann. Yes, Thérèse.

Thérèse. Happiness is a knack the clever ones have; the
ones who know the ropes. But don't worry, I'll learn it
too.

Hartmann [*with a hint of nostalgia*]. Yes, Thérèse, you'll
learn it too.

The HEAD HOUSEMAID *comes rushing in.*

Head Housemaid. Mademoiselle! Mademoiselle! Your
father has just arrived!

Thérèse [*turning pale*]. My father?

Head Housemaid. Yes, mademoiselle. He looks most upset. He says he must see you at once.

Hartmann. I'll leave you, Thérèse. If you should need me, I'll be in the garden.

He goes out. TARDE *comes in greatly agitated. He makes a sweeping gesture which* THÉRÈSE'S *attitude cuts short. The* HEAD HOUSEMAID *goes.* TARDE *repeats the same gesture with rather less abandon.*

Thérèse. Well, what is it?

Tarde. It's horrible!

Thérèse. What is? I told you you weren't to come here.

Tarde. It's horrible—horrible I tell you! Your poor mother. . . .

Thérèse. What about her?

Tarde. Oh, my God!

Thérèse. Speak, can't you? Is she hurt? Dead?

Tarde. All but! She fell on the corner of the piano.

Thérèse. And you've come all this way to tell me that?

Tarde. Oh, you are a heartless girl! She fell on her head, half dead—and why? I'll tell you why! Oh, the shame, the disgrace! She had a lover.

Thérèse. What?

Tarde. Gosta.

Thérèse. But you've known that for the last thirteen years!

Tarde. Nobody else did. Now every Tom, Dick, and Harry knows it. A public scandal—a ghastly shindy right on the bandstand—a shouting and a yelling such as you never heard! I feel hot with shame now as I think of it. Gosta gave her a punch on the nose. It was on account of you, needless to say. I wasn't there, Lord be praised. [*A pause.*] When I came out of the toilet——

Thérèse. You mean when you were hiding in the toilet?

Tarde. I happened to be in the toilet, that's all. When I came out, he'd left—in the middle of the performance, as usual—and your mother was coming to. It seems he said he was going to kill your young man. He took his revolver. You know me. Quick as a flash, I leaped into a cab! A train! Another cab! There's two hundred francs for the first cab, five hundred and fifty for the train fare—had to take a first class. It was an express—no seconds and thirds. Taxi number two from the station, three hundred and twenty, plus tip . . . it's waiting outside. In the excitement I came away without a cent. [*He pats his pockets for the look of the thing.* THÉRÈSE *does not move. He pats his pockets again.*] The clock's ticking up. If you could let me have . . . I'll just go and settle up with him.

Thérèse. Oh, be quiet. You'll get your money.

Tarde [*frantic at the thought*]. But . . . the meter's running——

Thérèse. Let it run.

Tarde. You don't seem very pleased to see me. You might thank me for missing a show to come and warn you. You know how the management feels about replacements. Gosta flinging out—now me—your mother with her head done up in gauze and sticking plaster. . . . We'll get the push from there too, I shouldn't wonder.

Thérèse [*almost imploringly*]. Be quiet. Please be quiet. I'll give you all the money you want, only be quiet!

Tarde. Right.

Thérèse [*after a pause*]. Has Gosta been very unhappy since I left?

Tarde. A wreck. He hasn't stopped drinking. He'd even given up knocking your Ma about, that shows you! This'll make you laugh! —One night, I found him crying like a baby over the little quilted cover you used to put over your fiddle—you remember, that red satin thing he gave you years ago.

Thérèse. Is that true?

Tarde. What a character! That makes two fights he's had over you. The first time was with old Lebonze, over some remark he made about you. Between you and me, I wasn't at all sorry at his giving that old bloodsucker his ticket. Do you know the old bastard didn't pay us our full money? We had to drag him to court over it. Anyhow, that's another story. The second time was with the waiter over at the Royal. You know, the lanky dark fellow—big chin, flat nose. Sniggered and asked Gosta how you were keeping. That time it wasn't funny. Gosta seized a soda syphon, the other one pulled out a knife. They ended up in the police station. Imagine the name the band is getting with all this. And here am I, working my fingers to the bone. However, after that little flare-up, I thought we'd have a bit of peace. What a hope! This afternoon, your ma, the great fool, goes and tells him you were very happy down here.

Thérèse. And he hit her because of that?

Tarde. Just because of that, girlie, without a word of a lie.

Thérèse. But what business is it of his whether I'm happy or not!

Tarde. You took the words out of my mouth, girlie. [*Suddenly remembering the taxi.*] But look, there's no point in keeping the taxi waiting. The meter's ticking up. If you could give me——

Thérèse [*in sudden anguish*]. Why did you have to come and tell me all this, Father?

Tarde. Are you serious? You're my daughter. He's my son-in-law, at least, my future son-in-law. I wasn't going to stand by and see you murdered! We must call the police! Personally, I don't mind telling you I'd as soon Gosta didn't know I came. So if you could give me. . . . There's a train back in half an hour . . . [*A pause. He adds, in spite of himself.*] and the taxi is outside. I shan't have to pay the starting charge because, as I said, he didn't stop his. . . . [*He mimes the action.*]

Thérèse [*looking up, vacantly*]. What?

Tarde [*repeating it with an effort*]. I said if I took the taxi on to the station now, I shouldn't have to pay a second starting charge, because he didn't stop his meter.

Thérèse [*incoherently*]. Why did you come, Father?

Tarde. You are a funny girl. I came here, regardless of danger and at considerable expense, because I thought it was my duty. If you could give me 250 plus 650 plus 320 plus, say, 400—that comes to——

Thérèse. Here's two thousand. Now be quiet.

Tarde [*the shrewd businessman*]. But you're forgetting the return journey, my lass.

Thérèse. Here, here. . . .

Tarde. Now you've given me too much! [*He pats his pockets.*] I haven't any change. I'll send you a postal order, or would you rather have cash?

Thérèse. He was weeping on my little red cover?

Tarde [*wheezing with mirth*]. Like a baby! [*Seeing that* THÉRÈSE *is not laughing.*] Well, like a desperate man . . . [*Anxious again*] a desperate man who'll be here in five minutes! With those automatics they use nowadays, they're none too fussy about the number of corpses. If you don't want a blood bath, you'd better do something! [*He pulls out his watch.*] As for me, if I don't want to miss that train.

Thérèse [*murmuring*]. Gosta is on the march now too. All the figures of my past will have come here, one by one, to take me back.

Tarde. I hope, when he does come, you'll see to it he'll find a couple of coppers ready to slip the bracelets on! Blubbing is one thing, but larking about with loaded firearms is another. Who does he think he is?

Thérèse. Yes, who does he think he is, who do you think you are, all of you?

Tarde. He's your mother's fancy man—all right. Let him act his love drama with her—God help us!—if he's that short of fun. But you, my little pretty! To come badgering *you*, under your fiancé's roof, the night you're trying on your chaste white dress! It's gorgeous, by the way. But I'm beginning to have doubts about everything now. You're sure you never slept with Gosta?

Thérèse [*smiling despite herself*]. Quite sure, Father.

Tarde. Then what does he hope to achieve? When he's fired his shots here, whether he hits your young man or not—I ask you, where will it get him? What will he gain by it?

Thérèse. The certainty of having lost me, irrevocably, at last. Of having reached the farthest limits of his pain. You may not know it, but at the far end of despair, there is a white clearing where one is almost happy.

Tarde. Queer sort of happiness.

Thérèse. Yes, Father, a frightful happiness. A foul, a shameful happiness. [*She clings to him, suddenly, seized with panic.*] But I don't want it any more! I want to be happy! I want to be happy like everybody else! I don't want to know anything more about you all!

The HEAD HOUSEMAID *comes in.*

Head Housemaid. Mademoiselle, there's another gentleman asking to see you.

Tarde [*yelling*]. Gentleman?—what sort of gentleman? Who is it, for God's sake?

GOSTA *appears.*

Gosta. It's me, Thérèse.

Thérèse [*to the maid*]. Leave us.

The HEAD HOUSEMAID *goes out.*

Gosta [*dully*]. Where's your fiancé? [*He steps forward.* TARDE *backs away and puts up his hands.*]

Tarde [*yelling*]. Not me, Gosta! Not me! I haven't done anything! I just dropped in—by chance—by chance— quite by chance! [*He tries to scream, but his voice breaks.*] Help! Police!

Gosta. Shut your trap, you!

Tarde [*cringing behind* THÉRÈSE]. Yes, I will, I will! This is none of my business! I'll just keep my trap shut!

Gosta. Where is your fiancé?

Thérèse. Take your hand out of your pocket, Gosta.

Gosta. Where is your fiancé? I want to talk to him.

Thérèse. Gosta, do as I say.

Tarde [*safe in his corner*]. Go on, do as she says!

Gosta. Where's your fiancé, Thérèse?

Thérèse [*struggling with him*]. Take your hand out of your pocket, I tell you! Take your hand out and give me that!

Tarde [*from the other end of the room*]. Careful, girlie —careful, now!

Gosta [*trying to shake her off*]. Thérèse, let me alone.

Thérèse [*panting*]. Give me that gun! Don't fight with me, Gosta, or I'll send a bullet through my heart! That's what you want, isn't it? Isn't it? [*She snatches the gun away.*]

Tarde. Phew!

Thérèse. Now look at me. [GOSTA *hangs his head.*] Look at me, Gosta. [GOSTA *looks up.*] You wanted to kill him.

Gosta. Yes.

Thérèse. Why? [*A pause.* GOSTA *looks away.*] Why? Answer me.

Gosta. I don't know.

Tarde [*exploding, now quite reassured*]. Oh, that's rich, that is! He doesn't know! Give me that gun, girlie, give it to me. [*He takes the weapon and puts it in his pocket.*]

A pause.

Gosta [*in a murmur*]. I'm a brute to have come, Thérèse. Call your young man and tell him to kick me out. It's all I deserve.

Thérèse [*in a hard voice*]. No, I won't have him think that someone had sufficient claims on me to come here and make a scene. Go of your own accord.

Gosta. You're right. I'm not even worth a scene.

Thérèse [quietly]. I've never loved you, Gosta. Even if I'd never met him, I could never have loved you. Did you think of that when you came here?

Gosta. Yes, I thought of that.

Thérèse. And you came just the same?

Gosta. I've been hanging about outside the drive gates for half an hour.

Thérèse. Then why did you come in? I don't want to see you. I'm happy, do you hear? I don't want anything more to do with you and your bundle of woes! I love him, do you hear? I love him. What are you doing here, with your wretchedness exposed for all to see? And how dare you smile when I say I love him? You're ugly, Gosta, you're useless, you're lazy. You're always saying you could have done better than anybody else, but you've never done a thing.

Gosta [looking intensely at her]. No, Thérèse.

Thérèse. You spend all your money on liquor because when you're drunk you imagine you could do something in life. You've only one suit left to wear and you're proud of that, too, because you think a coat that's out at elbows and covered in stains is the hallmark of a genius. Well, that courage, that strength you feel so full of, might perhaps consist in giving up drink and buying yourself some shoes.

Tarde. Girlie, girlie, don't exasperate him!

Thérèse. Your hands shake on the keyboard, you strike wrong notes more and more often, don't you? Well, your love, your great love of music, might perhaps be to stop drinking and to practice every day.

Gosta. Yes, Thérèse.

Thérèse. Your love for me might have prompted you not to come here, too. You seized that revolver and you set out, like an avenging hero bent on justice. Well, I'll tell you what that justice of yours was, if you don't already know it. It was your hatred. The hatred of a failure for all that's finer and cleverer than you!

Gosta. That's not true, Thérèse!

Thérèse. It is true! [*Crying out.*] Do you think I don't know everything that goes on in your mind? I know it all, better than you do yourself! [*A pause.* GOSTA *hangs his head. She goes on in a strange, hoarse voice.*] The vanity —the odious conceit of it! I'll sympathize, I'll willingly feel sorry for you, but if you thought our squalor, our misery, our grime were tokens of nobility you made a big mistake.

Gosta [*dully*]. And you can say that, Thérèse?

Thérèse. Yes. I can and I do. What else have you to say to me?

Gosta. Nothing. You're right, Thérèse.

Thérèse. Then go away! Get out, both of you! I want to be happy and never think of you again! You're unhappy but I don't care! I found my own way out of it! You're ugly and unwashed and you're full of dirty thoughts and the rich are quite right to hurry past you in the street! Get out! Get out quickly! Get out of my sight! [*Suddenly she collapses on the sofa, sobbing, and moans.*] Oh, go away for pity's sake! Can't you see I'm weak with the ache of carrying you in my heart!

She slips on to the floor, sobbing like a child. The two men look at her, speechless, not daring to move. The music starts again next door. GOSTA *stands listening. Gradually,* THÉRÈSE's *sobs die down.*

Gosta. Who's that playing?

Thérèse [*softly*]. It's he.

A pause.

Gosta. Is it his own stuff he's playing?

Thérèse. Yes, it's his.

Gosta [*after another pause*]. How does he do it?

Thérèse. That's the way he does everything, Gosta—without taking pains, without spoiling it or starting again. Without heartache. . . .

Another pause. The music sweeps over them.

Gosta. How does he do it, Thérèse? I sweat and strain and score out and start afresh and everything slips through my fingers. [*Another silence, filled with music.* GOSTA *moves at last. He goes to* THÉRÈSE *and says soberly.*] You must forget us. We ought never to have shown our ugly faces here. But it won't be long now. We'll go out into the garden, you'll see us walk through that patch of light and then the dark will close around us. We'll be dead and you'll have peace at last. [*They stand listening a while longer, as the music swells. Then* GOSTA *breaks out of the spell and goes to the door.*] Thérèse, one day, later on, tell him I came to kill him and that I went away again.

TARDE *follows him, an old, decrepit figure suddenly.*

Tarde. And you can tell him, girlie, that I've been thinking it over about the money and I'll try and give him back a part of it. . . .

The FITTER *and her girls come in again.* TARDE *sees them and takes* GOSTA *by the arm.*

Tarde. Come on, let's go. No need for anyone to see us here. [*He pulls* GOSTA *away and they both disappear.*]

Fitter [*very bright and talkative*]. There we are! I kept you waiting, mademoiselle. I do apologize. We'll just slip the little jacket on, then you can see the whole ensemble. It simply makes the dress! [*To the little workgirl.*] Come along, wake up! [*They set to work.*] Oh, this will be the wedding of the year!

Thérèse [*like a sleepwalker throughout this scene*]. Yes.

Fitter. What color are the bridesmaids wearing?

Thérèse. Rose pink.

Fitter. M. Lapérouse was so sorry not to be doing their dresses. I must tell you he had an utterly entrancing idea for them! But he quite understands, Mlle. France has her own loyalties. There are six of them, I believe?

Thérèse. Yes.

Fitter. Too enchanting! They manage to achieve quite deliciously elegant ceremonies in those little country churches. There will be little children to carry the train, no doubt?

Thérèse. Four little boys.

Fitter. Oh, how adorable! And the flowers, and the music and the color! You'll have planned a divine honeymoon trip, I'm sure? Oh, I'm being very indiscreet—do forgive me!

Thérèse. Switzerland and Italy.

Fitter. Switzerland and Italy. The classic honeymoon, but there's still nothing to touch it. May I wish you both joy? I'm sure you'll be quite blissfully happy!

Thérèse [*murmuring*]. Blissfully happy, yes. . . . [*She shudders and slips away from them.*] Please—leave me for a second, could you? I'd like to be alone.

Fitter. But, mademoiselle——

Thérèse. Please . . . leave me alone. . . . The dress is fine. Please. . . .

Fitter. But our train goes in half an hour and this is the final fitting!

Thérèse. I tell you it fits very well. Go up to the linen room, I'll join you. I'll come straight up, I promise. Only leave me now—leave me. . . .

Fitter [*tight-lipped*]. As Mademoiselle wishes. [*Venting her irritation on the little girl.*] Well, don't sit there dreaming! Pick up your pins! You'll make us miss that train!

They go out. THÉRÈSE *takes off her bridal wreath and goes out, quickly. Next door, the music stops. A pause.* FLORENT *comes in.*

Florent. Who are you talking to, Thérèse?

He glances round the empty room, then goes on to the veranda and looks out. When he comes back, THÉRÈSE *has come in again, wearing her outdoor clothes, and carrying the wedding dress over her arm. She lays it on the sofa.*

Florent. I was looking for you. Where are you going, darling?

Thérèse. Only into the garden for a minute.

Florent. You've put your coat on. But it's so warm. . . .

Thérèse [*softly*]. I felt a little chilly.

Florent [*drawing her to him*]. I went through the details of our trip with Hartmann this afternoon. I want to take you to all the places that I've loved. There's a rock I know on Lake Lucerne where we'll go and sit, early in the morning, before the sun comes up. And there's a painting of a little Renaissance princess, who looks like you, that we'll go and look at in the Uffizi together.

Thérèse. Yes, my darling. . . .

Florent. Oh, I feel so happy tonight. . . . It's a beautiful evening. And you?

Thérèse [*smiling with difficulty*]. Yes, my darling, I'm happy too. Were you working?

Florent. Did you hear me? The Andante is shaping well.

Thérèse. Go back and play, darling.

Florent. Will you listen to me out in the garden?

Thérèse. Yes, my darling. Go quickly, go and play. You're dying to—I can tell from your eyes.

Florent [*giving her a light kiss*]. It's going beautifully. I'm very happy. . . .

Thérèse. Yes, my dearest.

He goes. THÉRÈSE *stands a moment without moving. Then she says gently:*

You see, Florent, it wouldn't be any use cheating. However tight I shut my eyes, there will always be a stray dog somewhere in the world who'll stop me being happy. [*The music starts again next door. She touches the beautiful white dress in a brief, unfinished caress and murmurs, turning toward the room where* FLORENT *is playing, as if she still had many things to say.*] You see. . . . [*But she stops, turns abruptly and goes out into the night. The wedding dress lies on the couch, a dazzling patch of whiteness in the gloom.*]

HARTMANN *has appeared, unobtrusively, at the top of the stairs. He has watched* THÉRÈSE *go, without a word. He stands quite still a moment, looking through the windows and following her with his eyes as she disappears through the dark grounds.*

Hartmann [*in a murmur*]. There she goes, small, and strong and lucid, to pit herself against all the sharp corners in the world.

The music swells next door as the Curtain falls.

TIME REMEMBERED

English Version by

PATRICIA MOYES

Time Remembered by Jean Anouilh, English version by Patricia Moyes, reprinted by permission of Coward-McCann, Inc.

CHARACTERS
(In order of appearance)

AMANDA, *a milliner*
DUCHESS OF PONT-AU-BRONC
THEOPHILUS, *a butler*
LORD HECTOR
ICE-CREAM MAN
TAXI DRIVER
PRINCE ALBERT
FERDINAND, *a headwaiter*
SINGER
PIANIST
VIOLINIST
CELLIST
LANDLORD
GERMAIN, *a gillie*
FOOTMEN AND WAITERS

SCENE: *The action takes place in the Chateau and Park of the Duchess of* PONT-AU-BRONC.

ACT ONE

SCENE I: *A study in the Chateau. Late afternoon.*
SCENE II: *A Clearing in the Park. Immediately afterward.*
SCENE III: *The Study. The following morning.*

ACT TWO

SCENE I: *The Blue Danube night club. The following evening.*
SCENE II: *Outside the Chime of Bells. The next morning.*

ACT ONE

SCENE I

A study of stupefying elegance. In the midst of the splendor sits a young girl, AMANDA, *with a little cardboard suitcase at her feet. She yawns, fidgets, looks at her watch, then finally gets up and starts toward the door. Suddenly the door opens, and a little old lady bursts into the room, preceded by her lorgnette. It is the* DUCHESS. *She bears down upon* AMANDA.

DUCHESS. So, you've arrived, have you?
  Amanda. Yes, madame. Two hours ago.
  Duchess. Stand up straight, child. Chest over toes.

    AMANDA, *bewildered, straightens her back.*

[*Examining her.*] How do you contrive to be so absurdly small?
  Amanda. I don't know, madame. I do my best. . . .
  Duchess. Not good enough. You must make a serious effort. [*Continuing her examination.*] My child, I am sixty. I have improved upon nature all my life, and intend to go on doing so. [*Seeing* AMANDA's *comparatively low heels, she extends her own leg, encased in harem trousers, showing that she is wearing elegant high-heeled shoes.*] You must wear higher heels, child. Very high. . . . How tall do you think I am in bare feet?
  Amanda [*still startled*]. About five foot two, I should say, madame.
  Duchess [*annoyed*]. Not a bad guess. I am five foot one and three-quarters. However, it is of no consequence, as you will never see me in bare feet. I am glad to say nobody has ever seen me in bare feet, except the dear duke, of course. And he was as blind as a bat.

The results of her scrutiny obviously satisfy her. AMANDA *extends her hand in an attempt to interrupt. The* DUCHESS *seizes it.*

Good. You have pretty hands. As I thought. They may be accustomed to making hats, but they have a certain air about them. In any case, who doesn't make hats these

days? I don't, of course. But then I belong to a different
world altogether. [*Seating herself in an attempt to get down
to business.*] Now, I trust that the telegram explained quite
clearly why I want you here.

Amanda. I gathered you had a situation here in the
household, madame.

Duchess. A situation . . . what a delicious expression.
The child is quite enchanting. [*She thrusts her face to
within an inch of* AMANDA's *and repeats.*] Enchanting.
[*Without taking her eyes off* AMANDA, *she adds.*] Is she
not, Gaston? [*Since there is nobody else in the room,*
AMANDA *looks round in some surprise.*] I was talking to
the duke. He died fifteen years ago, but I have never been
able to break myself of the habit of talking to him. [*She
studies* AMANDA *again.*] Enchanting. [*Suddenly she adopts
a coaxing tone, as though speaking to a pampered lap
dog.*] And is the little girl pleased to have found a situation
then?

Amanda. Oh, yes, madame. You see, two days ago I lost
my job at Mme. Rensada's hat shop, and——

Duchess. I know all about that, dear. I arranged it.

Amanda [*in angry astonishment*]. You did! Well, of
all the cheek!

Duchess [*laughs delightedly and sweeps out of the room,
saying*]. Cheek! Cheek, she says! Gaston, didn't I tell you
she was adorable . . . ?

She has gone. AMANDA *grasps her little suitcase and looks
desperately around, on the verge of tears. She starts to
leave. A butler comes in and blocks her exit, bowing to
her elaborately.*

Butler. Her Grace the Duchess wishes me to inquire
whether it will be convenient for mademoiselle to partake
of a cold collation while awaiting Her Grace's return.

Amanda. I'm not hungry, thank you.

Butler. I beg mademoiselle's pardon, but my inquiry was
purely rhetorical. Her Grace has given orders that the cold
collation will be served. [*He claps his hands.*]

To the accompaniment of lilting music, a procession of
FOOTMEN *stream into the room, bearing dish after elaborate
dish amidst a dazzling welter of silver, cut glass and gleam-
ing napery.* AMANDA *is confronted by a display of cakes,*

fruits and sweetmeats extravagant enough to daunt the
staunchest appetite.

Butler. We feel sure mademoiselle will find something
to her taste here. [*Calling out as* FOOTMEN *proffer the
dishes. They present these as the* BUTLER *leads* AMANDA
to a table.] Cucumber Mousse on Hearts of Palm? Filets
of Sturgeon in Even Tail? Artichoke Bottoms in Ham
Mimosa? Crayfish in Dill? Stuffed Lettuce Flamande?
Woodman's Grouse? Turban of Sole Carmelite? Glazed
Ox Tongue? Salmon in Jelly Norwegian? Cream Puffs,
Snow Eggs and Honey Ice Cream?

Amanda. Stop! Please stop! Honestly, I'm not hungry.
I'll just have a tangerine. . . .

She takes a tangerine and begins to peel it. The DUCHESS
returns like a whirlwind, followed by LORD HECTOR, *a tall,
thin and tweedy individual redolent of the countryside and
its pursuits. The* DUCHESS *bears down upon* AMANDA,
*snatches the tangerine away from her, and throws it into
the fire.*

Duchess. No tangerines, no oranges or lemons. They
make you thin, and you cannot afford to lose a single
ounce. Now, look at her, Hector. Would she not be quite
striking . . .

Hector. Striking. . . .

Duchess. . . . if we could fill her out a little? [HECTOR,
who has placed a monocle in his eye the better to study
AMANDA, *has no time to reply. The* DUCHESS *sweeps on
relentlessly, examining the dishes.*] Eggs and pastry, pastry
and eggs. [*Calls.*] Theophilus!

The BUTLER *materializes discreetly.*

Butler. Your Grace?

Duchess. Remove all this paraphernalia and bring the
young lady an egg.

Amanda [*jumps up, pale but determined*]. No, madame!

Duchess [*turning to her, astounded*]. Did I understand
you to say "No"? [*To the others, who have turned to
stone.*] What does she mean?

Amanda [*desperately bold*]. I'm not hungry and I don't
like eggs!

Duchess [*to* HECTOR]. I told you so. Adorable.

She turns and sweeps out, followed by HECTOR, *who echoes:*

Hector. Adorable.

They have gone. AMANDA *can stand no more. She grabs her suitcase, and seems on the point of either smashing something or else bursting into tears. She shouts at the* FOOTMEN *who have begun to take away the dishes.*

Amanda. What's happening! Why won't anybody tell me? Why was I brought here?

Butler [*as he goes, bringing up the rear of the procession of* FOOTMEN]. Mademoiselle must excuse us, but these matters are not confided to the domestic staff. To obtain a reply, mademoiselle must address herself directly to Her Grace—or, as a last resort, to Lord Hector.

He goes. AMANDA, *left alone, throws her case down on the ground and stamps her foot in fury.*

Amanda. Crud! Crud! Crud!

Duchess [*coming in by another door*]. What a hideously inelegant word! Say "*merde*," my dear, it's so much more explicit. Crud is not only ugly, it is inexact. [*She addresses* AMANDA *in a sophisticated drawl.*] I must apologize, my dear, for keeping you shut up in this room so long—but the fact is that there is a certain person whom I am particularly anxious should not see you, and he is due back from his walk at any moment. [*She looks out into the garden, suddenly serious.*] It might jeopardize all my plans should you meet him just now.

Amanda [*using this excuse to finish the interview*]. Well, I'd rather tell you straight out, madame, that if the vacancy is for a housemaid, or even a lady's maid . . . I . . . well, I'm a skilled milliner, madame, and I'm determined to carry on with my profession.

Duchess. You were quite right, Gaston. The girl has spirit. [*She goes to the door, saying to* AMANDA *as she passes.*] A good point!

Amanda [*stopping the* DUCHESS]. No, madame! This time I'm not going to let you go!

Duchess. Not let me go? Did you hear that, Gaston? We are to be prisoners in our own home—just as we were under Francis the First.

Amanda [*a little taken aback*]. Francis the First?

Duchess. Yes, in 1520 we were confined to our estates after an abortive attempt to seize power. Apparently we died of boredom. [*She sits at a desk in front of the book-case.*]

Amanda. I promise you, madame, I have no intention of keeping you prisoner. But I arrived here on the 2.17 train from Paris, and it's nearly five o'clock now, and the last train back to Paris tonight is the 6.19. If I'm not going to be of any use to you here, I really must catch it.

Duchess. No, child, you will not travel by that train.

Amanda. Why not, madame?

Duchess. Because it is not running.

Amanda. But I looked it up in the timetable!

Duchess. I have no doubt that it appears in the time-table. Nevertheless, it is not running—as from yesterday.

Amanda [*to whom anything seems possible by now*]. You stopped it running so that I couldn't get away, didn't you?

Duchess. A hundred and fifty years ago, my dear, I would most certainly have done so. Unfortunately, since 1789 my family has lost much of its influence over the Administration. No, it was not I who canceled the train. [*Darkly.*] It was the freemasons. They realized that the train enabled the good people of the neighboring towns to come and visit our basilica. We've opened it to the public, you know. Twice a week, ten till six, fifty francs admission. [*She hands* AMANDA *a brochure.*] And very nicely we were doing—I had started a line of souvenirs—medals, rosaries, small blessed candles. [*She indicates stacks of them in the bookcase.*] Oh, yes, I move with the times. I realize the value of publicity. And then—out of a blue sky, before I could lift a finger—[*she snaps her fingers*] they canceled my train. Just like that. Ah, but I'm too clever for them. Do you know what I'm going to do? [*In a confidential whisper.*] Motor coaches! What do you think of that?

On this triumphant note, she gets up to go. AMANDA, *at the end of her tether, follows her tearfully.*

Amanda. But I don't understand, madame. I don't know what you're taking about—basilicas and trains and free-masons. I've been waiting for over two hours and I didn't even have time for any lunch before I left home——

Duchess. No lunch? No lunch? What can have happened to that egg? I will go and investigate. [*She makes as if to go again.*]

Amanda [*raises her voice in a wail of desperation*]. Oh, madame, please, please don't go away again without explaining things to me, or I'll go mad!

The DUCHESS *stops.*

Duchess [*serious*]. You are cleverer than you look, child. I will make a confession to you. I am not sixty. I am sixty-seven. I have survived the birth of the airplane, the death of the corset, short hair and World Wars. So if I say that I'm an old woman who has seen many bizarre and exciting things in her time, you believe me, won't you?

Amanda [*at a loss*]. Yes, madame. . . .

Duchess. Well, then, you must take my word for it that the reason I have been popping in and out of this room like a jack-in-the-box for the last ten minutes is simply that I cannot summon up the courage to tell you the truth of why I made you come here.

She goes out, leaving AMANDA *more dumfounded than ever.* AMANDA *picks up her case, half tearful, half angry, and announces almost hysterically to the empty room:*

Amanda. Mad! They're all stark staring mad! I'll . . . I'll *walk* back to Paris!

She opens the french window, looks round anxiously to see if she is observed, and then runs out into the garden. The orchestra strikes a mysterious chord. The stage is empty for a moment. Then the DUCHESS *comes in, covering her eyes, followed by* HECTOR.

Duchess. Hector! Hector, where is she? I have a most frightening presentiment——

Hector [*looking round the empty room*]. For once your presentiment seems to be correct. She's evaporated.

Duchess. She's what?

Hector. She's gone.

Duchess. Well, obviously. Hector! If she meets him in the park, we are lost! Hurry! Hurry!

They rush out into the garden. The lights dim. The music swells up.

SCENE II

When the lights go up again, we are in a clearing in the park. It is wild and overgrown. There is a small obelisk surrounded by a circular stone bench. At one side of the scene, pulled up near a large tree, stands an ancient taxi. Two legs stick out from under it. A closer inspection reveals that this taxi is filthy and antiquated, and overgrown with ivy and honeysuckle. Not far away stands an ice-cream cart displaying its gaudy pictorial representations of strawberry and vanilla cones and bars. Two legs are also visible under the cart. AMANDA *runs in, carrying her suitcase. When she sees the taxi, she stops, and exclaims joyfully.*

AMANDA. Oh, thank heavens! A taxi! [*She looks round, sees no one, and then notices the legs.*] Oh . . . excuse me. . . .

    A Voice. Who are you talking to?

    Amanda. I . . . I don't know . . . are these your legs?

A benevolent old man appears from behind the ice-cream cart. He adjusts his spectacles, and says:

Ice-Cream Man. Which legs?

AMANDA, *mute by now, indicates the legs which protrude from under the taxi.*

[*Simply.*] No. Those aren't mine. [*He disappears behind his cart again, newspaper in hand.*]

    Amanda [*as he goes*]. Oh, sir . . . please. . . . [*He reappears.*] Am I still in the park? I've been walking for ever so long.

    Ice-Cream Man [*lugubrious*]. Yes, miss. You can walk as long as you like and you'll still be in the park.

A mockingbird's song shrills out as though to taunt AMANDA. *Suddenly she snatches up her case and runs to the taxi.*

    Amanda. Taxi! Taxi! Driver, are you free?

At these words, the DRIVER *emerges from under his cab, furious.*

    Driver. Of course I am free. Am I not a Frenchman? [*He slides back under his taxi.*]

Amanda. Oh, thank goodness, I am saved. [*She opens the door of the taxi and jumps in, crying:*] Take me to the railway station, please! As fast as you can! [*She emerges almost immediately from the door on the other side.*] Driver!

Driver. Yes?

Amanda. There are rabbits in your taxi!

Driver. Of course there are rabbits in my taxi! [*He comes sailing out from under the cab, terribly concerned that his rabbits have been disturbed. He picks up the most distressed rabbit, and comforts it.*] So now I'm not allowed to keep rabbits, is that it? Eh? Have I or have I not got a right to keep rabbits if I want to?

Amanda [*retreating a step*]. Of course you have a right to keep rabbits. . . .

Driver [*advancing angrily*]. Am I a human being or am I not? I'm only asking.

Amanda. Of course you are.

Driver. Just because they pay me thirty thousand francs a month for doing nothing? Well, I'm not denying it, am I? That has absolutely nothing to do with it. Huh! Well?

Amanda [*retreating rapidly*]. I assure you I never meant——

Driver. All right then.

AMANDA *takes another step back and trips. She cries out, for by now everything scares her. Then she smiles timidly at the* DRIVER, *as if to excuse her exclamation.*

Amanda. I'm sorry . . . I'm a bit nervous today. . . . [*She sees what she has tripped over, and breathes again.*] Oh . . . it's only a bit of ivy. . . .

Driver [*calmer*]. Of course it's ivy. Any objection? [*He returns the rabbit to its place inside the cab.*] It's easy to grow, ivy is. I tried rambler roses once, pruned 'em, watered 'em every day—no good. Wouldn't grow.

Amanda [*still looking at the ivy*]. It must be awkward when you want to drive away.

Driver. What d'you mean, awkward?

Amanda. Well . . . the . . . the ivy. . . . [*By now anything seems possible. She asks him, with a timid smile.*] Do you . . . take it with you?

Driver [*delighted at the idea*]. You're a comic, you are.

What d'you think the ivy's made of then—elastic? [*He
calls.*] Hey! Joseph! [*The* ICE-CREAM MAN *reappears.*]
D'you know what she just said? Asked me if the ivy follows me around! She's a character, she is. Can't you just
see me taking it out for a walk every day to make weewee
on the boulevard. [*Calls, as if to a dog.*] Come along,
then! [*Whistles.*] There's a good little ivy . . . heel, sir,
heel! [*He roars with laughter.*]

Amanda [*continuing her inspection*]. But your taxi can't
possibly go at all! There are creepers growing all over it!

Driver. What's that? My taxi not go! D'you hear that,
Joseph? So my taxi won't go, won't it? [*He rushes to the
taxi, livid, and turns on a switch viciously. A hiccough,
and the motor starts.*] There! Now who says it won't go!

Amanda. No! No, please! Don't make it move! Not
with the ivy! I couldn't bear it! I think I'm going mad
. . . everything is absolutely crazy today. [*To the* ICE-
CREAM MAN.] You . . . are you really an ice-cream man?

Ice-Cream Man. Yes.

Amanda. Well, sell me an ice cream then. I'm terribly
thirsty.

Ice-Cream Man. An ice cream! My dear young lady, it's
two years since I had any ice cream to sell.

Amanda. Just as I expected. Thank you. You've set my
mind at rest. I'm beginning to see a mad sort of sense
in all this. I'd have been really worried if you'd *had* an
ice cream to sell—a real, freezing ice cream. Will you do
one more thing for me? [*She hands him something.*]

Ice-Cream Man. What's this? A pin? What d'you expect me to do with a pin?

Amanda. Prick me, please—not too hard, just enough
to make sure I'm not dreaming.

Ice-Cream Man [*pricking her*]. She's a character all right.

Driver [*a little apprehensive*]. She's worse than a character. She's loony.

Amanda. Ow! Thank you. May I have my pin back,
please? [*She takes the pin, and pricks her own hand,
gently, experimentally, as if to confirm her previous opinion that she is awake. Having done so, she suddenly turns
to the two men, who are stealing away, whispering to each
other.*] I *am* awake—and alive! I'm alive and when I'm
pricked with a pin, I feel it. I've got two legs and two
feet, and I can walk on them. I'm not even going to ask
you the way to the railway station. I'm going to follow my

nose till I find the main road. And on the road I'll find a signpost—because in the world I come from—the real world—there are real signposts on the road, pointing to real places! And I'll read it with my own two eyes and then I'll walk to the station, and I'll find the station-master—and he'll be a real live stationmaster, made of flesh and blood! [*She picks up her case with a sigh which is very close to tears, and adds.*] I hope.

As she goes off, she collides with the DUCHESS, *who arrives at a canter, followed by the faithful* HECTOR.

Duchess. Oh, thank heaven, we've found her! [*She sits heavily on the circular bench.*] Oh, child, what a fright you gave me! I nearly died . . . and I am prostrate with exhaustion.

Amanda. Don't try to make me feel sorry for you. What about me? I'm exhausted too, and I nearly died of fright.

Duchess. Fright? What on earth is there for you to be frightened of?

Amanda. Everything, madame—especially you.

Duchess. Me? What an extraordinary notion. D'you hear that, Hector?

Amanda [*lively*]. Yes—you! And the taxi driver who keeps rabbits in his taxi, and the ice-cream man who hasn't sold an ice cream for two years, and this awful park with no way out of it. . . . What do you want of me? Why did you entice me out here by promising me a job—what sort of job could I possibly do in this madhouse? I suppose you want a milliner who doesn't make hats! [*Determined.*] Well, I'm not frightened of you any more. Which is the way to the station? I demand that you tell me the way to the station!

Duchess. Hector, she is adorable.

Hector. Adorable.

Amanda [*worn out, sinks to the bench, crying amidst her sobs*]. Tell me the way to the station!

Duchess [*concerned*]. No, no! You must on no account cry! I am incapable of seeing anyone cry without bursting into tears myself. The moment has come for plain speaking, however painful. [*She indicates that the* TAXI DRIVER *and the* ICE-CREAM MAN *are to leave. They do.*] I will be brief. I have a nephew, mademoiselle. A nephew whom I idolize above everything else in the world. His name is

Albert. The poor boy is the victim of a most strange
melancholia, which——[*She stops.*] The story is so poignant
to me that I really cannot bear to repeat it. Hector, you
go on.

HECTOR *stands up, ceremoniously. The* DUCHESS *intro-
duces him in a brisk tone.*

Allow me to present my cousin, Baron Andinet of Andaine.

HECTOR *bows.* AMANDA *drops a little curtsey.* HECTOR *is
about to speak, but the* DUCHESS *forestalls him.*

Lord Hector. He is not to be confused with Lord Jerome,
who is first secretary at the consulate in Honolulu, nor
with Lord Jasper, the General's son. [*With a gesture.*]
Lord Hector.

HECTOR *bows again, and opens his mouth to speak. Once
more he is too late.*

There is very little likelihood of your confusing him with
Lord Jasper. He has been dead for some years, poor fellow.
　　Hector. Poor fellow!
　　Duchess. Go on, Hector.
　　Hector. Well, mademoiselle, my cousin, Prince Trou-
biscoi. . . .
　　Duchess. Yes, my sister became a Troubiscoi by her
fourth marriage, the silly girl. The Tsar was visiting Paris
at the time—Slavonic charm, I am afraid, quite fatal—
however, we've been into all that . . . go on, Hector.
　　Hector. My cousin, Prince Troubiscoi——
　　Duchess. Call him Prince Albert, or she may think you
are referring to the other one—that imbecile who married
the Englishwoman—Patrick Troubiscoi. [*To* AMANDA, *perfectly naturally.*] You may have met him?
　　Amanda. No, madame.
　　Duchess. You amaze me. One meets him absolutely
everywhere. Go on, Hector.
　　Hector. Well, mademoiselle, some years ago my cousin,
the Prince Albert, visited Dinard, where he met a young
woman who——
　　Duchess [*interrupting*]. No, no, no! Be quiet, Hector.
You manage to invest the story of this exquisite romance
with such a flat-footed platitudinous boredom that I prefer
to make the sacrifice and tell it myself. Two years ago,
mademoiselle, my beloved Albert became deliriously en-

amored of a lady of incomparable beauty and impeccable
aristocracy . . . a lady of whom you will certainly have
heard. I will tell you her name. Léocadia Gardi.

Amanda. The ballerina?

Duchess. Yes, child. The great and glorious ballerina.
The divine Gardi, as they called her. Ah, the exquisite,
ethereal grace of that first entry of hers in *Swan Lake.*

*Carried away by the memory of it, she runs into the wood
and returns dancing the entrance.* HECTOR *joins her and
they dance a few measures. The* DUCHESS *stops.*

Unhappily I am no dancer. When I was a girl I was as
light as thistledown on my feet—but thirty years of waltz-
ing with the dear duke proved too much for my delicate
talent . . . a pity, but there it is. Where was I?

Hector. In the *Swan Lake.*

Duchess. Oh, yes . . . Léocadia. Dear Léocadia. You
say you knew her well. That will be the greatest help to
us.

Amanda. Oh, no, I didn't know her at all. I just read
about her death in the newspapers.

Duchess. Alas, yes! You know how she died?

Amanda. I think an accident.

Duchess. Yes. The poor darling always wore a scarf of
immense length; she had a different one for every costume
she possessed . . . very becoming they were, too . . .
they became quite a legend, Léocadia's scarves. As she
said good-by to you, she would fling her scarf around her
lovely neck, and knot it in her own inimitable way. . . .
Well, one evening she was knotting her scarf with the
grandest, most extravagant gesture of her career. Alas, she
realized too late that the knot was in the wrong place . . .
but art was stronger than nature. She could not bring herself to spoil that incomparable gesture. She flung out her
arm . . . uttered a single cry . . . a strangled one, of
course . . . and fell dead. [*She sniffs.*] Finish it, Hector.
I can't go on.

Hector [*who is under the impression that it is already
finished, merely repeats*]. Dead. . . .

Duchess. It was only three days before this tragedy that
poor Albert fell in love with her. He has never recovered
from those three days. Now do you begin to understand?

Amanda. No.

Duchess. Very well, I will proceed. When he heard the

ghastly news, his first thought was to fling himself from his balcony. For more than an hour I held him back by his coattails. But that was merely a temporary danger. I had to think of the future. I decided that he must travel. We went on a most expensive and enthralling cruise—one and a half times round the world—but all in vain. One hundred and twenty-two days we spent on that peregrination—Albert sitting in his cabin gazing at a photograph of his dear departed, and me sitting in mine gazing at him through the intervening keyhole, to make sure he did not jump overboard. [*Explaining, suddenly intimate.*] Do you wish me to describe to you in detail the agonies of my long martyrdom?

Amanda. No, madame.

Duchess. No. You are right. It would be too long and too painful. Suffice it to say that I, the very soul of curiosity, traveled one and a half times round the world with one eye shut and the other glued to a keyhole. Now and then, when we were in harbor, my gypsy nature became too strong for me, and I would snatch a peep through the porthole. Once I caught a glimpse of a turban—that was India. Another time, a pigtail—China, of course. The smoke of a volcano told me we were approaching Italy . . . only when we were on French soil once more did I dare to think of myself again. I found I had lost twenty pounds through worry and anxiety . . . fortunately, however, the lack of exercise had put it on again . . . we are now in Marseilles. Are you following me, or am I going too fast for you?

Amanda. No, madame. I'm with you.

Duchess. Good. We returned home with all speed—we both needed a rest. At last I seemed to detect a lessening of Albert's grief . . . but his melancholy was still deep enough to worry me. I set my spies on him, to report on his every movement. I learned that he spent his days in Dinard, chatting sometimes with a taxi driver, sometimes with an ice-cream merchant, sometimes with the landlord of a wretched little inn called the Chime of Bells. As for his evenings, he invariably went to a certain Viennese night club, sat always at the same table, and was served always by the same waiter. September came . . . Dinard was deserted.

Hector. Always is in September.

Duchess. All the cafés closed for the winter—except that

one. It remained open, and night after night Albert sat there in solitary state. I confess, I was baffled. I could not understand—and then, suddenly, I saw the light!

Amanda [*who is beginning to take an interest in the love story*]. Was it there that they first discovered that they loved each other?

Duchess [*regarding her admiringly*]. Oh, Hector! What a splendid thing it is to have a plebeian soul! The girl has understood instinctively what we, with our intelligence, took months to grasp. Yes, child, you are right. The taxi driver, the ice-cream man, the Chime of Bells, the Viennese café . . . all of them formed the background of poor Albert's love affair with his divine Léocadia, and day after day for three long months he returned to their enchantment, like a man possessed.

Amanda [*dreamy*]. It must be wonderful to love someone as much as all that. . . .

Duchess. I dare say. But think of my position. Albert is not only a Troubiscoi, but—far more important—he is an Andinet of Andaine, on his mother's side. Please don't think I am simply a reactionary old fossil—nothing could be further from the truth. In the war, I signed on in the nursing reserve without making any stipulation whatsoever about the social status of my patients. But all the same . . . all the same . . . you must admit that it hardly seems worth going to the trouble and expense of gaining control of half the kingdom in the reign of Louis the Gross, if a mere seven hundred years later one is going to have one's nephew gossiping on street corners with taxi drivers and ice-cream men. However . . . where was I?

Hector. You suddenly saw the light.

Duchess [*picking up the thread*]. Ah, yes. I realized suddenly that these people were merely the souvenirs of dear Albert's great love. Well, I am a collector at heart. I bought the taxi, the ice-cream cart, the park bench upon which they sat . . . that bench was the most difficult of all. . . . I had to go to court over it—but I got it. As for the inn and the Viennese night club, I had them rebuilt stone by stone in the park.

Amanda. It's . . . it's like a fairy story. . . .

Duchess. Nonsense. It was the least I could do. I confess I am thankful that the poor children did not visit the Eiffel Tower. . . .

Amanda. How you must love your nephew, madame!

Duchess. My dear, I worship him—and so will you, when you meet him.

Amanda. But I still don't understand where I fit in, madame. I promise you I've never set eyes on your nephew at any time—let alone during those three fatal days—I can't possibly be one of his souvenirs. I've never been in Dinard in my life.

Duchess [*to* HECTOR]. Hector, I find her quite delightful.

Hector. I must admit she's rather pretty.

Duchess. She is far more than just pretty. She has spirit.

Hector. That's what I meant.

Duchess. Hector, you're pathetic. [*To* AMANDA.] Pay no attention to him, dear. You have spirit. A quality all too rare these days.

Amanda [*lively*]. I am well aware that I have spirit, madame. But I was not aware that my reputation for it had spread all the way down from the Rue de la Paix. Don't try to tell me that *that's* why you sent for me!

Duchess. No, child. [*She suddenly seems uneasy.*] What time is it? Here we are, chattering away . . . it must be quite late. . . . [*She starts to rise.*]

Amanda [*desperate, pushing her down again*]. No, madame. Sit down and give me a straight answer for once. I don't know what time it is, and I don't care. I've missed my train back anyway, thanks to you. . . .

Duchess. Nobody has ever dared to use that tone with me—not even the dear duke!

Amanda. Well, nobody has ever dared to lure me into the wilds of Brittany by promising me a job, and then refused to tell me what the job is!

Duchess [*to* HECTOR]. This is painful for us, Hector, but we asked for it. [*Resolute.*] Hector, we must tell her.

Hector [*unenthusiastic*]. Yes, we must.

Duchess. We must.

A long pause. They stare into the distance, deeply embarrassed.

[*Suddenly.*] Hector.

Hector. Yes.

Duchess Are you a man or a mouse?

Hector [*without hesitation*]. A mouse.

Duchess. What?

Hector [*pathetic but firm*]. A mouse. You're always telling me so.

Duchess. Only in fun, Hector. Of course, you're a man. Tell the girl the truth, before she begins to suspect the worst.

Amanda. I suspect the worst already, madame.

Duchess. My dear child, what you call the worst is the least of your worries. It is far worse than the worst. Go on, Hector. We are waiting.

Hector [*after much preliminary clearing of the throat*]. Well . . . the fact is . . . if you. . . . [*Pause. In a strangled voice.*] No, I can't say it! It was all your idea, anyway!

Duchess. Very well. I will meet you halfway. Let us speak in unison.

Hector. In unison?

Duchess [*ironic*]. Unless you feel up to the descant. We will recite together the speech we prepared this morning.

Hector. Word for word?

Duchess. Word for word. Watch my hand. One, two, three . . . ready?

Hector. Yes, I suppose so.

Duchess. Go!

> *They take a step forward, and begin, together:*

Duchess and Hector. Mademoiselle . . . or rather . . . dear child, if we may presume so to address you. . . . [*They look at each other, and take a breath in unison. Then they continue.*] Dear child . . . what we have to say may shock you, coming as it does from such irreproachably respectable lips as ours. . . .

HECTOR'S *voice has trailed off miserably. The* DUCHESS *gives him an admonitory look.*

Duchess. Hector, where are you?

Hector. It's no good . . . I can't say it . . . not even in unison!

Duchess [*sad*]. To think that an ancestor of yours once defended a bridge singlehanded against the entire Albigensian army.

Hector [*stung*]. That has nothing to do with it! Show me the Albigensian army, and I'll defend a bridge against it with pleasure. But this is a different kettle of fish, altogether, and I want no part of it.

Duchess. Very well. In that case, go away. Since the head of my family turns tail at the first whiff of grapeshot, I shall have to carry the banner alone! Leave us!

HECTOR *goes, his head bowed in shame. The* DUCHESS *abandons her belligerent attitude, and speaks more quietly and with less buffoonery than before, a genuine sensitivity shining under the raillery which makes her suddenly warm and human.*

Duchess. Well, child. I suppose you think I'm a mad old woman . . . no, no, don't deny it . . . but I do assure you that I'm not. I know perfectly well that you will be offended by what I'm going to say. You will stand up in adorable affronted dignity, clutching your little cardboard suitcase, and slip away through my fingers into the dusk. [*She looks at* AMANDA, *then goes on.*] And the tragic thing is that if you were my daughter, that is just what I would want you to do . . . and yet . . . my dear . . . no one can overhear us . . . and even you and I are growing dim to each other, as the violet velvet of the evening falls tactfully between us. [*She stops, and dreams a little.*] If you were my daughter . . . but I have no daughter. I could never have a child. Was it poor Gaston's fault or mine? I never knew. And when he died it was too late for me to find out. I have no daughter. But I have a nephew. Perhaps it is naughty of me to be so indulgent with him . . . but it is only because I love him too well . . . and in any case, I am extravagant by nature. [*A little pause. She looks at* AMANDA *again.*] If you were my daughter . . . but there it is. Providence sends us good fortune and bad. Sometimes we have bitter roles to play, believe me. Here I am, near the final curtain of my life, playing a ridiculously unsuitable part for a woman in my position . . . but you . . . you are so young . . . standing in the wings of your life . . . waiting to make your entrance, tremulous on the brink of adventure . . . it would be so easy for you to come to the rescue of a poor old woman who is at her wit's end.

Amanda [*a murmur*]. I don't understand what you mean, madame.

Duchess. I did not intend that you should, my dear. I am only talking to myself—rambling on to spin out the tardy time until the dusk deepens to hide my blushes. How strange it feels to blush. I have not blushed since I was a little girl in a crinoline made to stand in the corner because I refused to kiss a field marshal with a black beard.

Pause. It grows darker.

Amanda [*a whisper*]. It is almost dark now, madame.

Duchess [*a sudden brisk voice from the gathering gloom*]. Tell me then, child—have you had many lovers?

Amanda [*taken aback*]. Lovers?

Duchess. Flirtations, I mean. Nothing serious. Snatched kisses in the shrubbery after a croquet party—oh, what am I saying! I simply cannot get my epochs right!

AMANDA *is silent. Pause.*

[*A little weary.*] Now I've frightened you. Or even disgusted you. I don't want to know whether you have ever been in love, child. I wouldn't pry into your secret heart. I am simply talking about flirtations.

Amanda [*soft, after a pause*]. Yes, madame. I have had flirtations, but I have never been in love.

Duchess. Life is full of delicious surprises, child. One day love will burst upon you out of a clear sky in a sudden golden glory. Until then, you must live as intelligently as you can from day to day, and when your moment of happiness comes . . . seize it with both hands—be greedy—don't waste it, for it will never come again. [*Pause.*] But I did not mean to speak of love. [*Pause.*] Albert is a fine handsome boy—but all his youth and gaiety have been numbed by his sorrow. Day by day I see him grow more melancholy and more desperate. One day he will take his own life, tomorrow perhaps, perhaps the day after . . . I don't know. But one day he will do it, unless I can bring Léocadia back to life for him.

Amanda. Bring her back to life?

Duchess. My dear, I'm a very influential old woman, even in these democratic days, and ludicrously rich. I have done everything in my power for him—but I have failed. And now I cannot lift a finger to save his life—unless you will help me.

Amanda. But how, madame? I dare not think that you mean . . . well, in any case, why me? I'm not very pretty, and even if I was, how could anyone come between him and his memories?

Duchess. Nobody could—except you.

Amanda [*amazed*]. Me?

Duchess. The first time I saw you in Mme. Rensada's shop, child—I wept. Because, to anyone who knew her as she really was, you are the living image of Léocadia.

Silence. The park is vibrant with rustling leaves and chasing shadows.

Amanda [*very soft*]. Even so, I'm afraid I can't do it, madame. I may be poor and insignificant, but at least my flirtations have been my own. . . .
Duchess. Of course. I beg your pardon.

She gets up slowly. For the first time, we realize what a very old lady she is. Suddenly there is the sound of a bicycle bell. The DUCHESS *trembles.*

Listen! There he is! Oh, let him see you standing beside the obelisk, where he first met her! Let him see you just once—and cry out, be horrified, anything! I swear I will tell him tomorrow that it was a trick I played on him, even though he may hate me for it. It's worth it, if only I can see him stung into feeling again by something alive. [*She grasps* AMANDA's *arm.*] I beg you, mademoiselle . . . on my knees. Take pity on me. [*She looks at her imploringly then adds quickly.*] And you will see him, too. And . . . great heavens, I'm blushing again . . . the third time in sixty years and the second time in ten minutes . . . how gloriously illogical life is. My dear, he is handsome, he is charming. Why shouldn't he be one of your very own flirtations—for a moment?

The bicycle bell sounds again, closer.

Amanda [*a whisper*]. What shall I say to him?
Duchess [*embracing her*]. Just say, "Excuse me, can you tell me the way to the sea?"

She disappears into the deep shadows under the trees— just in time. Out of the darkness, the shadow which is the PRINCE *on his bicycle passes close to the shadow which is* AMANDA *standing by the obelisk.*

Amanda. Excuse me. . . .

The PRINCE *stops, gets off his bicycle, and sees her.*

Prince. Yes, mademoiselle?
Amanda. Can you tell me the way to the sea?
Prince. The second turning on the left, mademoiselle.

He bows, remounts and cycles off. The DUCHESS *emerges from the shadows. Pause.*

Amanda [*soft*]. He didn't recognize me. . . .

Duchess. It is very dark . . . and then he may remember her differently after all this time. [*Pause, then she says, almost shyly.*] The last train has gone, mademoiselle. Won't you change your mind and stay with us tonight?

Amanda [*after a pause, softly*]. Thank you, madame. . . .

The darkness has really closed in now, and the figures of the two women can no longer be distinguished in the gloom. Only the wind can be heard sighing in the tall trees. The curtain falls.

SCENE III

The DUCHESS's *study. Morning. The* BUTLER *is seated at a table paying the* ICE-CREAM MAN *and* TAXI DRIVER. *They sign and exit. The* BUTLER *appears to be waiting for something. The door opens and a man comes in. In dress, deportment and manner, he as like the* BUTLER *as two peas in a pod. He is the* HEADWAITER. *The two regard each other with hostility.*

HEADWAITER. Good morning.

Butler. Good morning. [*Pause. He pays the* HEADWAITER, *who, after receiving his money, makes no effort to leave. Pause.*] Is there anything further I can do for you?

Headwaiter. Her Grace requested me to wait upon her here at nine o'clock, in order to discuss certain details relating to the entirely imaginary Viennese night club which I run in the park.

Butler [*with a tinge of bitterness which he takes pains to conceal*]. In that case, won't you take a seat?

Headwaiter. I am much obliged to you.

He sits down, stiffly. The BUTLER *makes as if to leave the room, pausing as he goes to adjust the position of a Venetian blackamoor, with an authority calculated to drive home the fact that this is his domain. At the door, however, he changes his mind and comes back.*

Butler. I wonder if I may have a word in your ear?

Headwaiter. You may.

Butler. I myself have been in service all my life with high-class families—representing, I flatter myself, all that is best in the upper reaches of society. But I have a brother-in-law who has elected to pursue his profession in the hotel and restaurant side of our calling—for the sake of money. He has been employed at the Waldorf, the Savoy, the Excelsior . . . perhaps you may have heard of these establishments?

Headwaiter. I have heard of them.

Butler. Now, I must confess that in him, and in his colleagues, I have always detected a certain slackness . . . a tendency toward familiarity, typical of those who serve a customer rather than a master.

Headwaiter [*inscrutable*]. I fear I cannot follow your train of thought.

Butler. I will elucidate. I have failed, to my great astonishment, to observe in you any sign of this degeneracy. I understand you used to work in Dinard, in a short-lived establishment, which, if I may say so, could not in the nature of things have been . . . shall we say . . . five star.

Headwaiter [*pale*]. It was an excellent restaurant of its kind . . . excellent . . . but five star, no. Three, say. But not five.

Butler. As I thought. So I would like to put a question to you. Did you not spend long years of service in a private household before——

Headwaiter [*bowing his head, with a stifled sob*]. Yes, you are right. I did . . . before . . . but then one day——

Butler [*silencing him with a gesture*]. Please. Please. Far be it from me to pry into the reasons for your downfall. I merely wished to verify my contention that a butler who is worthy of the name can always be distinguished by a standard of etiquette which no degradation can eradicate.

Headwaiter [*raising his head*]. Thank you.

Butler [*affable and superior*]. Think nothing of it, my dear fellow. You must forgive me if I have twisted the knife in an old wound. The subject will never be mentioned again. [*Formal.*] I will inform Her Grace of your arrival.

He goes. The DUCHESS *enters in a whirl as usual, followed by* HECTOR *and* AMANDA. *The latter is dressed in the flamboyant style which one would associate with Léocadia.*

Duchess [*to the* HEADWAITER]. Ah, there you are, Ferdinand.

Headwaiter [*rising precipitately*]. Good morning, Your Grace.

Duchess [*a cry*]. Don't say good morning to me yet! Turn around. [*He does.*] I have something to show you. Don't look yet! Well, what have you to say to me now?

The HEADWAITER *looks at* AMANDA, *bewildered, and then suddenly, realization breaks upon him.*

Headwaiter. Aaaah!

Duchess [*forgets herself to the point of seizing his hand in her enthusiasm*]. Thank you! Oh, thank you for that Aaah! [*To* AMANDA.] We have succeeded, child. Come and kiss me. [*She kisses* AMANDA. *Then she turns to the* HEADWAITER *again.*] Now you may wish me good morning.

Headwaiter. Good morning, Your Grace.

Duchess [*in her usual, aloof tone*]. Good morning, Ferdinand. [*She indicates* AMANDA.] Well? Is it not truly amazing?

Headwaiter. It's . . . it's phantasmagoric, Your Grace.

Duchess [*a cry*]. Phantasmagoric! The very word I have been searching for since yesterday! Phantasmagoric! That is exactly it. Where did you find it?

Headwaiter. What, Your Grace?

Duchess. That word! Where did you find it?

Headwaiter. I really don't know, Your Grace . . . in a newspaper, I think. . . .

Duchess. Ah, I never read the newspapers. That accounts for it. Phantasmagoric. [*She is delighted.*] Phantasmagoric! You are phantasmagoric, child!

Amanda. I don't much like the sound of it, madame.

Duchess. Oh, what a quaint girl it is! Don't worry, child, you may appear phantasmagoric to us, but in reality you are a Greuze. A little living Greuze.

Hector. I'd say she has more of the piquant, provocative quality of a Boucher.

Duchess. Fiddlesticks. Don't talk nonsense, Hector. She is not at all a Boucher, she is a Greuze. When she smiles, I will grant you a fleeting glimpse—no more—of a Le Nain shepherdess. . . . [*To* AMANDA.] Has nobody ever remarked on it before?

Amanda [*simply*]. No, madame. I've never heard of any of those people.

Duchess. She is adorable, Hector.

Hector. Adorable.

Duchess [*to* AMANDA, *as though explaining to an imbecile child*]. They are painters, dear. Great artists who lived long ago, and painted pictures . . . with paint brushes.

Amanda [*a little smile*]. Yes, I know what a painter is.

Duchess [*offhand*]. I have a couple of dozen of their best canvases in the picture gallery. That will settle the argument. But meanwhile, we have work to do. [*She approaches the* HEADWAITER.] Ferdinand, we need your help. That is why I asked you to come here. The Prince has not yet had the opportunity of being presented to this young lady, and I am determined that when he sees her, he shall be thunderstruck. Absolutely thunderstruck! But, alas, we cannot work miracles. It would be so much easier if we could—frankly, we need one.

Amanda. Oh, don't say that, madame! I'm scared enough as it is!

Duchess. There's no sense in minimizing the difficulties of our task, dear. We have a physical resemblance. That goes a long way, but not far enough, especially in the case of a woman like Léocadia. We must create an atmosphere. First of all—[*to* HECTOR, *a scream*] where are the orchids?

Hector [*jumping up, as though afraid that he might have been sitting on them*]. The orchids!

Duchess. Have you forgotten that Léocadia never went anywhere without a sheaf of orchids? I must telephone Dinard and have a selection sent along immediately.

She goes out. He follows. AMANDA *is left alone with the* HEADWAITER. *They look at each other for a moment, embarrassed. Then she says, with a smile:*

Amanda. Phantasmagoric, am I . . . ?

He hesitates, as though unsure what attitude to take—then makes a vague and noncommittal gesture.

We've got a funny profession, you and I, haven't we?

Headwaiter [*stiff and formal*]. There is no such thing as a funny profession, mademoiselle.

Amanda [*gently*]. No, I suppose there isn't. [*Pause.*] Well, we all have to eat, don't we? How long have you been at it?

Headwaiter. At what, mademoiselle?

Amanda. Being a memory.

Headwaiter. Nearly two years now, mademoiselle.

Amanda. D'you get decent pay?

The HEADWAITER *is shocked by this question. He makes*
a gesture reminiscent of a butler refusing a tip.

Headwaiter. Mademoiselle! [*Then, abashed by* AMANDA's
clear gaze, he adds.] Yes, mademoiselle, very good pay. . . .
[*At once he is overcome with remorse at having given*
away forbidden secrets of his profession. He adds shame-
facedly.] Well . . . that is . . . when I say "good" . . .
I don't mean. . . .

Amanda [*amused at his embarrassment*]. Is it tiring?

Headwaiter. What, mademoiselle?

Amanda. Being a memory. [*The* HEADWAITER *makes a*
negative gesture.] What do you do all day?

Headwaiter. Nothing. I just wait. I wait for him to come.
I walk about among the empty tables. I think. [*He adds,*
in a burst of confidence.] It's strange, isn't it, when you
consider it. Strange, and a bit sad, really.

Amanda. I only saw him for a moment last night—and
it was very dark. What's he like? Is he nice?

Headwaiter. He's neither nice nor not nice. He just
doesn't seem to be there at all, if you know what I mean.

Amanda. What does he do when he comes into your
restaurant?

Headwaiter. He sits down at a table—always the same
one—the table they had that night. Then he orders what
they ordered then—a bottle of Pommery. I bring the champagne and two glasses. Then he sits and stares at the empty
chair opposite him, without saying a word. Sometimes for
five minutes. Sometimes all night. And then he goes away.

Amanda [*dreamy*]. Poor fellow.

Headwaiter. And we drink the champagne.

Amanda [*ingenuous*]. Ooh! Aren't you lucky!

Headwaiter. I don't know so much about that, mademoiselle. It's beginning to affect my liver.

Amanda [*after a pause*]. What's so funny is that they
only knew each other for three days. I should have thought
it took longer than that to fall in love . . . properly, I
mean. . . . [*Suddenly she demands of the* HEADWAITER.]
Were they lovers?

Headwaiter [*after his first shocked reaction*]. That I
can't say, mademoiselle. They certainly didn't spend the
night together in *my* establishment. [*Pause. Unbending a*

little.] The people who run the Chime of Bells—they've been brought here too, you know—they maintain . . . but then I have reason to believe that they circulate the story simply to try to look important themselves. . . .

Amanda [*very soft*]. And even if they were lovers . . . they had so little time together . . . just one night. [*Urgent again.*] Do you think he's *really* heartbroken, really and truly?

The HEADWAITER *indicates by a gesture that he does not intend to commit himself.*

know people do suffer terribly from broken hearts. But . always thought that they either bottled it all up so that nobody knew about it, or else went really crazy. I've never known anyone behave as he does.

Headwaiter [*infinitely lofty and patronizing*]. How can one presume to analyze the grief of the aristocracy?

The DUCHESS *has returned, followed by* HECTOR.

Duchess. There! Two hundred orchids will be here in ten minutes.

Amanda [*smiling*]. Surely that's far too many?

Duchess [*turning surprised*]. What do you mean, too many? I very much doubt whether it will be enough. Léocadia used to nibble them ceaselessly. How long do you think it takes a person of sensitivity to nibble the heart out of an orchid? —Naturally, she discarded the outside petals.

Amanda. I've no idea. If I wanted to eat flowers, I'd buy daisies. They're cheaper.

Duchess [*not even hearing this last remark*]. Now, we must plan. I have decided to reconstruct a specific incident for the child. I think that the arrival of Léocadia at the Blue Danube restaurant would be the most vivid. [*She seizes a chair.*] First of all, we must set the scene. [*To* AMANDA.] Sit there for a moment. [*To* HECTOR.] Isn't she ravishing? And she is getting the idea of it already. [*She inspects* AMANDA'S *face at very close quarters, and adds.*] Ravishing!

Amanda. I suppose I'd better try to look distinguished.

Duchess [*bustling away*]. No, no. Don't try to look anything. We will tell you what to do. [*To the* HEADWAITER.] I don't want to rehearse in your café, because Albert is out riding in the park and he might come in and catch us at it. Here we are perfectly safe. He never comes into the house in the morning, and in any case Theophilus is keeping watch at the door. [THEOPHILUS *pokes his head in.*] Right. [*She goes to* AMANDA.] Now, child, I have come to the conclusion that the secret of Léocadia's fascination lay in her eyes. She had a way of looking at one—something like this—which was absolutely irresistible. Between ourselves, she was extremely nearsighted. While we are arranging the furniture, I want you to practice screwing up your eyes, as I showed you. . . . Let me see. This will be the entrance. [*To the* HEADWAITER.] You can help me move this blackamoor. Léocadia loved him. She always called him her coal-black Ariel, as fickle and insubstantial as a fugitive shadow. . . . [*She lifts the figure with the aid of the* HEADWAITER.] Heavens, what a heavy brute he is. [*As she passes* AMANDA, *she says.*] Screw up your eyes, child. Screw up your eyes and incline your head slightly forward. That's better. You're coming on splendidly.

The door half-opens noiselessly, the BUTLER *peeps in, and is shattered to see that his rival, aided by the* DUCHESS, *is flaunting the most sacred conventions by moving the statue, while in a corner the strange young person is screwing up her eyes and bowing her head incessantly, and for no apparent reason. He trembles with horror and disappears.*

Duchess [*rearranging the furniture*]. If this is the stage where the orchestra is, then the table where they sat should go here. Is that right?

Headwaiter. Approximately, yes, Your Grace.

Duchess. Well done. [*As the* HEADWAITER *looks up in surprise.*] I was talking to myself. [*To* AMANDA.] Stop screwing up your eyes now, child, you'll get cramp, and the knack will desert you when you need it most. [*To the* HEADWAITER.] Ferdinand, I will tell you what I want you to do. I knew Léocadia too well. It would be of the greatest value to us if you, as a stranger, would describe to the young lady your instinctive, overwhelming impression of the divine Léocadia when she entered the Blue Danube night club for the first time.

Headwaiter [*delighted to be asked to play such an important role*]. My impression?

Duchess. Your instinctive impression. Don't be afraid. Take your time. We are all comrades here, seeking only to unearth the truth, the whole truth and nothing but the truth.

Headwaiter [*instinctively raising his hand*]. So help me God.

Duchess. What's that?

Headwaiter [*blushing*]. Nothing, Your Grace. Forgive me.

Duchess [*to* AMANDA]. I said stop screwing up your eyes, girl. For heaven's sake, stop!

Amanda [*whose eyes are screwed up in a desperate effort to hide her laughter*]. I wasn't aware I was doing it, madame.

Duchess [*delighted*]. Excellent! You are really beginning to feel like Léocadia. In that case, screw them up by all means, dear. [*To the* HEADWAITER.] We are waiting.

Headwaiter [*who has had time to think it over*]. Very well then. To be honest, Your Grace, when Mademoiselle Léocadia Gardi first came into the Blue Danube, I think I am speaking for all of us there when I say that we received a profound shock.

Duchess. A shock? How very interesting. A shock. [*To* AMANDA.] Remember that, child. Have you a pencil?

Amanda [*who can hardly suppress her mirth*]. No, but I'll remember. [*Imitating the* HEADWAITER.] A shock.

Duchess [*repeats, entranced*]. A shock.

Hector. A shock.

Headwaiter. A shock. First of all, Mademoiselle Léocadia was beautiful—very beautiful indeed. But she had a most disturbing way of looking you straight in the eyes, walking right up to you, and then looking away at the very moment when you expected her to speak to you . . . she did it with an air of arrogance, of distinction . . . which reminded me more than anything of . . . may I speak frankly, Your Grace?

Duchess. Please do.

Headwaiter. A dog! A mad dog! A demented borzoi!

Duchess [*enthusiastic*]. A demented borzoi! [*To* AMANDA.] Remember all that. It is surprisingly accurate. This fellow has a rare and courageous gift of observation. It's quite true—the whole of Léocadia's character was revealed in that particular and inimitable manner of walking. [*She demonstrates.*] Holding your eyes with hers until your noses were in imminent danger of collision, and then —suddenly—losing interest and passing you by without another glance. There is her whole personality in a nut-shell. [*She bumps into* HECTOR.] I am quite different, of course. With my height, I have to stand on tiptoe to look anybody in the eyes. It's very provoking. [*To the* HEAD-WAITER.] Do you know what you must do now, my good man, to make a lasting impression on the child? You must give us a demonstration.

Headwaiter. A demonstration of what, Your Grace?

Duchess. Of Léocadia entering the Blue Danube, of course.

Headwaiter [*who is dying to*]. I really don't know if I can, Your Grace. . . .

Duchess. It is an order.

Headwaiter. Very good, Your Grace. But Your Grace must understand that I mean no disrespect by anything I do . . . after all, I'm a man . . . it's not easy for a man to imitate a lady.

Duchess. Bah! Don't worry about that. We are here simply and solely to build up an atmosphere for the girl.

Headwaiter. All right, then. When Mademoiselle Léocadia Gardi came in, the orchestra had just started to play, by special request, a tango which was very popular that year—"The Chains of Love." And then. . . .

Duchess. One moment! I have an idea. Hector, you can be the orchestra. Go up on the stage—that's right. You know "The Chains of Love"—two years ago you nearly drove us all mad whistling it. Hum it. It will help this good fellow.

Hector [*delighted*]. May I mime the violinist as well?

Duchess [*uninterested*]. If you wish.

HECTOR *hums the tango and debates mimically upon the desirability or otherwise of accompanying himself upon an imaginary violin.*

Headwaiter. If you are agreeable, Your Grace, I will direct my entrance at you.

Duchess. An excellent idea.

Headwaiter. Right! Orchestra!

HECTOR *attacks* "The Chains of Love." *The* HEADWAITER, *with great seriousness, begins to mime Léocadia's entry into the Blue Danube. At this moment, the* BUTLER *enters precipitately, much agitated.*

Butler. Your Grace!

He stops, rooted to the spot, as his rival passes him, oblivious and apparently performing the steps of some outlandish tango, with his eyes fixed hypnotically on those of the DUCHESS, *who exclaims as he reaches her:*

Duchess. That's it! That's it! That's absolutely right! This man is a mimic—a born mimic! Do it again, quickly, while you are in the mood. And you, child, walk behind him and copy everything he does.

HECTOR *starts the waltz again. The* HEADWAITER *repeats his performance, with* AMANDA, *who is bursting with laughter, following behind and imitating him. The* HEADWAITER *finishes his promenade and turns to watch his pupil. He cries ecstatically:*

Headwaiter. Bravo, mademoiselle! Just like that! Now, come right up to me—look me in the eye! Be arrogant! Be haughty! I'm only a headwaiter! I'm lower than mud! You don't even see me any more!

But AMANDA *has suddenly stopped dead, covered in confusion. For the* PRINCE *has pushed aside the* BUTLER, *who since his entrance has stood as though petrified, and stands there in the doorway, pale with anger.* HECTOR *stops humming, and the* DUCHESS *and the* HEADWAITER *turn round, dumfounded.*

Prince. Aunt Melisande!
Duchess. Albert!
Prince. What is the meaning of this masquerade?
Duchess. Theophilus, what have you done?
Butler [looking ten years older, as he bows his head]. I came to warn Your Grace, but I was so dumfounded by what I saw that I fear I——
Duchess [terrible, with an imperious gesture]. Theophilus, you are dismissed!

The BUTLER *creeps out, a hundred years older.*

Prince [dry, to the others]. Perhaps the rest of you would be kind enough to leave us also. I wish to speak to this young lady alone.

HECTOR *and the* HEADWAITER *beat a hasty retreat. The* DUCHESS *also prepares to go. The* PRINCE *looks at* AMANDA *for the first time, to her great embarrassment. Suddenly he sees the Venetian blackamoor. He leaps to it.*

Who has dared to lay hands on this statue?

Duchess [*at the door*]. I did, Albert. I wished to clear a space for——

Prince [*in a fury, as he puts the statue back in its original place*]. I gave orders that nobody, under any pretext whatsoever, was to touch anything that she had touched!

The DUCHESS, *who is really not very intimidated by this display of temper, is making complicated signs to* AMANDA *behind the* PRINCE'S *back. He turns and catches her. The* DUCHESS *goes.*

Prince. I am afraid that my aunt has placed you in an embarrassing position, mademoiselle.

Amanda [*simple*]. I'm afraid she has, sir.

Prince [*unkind*]. I don't doubt that you were desperate to find employment of some sort——

Amanda. No, sir. That is to say, yes, sir. You see, your aunt had taken the trouble to get me dismissed from the milliner's where I worked before she summoned me here.

Prince. She's an amazing woman.

Amanda [*a little bitter*]. Amazing is right. [*Pause.*] But since yesterday I've got to the point where nothing amazes me any more.

Prince. You have been here since yesterday?

Amanda. Yes. You even spoke to me last night, in the park, by that obelisk with the stone bench round it——

Prince. Was that you? I must beg your pardon for not recognizing you. It was very dark. Why did you ask me the way to the sea?

Amanda [*soft*]. Apparently that was the particular phrase of which you had to be . . . reminded. . . .

Prince [*stops as though thunderstruck, and murmurs*]. Excuse me, can you tell me the way to the sea?

He sits down in an armchair, saying nothing, as if in a trance. Endless pause. AMANDA *clears her throat. No effect. She starts to tiptoe out. He suddenly cries:*

Don't go! Come back, where I can see you! You are plain. You walk badly. You are not in the least like her. You never could be like her. You're just a common little milliner, with no mystery, no aura——

Amanda. What's that?

Prince [*stops surprised*]. What?

Amanda. An aura?

Prince [*exploding*]. If you imagine that I'm going to give you lessons in your own language into the bargain——!

Amanda [*looking him straight in the face. With dignity*]. I only wanted to know if it's an insult.

Prince [*looking at her, he cannot repress a little smile. He says quietly*]. No, it is not an insult.

Amanda. I'm glad.

Pause. She looks him up and down and then walks toward the door with as much dignity as she can muster. The PRINCE *cannot help asking:*

Prince. What would you have done if it had been an insult?

Amanda [*turning*]. I would have told you just what I think of you.

Prince [*quiet and suddenly very weary*]. I don't care what anybody thinks of me. [*He retires into his huge armchair and relapses into silence.*]

AMANDA *watches him from the doorway with a suspicion of pity in her eyes. Suddenly he begins to mutter with closed eyes:*

Prince. Excuse me, can you tell me——? [*He stops, then tries again in a different tone.*] Can you tell me the way——? [*He tries another tone, but his voice is not flexible.*] . . . the way to. . . . [*He stops, weary. His features relax in sheer exhaustion.*]

AMANDA *sees that he is really distraught, and she murmurs softly, as she did in the park:*

Amanda. Can you tell me the way to the sea?

Pause.

Prince [*soft, almost humble*]. Who taught you to imitate that voice?

Amanda. Nobody. It's my own voice.

Prince. Would you mind very much repeating that sentence once more?

Amanda. Can you tell me the way to the sea?

Prince [*soft, eyes closed*]. The second turning on the left, mademoiselle.

Amanda. Thank you.

Prince [eyes still closed—suddenly]. Mademoiselle——
Amanda [surprised]. Yes?
Prince. You have dropped your glove.

AMANDA *looks at her feet, surprised, and then realizes that
he is reliving his conversation of two years ago. Timidly,
hazarding a guess, she says:*

Amanda. Thank you. That is very kind of you.
Prince [opening his eyes]. No. She didn't answer me.
She just smiled, a tantalizing half-smile, and disappeared
into the dusk. [*He stands up, not looking at her.*] Forgive me.
Amanda. It's you who must forgive me for being here.
[*Pause. Looks at him, then says gravely.*] What I don't
understand is that last night I said the same thing to you
and you answer me quite calmly, as though it was the
most ordinary thing in the world for someone to ask you
the way to the sea.
Prince. That's strange, isn't it?
Amanda. Yes. It is strange.
Prince [with difficulty, not looking at her]. Mademoiselle, I wonder whether—in spite of what I have said to
you—in spite of what you must think of me—you would
consider accepting my aunt's proposition, and for a little
while—say for three days—you would. . . .
*Amanda [bows her head. With all the dignity she can
manage, she says].* Last night, I refused. This morning, I
said "yes." Just now I was on the point of going out to say
"no" again. . . .
Prince [turning to her, kindly, for the first time]. Please
say "yes" again. It will make the score even.
Amanda. But it makes me look such a fool, always
changing my mind.
Prince. And how will I look?
Amanda. Oh, but—it doesn't matter for you. I can't
afford the luxury of going nuts about anybody at the
moment.
Prince. And what would happen to you if you did "go
nuts," as you say, about someone?
Amanda. Oh, dreadful things! I'd run my stockings and
lose my gloves and miss my train and lose my job——
[*She stops and sighs, laughing in spite of herself.*] Anyway,
all those things did happen to me yesterday.

Prince [*on the defensive*]. You have doubtless heard my story. I agree that for someone who leads your sort of existence, in which the small material considerations of everyday life loom so importantly, it must be somewhat galling to think of so much money, time and trouble expended on the worship of a memory.

Amanda [*quiet and simple*]. Oh, no, you're quite wrong. When we got the telegram saying that my father would never come back from the war, my mother, who was just an ordinary housewife, went and slept on a camp bed in the kitchen. And in their room, she laid out everything that had belonged to him—the suit he was married in she placed on the bed next to her white wedding dress, and every year, on the anniversary of his death, the flowers she used to buy cost her far more—comparatively—than you could ever spend even if you rebuilt a whole town in your park.

Prince. I beg your pardon.

Amanda [*very kind*]. Granted. But I don't want you to think——

Prince. I no longer think it, mademoiselle. And I am very grateful to you for what you have just told me, because it makes it possible for me to confide in you— a terrible confidence which I have never before entrusted to anyone. My aunt is a lunatic—a charming one perhaps—but a lunatic all the same. I am saner than she is. The only reason I have submitted to the caprices of her folly, and allowed her to rebuild in the privacy of the estate every place that I visited with Léocadia—the only reason was the hope that this very privacy and isolation would help me a little in my terrible struggle.

Amanda [*bewildered*]. Your struggle?

Prince [*with a smile*]. Yes. It's extraordinarily difficult to tell you this. And now that I am on the point of making my confession, I can see that it is almost comic. Please don't laugh at me . . . I agreed to all this simply because I am on the verge of forgetting.

Amanda. Forgetting what?

Prince. The woman I loved. I can't even remember the exact color of her eyes. I had completely forgotten her voice until just now. . . . [*He taps his forehead.*] To think that you could have stood there, in the same twilight, and asked me in that very voice the way to the

sea . . . and I didn't cry out . . . I wasn't even surprised. . . . I simply didn't notice. It's terrible . . .
it's laughable . . . Prince Albert Troubiscoi rebuilds a
whole town in his estate to preserve the memory of his
love, and he can't even remember the first words she said
to him. . . . [*He sits down, worn out.*]

Amanda. How can I help you, sir?

Prince [*low, after a pause*]. Stay here for three days,
and let me watch you moving through those memory-ridden
haunts where I seek for her, in vain. Try—forgive me for
saying this—but please try to be not yourself, but her—
just for three days.

Amanda [*who is standing with one hand caressing the
Venetian blackamoor*]. I will try.

Prince [*a sudden cry*]. Stay there! Don't move, I beg
you. . . . [*He runs to the door and begins to re-enact
this meeting.*] The next day she came to this house after
luncheon to ask my aunt if she could borrow the park for
a charity fete. My aunt was out, and so the butler called
me. I found her in here . . . standing just like that . . .
she told me she loved that statue . . . we spent the whole
afternoon together, and that evening she allowed me to
take her to the Blue Danube for the first time. That was
the restaurant where, the following evening, we discovered
that we loved each other. . . . [*Crossing back and forth
in his excitement as the memory is working.*] The Blue
Danube. The most pretentious and ridiculous place in the
world. With that fantastic headwaiter, and that ghastly
mock-Viennese music, which everyone was raving about
that year . . . she hummed it to herself all the evening. . . . [*He makes a poor attempt to sing the opening
bars of a waltz.*] Tra-la-la . . . how does that waltz go?

Amanda. Which waltz? I don't. . . .

Prince [*sings another phrase, rather ineptly, and then
says urgently*]. Help me! Help me!

Amanda. But I can't.

Prince. You can. . . . You must . . . you must *be*
her. [*He turns and faces her.*] You *are* her. . . .

Amanda [*slightly scared*]. I'm not. I'm Amanda.

Prince [*looking at her as if in a dream*]. No, you're not
. . . you're Léocadia. . . . [*He smiles at her, then walks
towards her and addresses her as if he's talking to the
real Léocadia.*] Léocadia. [*He will go on, but the curtain
falls as he reaches her.*]

ACT TWO

SCENE I

The clearing in the park where the DUCHESS *has rebuilt the Blue Danube café, which is brilliantly lit, the sparkling radiance from its tinkling chandeliers illuminating the old-fashioned charm of its baroque red plush and gilt décor. Three* GYPSIES, *who vaguely resemble skating instructors, ply their violins assiduously. An overzealous tenor sings* "The Chains of Love." *They remind one of ancient, dusty moths—once brilliant creatures of the night, now moldering neglected in a glass case, transfixed by pins. Indeed, so do the* HEADWAITER *and the* CLOAKROOM ATTENDANT— *the latter with her bun and frilly apron looking like a superannuated usherette. All of these people have just leaped to their posts at the arrival of* AMANDA *and the* PRINCE. AMANDA *is doing her own version of Léocadia's entry into the Blue Danube. She tosses the orchid on which she has been nibbling to the singer, stops her performance as she looks at the* PRINCE, *who has preserved his sober mien. The* CLOAKROOM ATTENDANT, *ravished with delight, helps* AMANDA *off with her furs. The* HEADWAITER *hovers expectantly. They sit down at their table.*

HEADWAITER [*as if he didn't know*]. And what may I bring you, sir?

Prince. The same as last night.

Headwaiter. Very good, sir. [*He writes down on his pad, then sotto voce repeats the order to one of his assistants, who repeats it to another.*] Pommery. '47.

Amanda [*without thinking*]. Oh . . . first of all . . . I would awfully like . . . I mean, I'm terribly thirsty, I do love it . . . a gin and lime with lots of water.

There is a moment of utter dismay. The music stops.

Headwaiter. But . . . that is . . . Mlle. Gardi did not . . . I'm sorry, mademoiselle, but. . . .

Amanda [*in confusion*]. No, no, I'm sorry. I must be crazy. Champagne . . . of course. The same as last night. Champagne it is.

Prince [stiff, after a pause]. If you are really thirsty . . . and if you're so very fond of it . . . bring the young lady a gin and lime.

Headwaiter [stunned]. A gin and lime. I'll go and see if we . . . yes, very good, sir. . . .

Amanda [calling after him]. With lots of water, please!

Headwaiter [more and more shocked]. Water! I've never heard of such a thing. . . . I suppose we can melt some ice. . . .

Amanda. Thank you—you're very kind. I'll drink it up quickly.

Headwaiter [as he goes, sotto voce]. I should hope so.

The music starts again.

Amanda [with an apologetic smile]. It's very difficult, you know, to have no will of one's own for two whole days.

Prince [dry]. Please try to be patient. The day after tomorrow you will be free.

Amanda. I don't need to be patient, you know that. It's thrilling being somebody else. . . . *[She fingers her bracelets.]* Somebody rich . . . somebody in love. . . .

Meanwhile, the gin and lime is being prepared—an elaborate and complicated ritual involving large numbers of people and much coming and going. At last, the precious glass is ready, and the HEADWAITER *brings it to the table, interrupting the* PRINCE.

Prince. You weren't at all bad yesterday.

Headwaiter. Your gin and lime, mademoiselle. *[He adds, in pain, for this is what upset him most.]* With lots of water.

Amanda [who really is thirsty]. Oh, thank you! *[She takes a mouthful and then suddenly looks at the glass.]* Ooh, it's lovely and strong!

She seems to be on the point of enjoying herself genuinely, reveling in the unaccustomed lights, music, perfume and jewels. But suddenly she notices that the PRINCE *and the* HEADWAITER *are watching her with icy impatience. Hastily she empties the glass in a single gulp, and cannot hide a grimace at the unwonted strength of the drink. She spills a little, which the* HEADWAITER *and his staff quickly mop up.*

Amanda. Pardon. [*She gives the glass to the* HEAD-
WAITER, *who takes it with a satisfied sigh.*]

Headwaiter. Ah!

Prince [*also relieved that this interlude is over*]. Ah!

*The orchestra, which had suspended operations during
the sacrilegious moment, breaks out again into the most
sentimental version of the waltz theme, and the* HEAD-
WAITER *brings on the champagne bucket and serves it with
all the ceremony fitting to a serious occasion, in an atmosphere restored to serenity.*

Prince. Yesterday was not at all bad, for a first attempt,
in spite of a few mistakes, and—how can I put it without wounding you?—a trace of the . . . plebeian in your
manner, which, I must admit, is not without a certain
charm of its own, but which, naturally, strikes a false note.

Amanda. I haven't said a single word of slang all day.

Prince [*offhand, to* AMANDA'S *horror*]. That's true. Of
course, Léocadia spoke nothing but slang—but nobody
could expect you to reproduce her language as well. The
important thing was to see you sitting there, on the other
side of the table, nibbling your flowers.

Amanda [*apologetically*]. I'm afraid I'm not much good
with flowers. I'm getting a bit discouraged about it.

Prince. Discouraged?

Amanda. Yes. Oh, I love to suck juicy blades of grass,
but these great big flowers . . . they're bitter and sweet
all at the same time . . . and having bits of them in my
mouth all evening—it's . . . well . . . [*She drains her
glass of champagne.*]

Prince [*dreamy*]. She used to say that they reminded
her of opium poppy and mandragora, and all the baleful
draughts of the inscrutable Orient.

Amanda [*trying to raise a smile from the* HEADWAITER,
who is pouring her another glass]. I don't know anything
about those things. I only know orchids give me a
stomach-ache. But I was better this afternoon, wasn't I?

Prince. Much better. When we took the boat and
idled away the long sunlit hours exploring the upper
reaches of the river, your evocation of the divine spirit of
Léocadia was nearly faultless.

Amanda [*pleased, with a triumphant look at the* HEAD-
WAITER]. Thank you.

Prince [*without malice*]. Of course, I realize that **on** that afternoon two years ago she deliberately dimmed the radiance of her blazing intellect to harmonize with my mood.

Amanda [*deflated*]. Thank you all the same.

She avoids the eye of the HEADWAITER, *who goes out shrugging.*

Prince [*oblivious*]. Yes, you were quite perfect. A touch livelier than she perhaps . . . a little too much flesh-and-blood.

Amanda. It's very difficult to be anything else when one *is* alive. But I'll do better this evening! I feel so light, as if I'm hardly weighing on my chair at all . . . but that's no wonder, considering the meals we've been having.

Prince. Léocadia always laid her glove down on her plate.

Amanda. I know . . . lucky I've got plenty of pairs of gloves.

Prince [*regarding her dreamily*]. Léocadia, blessed spirit.

Amanda [*afterthought*]. One day, you know, I'll eat one of them.

Prince. I beg of you, mademoiselle, out of respect to her sacred specter . . . even if your natural appetite overcomes you—as it must, as it has every right to—even if you do order huge meals to be sent up to your room each night after we have parted, I pray you, do not tell me about them.

Amanda. I may be only flesh and blood, but I am honest. I really am trying to be like her for these three days—even when I'm not with you. I promise you I've eaten nothing but orchids and champagne, and my plate has been empty except for embroidered gloves! I generally got to bed at ten, but last night I sat up as late as Mlle. Gardi used to. And if you'd walked past my window, you'd have seen me there in the small hours lying on a gilt chaise longue like she did, reading the poems of Mallarmé by candlelight. It was terribly uncomfortable.

Prince [*very surprised*]. But why? You knew there was not the remotest chance that I would pass your window after I had formally bidden you good night. Did you do it for fun?

Amanda. I should say not! I like books that make me

laugh, and I like to sleep. . . . Oh, how I'm going to sleep the day after tomorrow!

Prince. Then—why?

Amanda [*a little ill at ease*]. Because . . . well, when I do a job, I like to do it properly, that's all.

Pause. They have moved closer together, unconsciously. The Gypsies *feel obliged to strike up the waltz. When the* Prince *begins to speak again, they finish the music softly, and sit down again.*

Prince [*reverting to his original idea*]. That second evening was the turning point of our lives . . . that is, of all the life which was left to us. A precious morning together, and a last valedictory afternoon. . . .

Amanda. That was the evening when you discovered you loved each other, wasn't it?

Prince [*brusque*]. Who told you that?

Amanda. I can't remember—you, I think.

Prince. No, not I.

Amanda. Then it must have been your aunt—or perhaps I just sensed it when we arrived here tonight.

Prince. Yes, it was on the second evening. And as that strange night wore on——

Amanda [*interrupting*]. What did you talk about that night, before you began talking about yourselves?

Prince. We talked of nothing but ourselves.

Amanda. Did you do the talking, or did she?

Prince. Well . . . both of us . . . perhaps she more than I . . . why do you ask me that?

Amanda. No reason . . . just that it seemed to me . . . if I had fallen in love with you after that long sunny afternoon on the river, I'd have wanted to sit quite still, feeling the smooth satin of my dress against my sunburned skin, and the icy stem of my glass between my fingers . . . and just looked at you without saying a word.

Prince [*calmly*]. That is because you are a young savage, incapable of analyzing your own emotions.

Amanda. I suppose I am.

Prince. Which reminds me, I meant to thank you for the perfect tact and discretion with which you have played your part up till now. I presume that you are not talkative by nature?

Amanda. Oh, but I am. The girls in the workshop called me "Chinwag."

Prince. Chinwag?

Amanda. Yes, because I never stopped talking.

Prince. In that case, you must have great natural tact, which is even better.

Amanda [*laughing*]. Oh, goodness, no! In the shop before that, they used to call me Flatfoot.

Prince. Flatfoot?

Amanda. Because I was always putting my foot in things.

Prince. You do not appear to me to deserve either of those nicknames.

Amanda [*laughs*]. Oh, but I do . . . that's why I'd be so pleased if I made a success of these three days. And if I can't talk like Mlle. Léocadia, I do at least want to keep silent in the same way that she did. There are so many different ways of saying nothing to the man you love. How did she say nothing to you?

Prince. She spoke a little less loudly.

Amanda [*stupefied*]. But she went on speaking?

Prince. Oh, yes. She would always answer her own questions, or else finish your reply for you. At other times, she just murmured words at random—in Rumanian, as a rule—that was her mother tongue. That uninterrupted monologue was one of her greatest charms. She would punctuate her talk with deep, fascinating ripples of throaty laughter, thrown into the conversation at the moment when they were least expected, and dying away into what was almost a sob.

Amanda. I must seem very dull beside her.

Prince. No, no. You have done very well, mademoiselle, to present me with such an accurate and precious picture of her rare moments of silence. [*He has taken her hand quite naturally toward the end of this speech. Now he suddenly drops it.*] Forgive me.

Amanda [*looking at her hand*]. For what?

Prince. I took your hand. She hated anybody to touch her.

Amanda. Even you?

Prince. Especially me. She used to say that I had coarse peasant hands—hands made to hurt and destroy.

Amanda [*taking his hand quickly and looking at it*]. Peasant hands?

Prince [*a little embarrassed*]. The skin is hard, I know. **But what with** yachting and tennis . . . and then, I don't know if you agree with me, but I simply cannot play golf in gloves. . . .

Amanda [*still looking at his hand*]. How funny. You're a gentleman of leisure, and yet your hand does look like a peasant's. Hold out your arm so I can see it properly. [*He holds out his arm, a little unwillingly. She shuts her eyes and after a pause, murmurs.*] No. They are hard, but they would never do anybody any harm.

The PRINCE takes away his hand. Pause. The GYPSIES, terrified of being caught red-handed in idleness, leap to their violins. The Leader comes to the table, playing his seductive melody. The PRINCE says nothing, but stares at his hand. After a moment, AMANDA ventures timidly:

Penny for your thoughts?

Prince. I was thinking . . . if she had said—that evening—what you have just said—about my hands—I would have been wild with happiness.

Amanda [*soft*]. But if she talked so much, she must have told you, among other things, that she loved you.

Prince. Oh, yes. But I find it extremely difficult to remember the exact words she used to declare her love——

Amanda. Not the exact words, perhaps—but you surely remember the moment when she said them.

Prince. Even that is difficult. She was crazy that evening—she started a thousand topics—tossed them into the air and caught them as they fell in cascades of colored stars. She played at being every great lover in mythology—she compared me to a bull—to a swan. She even made me light an enormous cigar—a thing I detest—because she swore that some goddess or other was raped by Jupiter disguised as a puff of smoke! And all this intermingled with reminiscences of the ballets she had danced. That night I was Daphnis and Prince Siegfried, Jupiter and Mars. . . .

The violinist has rejoined his fellows, and the music dies softly into silence.

Amanda [*asks in a small voice*]. But you are sure that she didn't once say, simply, "I love you"?

Prince [*amused*]. Léocadia was incapable of saying simply "I love you"—even to her favorite greyhound or the little tame serpent which followed her everywhere.

Amanda. I'm not talking about a little serpent, tame or

not! I'm talking about you! I can't bear to think that she never said, "I love you, Albert."

Prince [*sarcastic*]. "I love you, Albert"! Really, mademoiselle, you are ludicrous. Please get it into your head once and for all that this was not a flirtation between a shopgirl and a butcher's boy on a park bench.

Amanda [*sharply*]. That's quite obvious. [*Then trying to console him, gently.*] I expect she did say "I love you" among all the other things, and you just didn't hear it.

Prince. I don't think so.

Amanda. But when you come here in the evenings, and try to imagine her sitting here opposite you, don't you imagine her talking?

Prince [*heavy*]. Of course . . . not straight away . . . it takes me several hours before I can conjure up the picture of her sitting there motionless . . . she used to move about such a lot! And even then, there are details which evade me . . . the eyes. . . . I can never quite remember the eyes. [*He looks at* AMANDA, *then turns away hurriedly.*] And then, when I have built up a complete picture of her in my mind, then, very cautiously, I imagine her talking. . . .

Amanda [*unable to refrain from a slightly malicious note*]. You imagine the monologue, do you?

Prince [*ingenuous*]. Oh, no, that would be far too difficult—almost impossible. I have to imagine her saying the simplest things. . . . "Yes . . . no . . . perhaps . . . this evening." I try to make her say my name . . . she decorated me with a galaxy of ridiculous nicknames . . . Florizel, Endymion, Prince Charming . . . she never called me by my real name—she found it unaesthetic . . . which it is, of course—but still, it is my name. So now I take my gentle revenge—I make her say "Albert." Once I sat here for a whole night, making her repeat over and over again "My darling Albert." But I am hoist with my own petard, for the only time she ever said that to me, she was making fun of me, and it is always that moment which I recapture when I visualize her lips forming my name.

Amanda. And do you never make her say "I love you"? That would be the moment when you had her in your power.

Prince [*lowering his eyes*]. No. I dare not. I cannot

really imagine that she ever did say it . . . I have no recollection of her lips forming those words.

Amanda [almost tenderly]. Look at me.

He raises his head, surprised, and looks at her. Looking him straight in the eyes, she murmurs softly:

I love you, Albert.

He looks at her, pale, his face working.

I love you, Albert. Watch my lips, and remember how they look. I love you, Albert.

Prince [a little hard, from a dry throat]. Thank you.

He tries to pour out some champagne but his hand is shaking, and he does not tip the bottle far enough. The HEADWAITER, *who is hovering like a hawk, misinterprets this, and arrives at a canter.*

Headwaiter. Another bottle of champagne, sir?

Prince. Yes, please. [*The* HEADWAITER *takes the ice bucket. At once the orchestra, who seem to regard this as a signal, attack a composition of great* brio *and gaiety. The* PRINCE *turns to them, suddenly angry, and cries.*] I don't want to hear that music.

Headwaiter [coming forward]. Forgive me, sir, but surely you have not forgotten that this particular piece of music was played at the exact moment when the second bottle of champagne was served? And that is exactly what happened on that particular evening, I can assure you, sir.

Prince [exasperated]. I don't care what happened that evening! Stop that music!

The players stop, amazed. There is a shocked silence at these blasphemous words. The HEADWAITER, *who is holding the ice pail, trembles like a leaf. In the ghastly pause, the only sound is the rattling of the bottle in the metal bucket. The* HEADWAITER *trembles so violently that the champagne, thoroughly shaken up, suddenly expels its cork with a tremendous explosion. The* CLOAKROOM ATTEND-ANT, *watching from the doorway of her lair, lets out a squeak of alarm. The champagne falls in a deluge of bubbles. The* WAITERS *mop it up.*

Headwaiter [in an agony of mortification]. Please forgive me, sir. . . . It's the first time in thirty-seven years that that has happened . . . it must have been a bad bottle. I will bring another immediately.

Amanda [calmly to the retreating HEADWAITER]. And another gin and lime for me.

Headwaiter [horrified, as he exits]. Another gin and lime!

Prince [between clenched teeth]. What is the meaning of this gratuitous insolence?

Amanda [calm]. It's not insolence. It's simply that I don't intend to put up with your stupid bad temper any longer. So I'm going back to being "me" for a bit. And "me," I'm thirsty. And "me," I don't like champagne.

Prince. Me! Me! Me! That's all you ever think about isn't it? Well, let me tell you that for the last two days you've never once stopped being "you." You've simply been making fun of something you are too ignorant to understand.

Amanda. That's not true. I've tried as hard as I can to be her. I've done my level best, and I can't go on a moment longer. Please excuse me, and let me have my gin and lime.

The WAITERS *have returned.*

Prince. Why did you hurt me by saying those words you knew she never said?

Amanda. I hoped they would help you.

Prince. You're lying.

Amanda. Yes, I'm lying. [*She stands up. Simply.*] Please forgive me what I'm going to say. But it seems to me that a love affair is too precious and beautiful a thing to play about with like this. I know you'll be furious with me, and probably drive me away—but I'll go back to Paris happier if I've told you what I think. She never loved you. But that isn't really important, because you can give all your heart to someone and get nothing in return—and anyway, I'm certain you know already, deep down, that she didn't love you. But there's worse to come, and I must say it before I go. You're young and rich and handsome and charming and your hands aren't really hard . . . just strong and useful . . . you ought to try to live, and be happy and forget the past—because I'm absolutely positive that you didn't love her either.

Silence. Nobody breathes. Then the PRINCE *says calmly:*

Prince. I'm afraid you are very stupid, mademoiselle, and unspeakably impudent into the bargain. Ferdinand, please bring mademoiselle's wrap. The path back to the house is rather dark, so someone will walk with you. My aunt's secretary will settle up with you in the morning.

Amanda. You're not hurting anybody but yourself by bringing money into this.

Prince [*a bitter smile*]. I had quite forgotten the admirably disinterested attitude of the proletariat toward filthy lucre. If you prefer it, we will pay you nothing.

Amanda. Oh, yes, you will. You'll give me the price of my return ticket to Paris, and three days' pay as a milliner at trade union rates, with overtime.

Prince [*icy*]. You may go now.

The HEADWAITER *creeps up, followed by the* CLOAKROOM ATTENDANT, *who carries* AMANDA'S *wrap.*

Headwaiter [*stammers with emotion*]. M-M-Mademoiselle's . . . wr-wrap. . . .

Amanda. You can take it back to the house yourself. Me, *I* don't wear furs in the summer. *I'm* quite warm enough, thank you. [*She moves toward the door with dignity.*]

Prince [*calling her back*]. Mademoiselle!

She stops. He indicates that everyone else is to leave. They do.

Mademoiselle. I belong to a class which is invariably represented in humorous fiction as consisting entirely of effete young half-wits and dithering dotards. . . . I suppose it's only to be expected that you should think me an imbecile.

Amanda. I never said that!

Prince. But you would have liked to. No, don't deny it, it is quite understandable. I have just accused you of being stupid—we always accuse people of being imbeciles if their views differ from our own. No. You cannot dispute that people are prejudiced against a man like me, who lives in a sixteenth-century mausoleum, and rejoices in twenty-two Christian names and a procession of titles, all of which lost their significance centuries ago. It may surprise you when I tell you that it is just as difficult for a man in my position to convince people that he is not a blockhead as it would be for the scion of a long line of village idiots. And even then, once the village idiot's son has proved his intelligence, he is laden with scholarships and encouraged to become Prime Minister. But I am not.

Amanda. I don't see at all what you're driving at.

Prince. Just this. You and I are neither of us idiots. Are we agreed on that? Nevertheless, my love story seems absolutely grotesque to you. You cannot imagine how I could possibly have fallen in love with such a weird creature as Léocadia.

Amanda. I never said "weird."

Prince. Only because you have been brought up never to speak ill of the dead. But if she had been here this evening, dressed like you, as like you in features as an identical twin, you would have been bursting with hysterical giggles all the evening at her behavior. Isn't that so? Admit it.

Amanda. Yes, I would.

Prince. But since we have agreed that neither of us is an imbecile, we are going to explain ourselves to each other, once and for all. Sit down.

Amanda. Why?

Prince. Because I am about to embark on an extremely long speech. [*And indeed he is.*] Right. Life is a wonderful thing to talk about, or to read about in history books— but it is terrible when one has to live it. It is almost impossible to sleep for more than twelve hours a day, and the remaining twelve hours have to be filled in somehow. There are, of course, the classic diversions—drink and drugs. But personally I have no taste for happiness induced by chemical compounds. There is, too, the determined brightness of the Boy Scout breed, who fill every second with some useless but efficiently performed task—but that sort of behavior requires a special talent which, mercifully, is disturbed by providence as parsimoniously as any other. As for the method which consists of leaping out of the right side of the bed every morning in the chilly dawn, and doing Swedish exercises in front of an open window, repeating incessantly that every day and in every way things are getting better and better. . . . [*He shudders.*] No. That's nothing but a spiritual laxative, and not for me. Consequently—I was bored. "But you have everything in the world," they used to say to me. "It's downright ungrateful to be bored when there's so much poverty about."

What gloriously muddled thinking! One might just as well
tell a man who can't afford the price of a loaf of bread
that he has no right to complain, but on the contrary,
is extremely lucky, for he has good digestion and so many
millionaires are dyspeptic. He'd throw you downstairs, and
quite right too. It's just the same with me. Comfort can
be taken for granted just as easily as a good digestion, you
know. And only a fool could find happiness in comfort
alone. I was bored. "Ah," they said, "if you had to work
eight hours a day for your living, young man——" I don't
doubt it. If I had been poor and confronted daily with a
factory bench or a pile of ledgers, I would have had the
precious opportunity of keeping my mind occupied all the
week, and only being bored on Sundays, like everybody
else. But it was my fate to be condemned to endure seven
Sundays every week. I really did try to fill them. But somehow I didn't seem cut out for sitting on the committees of
charity balls, or presiding over the meetings of societies
for the encouragement of those breeds of horses which
run faster than their competitors. As for the idea of working to amass a still larger fortune, I'm sure you'll agree
that would be positively immoral. What more can I say?
I have no artistic talent. I have no great gift of scholarship.
I have a fairly good memory, it's true, but I think it's
ridiculous to press it into the service of recording knowledge
which would never be of the slightest use to me. No, the
only thing that remains for people like me is an organized
and unremitting round of amusements. We all get caught
up eventually in the terrible roundabout of the fashionable
seasons, and, believe me, it's a dog's life. If the professional
classes put half the energy, imagination and tenacity into
their businesses that the idle rich do into being bored to
tears in exactly the right place on exactly the right date
all over Europe, they would soon make their fortunes. I
haven't even any vices. Vices are wonderfully strong, simple things. But I haven't even one. [Pause, *as the awful
truth of what he has said penetrates his mind.*]

    Amanda [*soft*]. Have you finished?

    Prince. Almost. Through the clammy mists of boredom
from which I had practically abandoned hope of escaping,
there flashed suddenly, like a will-o'-the-wisp, a brilliant
creature, whose light and warmth dispersed the fog for
three short days. A preposterous character, I grant you,

followed by her retinue of greyhounds and tame serpents, a creature who awoke at dusk and went to bed at dawn, and spent the night between in meaningless chatter. An orchid-eater who lived on champagne and passion, and who died for the sake of an extravagant gesture—strangled by her own scarf. And yet, this madwoman, with all her ridiculous affectations and frivolities, was intelligent. . . . [*Pause. He looks at her, insolent.*] Intelligence. Another goddess of whom you may have heard. Her quicksilver intellect—her sublime outrageous wit—her profound nonsense suddenly made my life worth living. In those three days, before the mists closed in again, this lovely lunatic taught me the value of so many things. Oh, yes—she taught me the value of your world, of your silence, and your simple love, so happy just to bask in the sun among the carnival litter of a picnic. But she taught me the value of my world too—my world and hers—a world of bitter joys, beyond the comprehension of your uncomplicated happiness. [*Pause. A cry.*] I do not love you, mademoiselle! You are beautiful—even more beautiful than she—you are desirable, you are gay and tender and compact of all manner of delights—youth, nature, life . . . and even common sense into the bargain. But I do not love you!

Amanda [*the tears streaming down her face but sitting erect*]. Have you quite finished now?

Prince. Yes, I have finished.

Amanda [*getting up with dignity*]. Well, personally, you leave me cold. [*She crosses the restaurant and goes out.*]

The PRINCE *looks around, and finds that he is alone. Automatically, he goes to his table and as the* HEADWAITER *approaches, he says, pathetically.*

Prince. You never doubted that I loved her more than all the world, did you, Ferdinand?

Headwaiter [*obsequious*]. Oh, sir! How can you ask such a thing! You worshiped her. We all remarked on it, amongst ourselves. Such great love was unforgettable, sir —even to us, who only stand and wait.

Prince. Thank you, Ferdinand.

As the PRINCE, *who has fallen into a reverie, puts his head in his hands, the* HEADWAITER *turns to the orchestra, and signals for music. The* SINGER *starts softly to sing.*

Singer.
>Ages ago, I believed in love
>But that was ages and ages ago,
>And still I try, now that I
>Am deceived in love,
>To stop the clock, and recapture the glow.
>I pace the street, and hope I'll chance to meet
>Someone I could completely and madly adore
>But I can't change, there's no danger
>Because I know
>I love the girl I loved ages ago.

The PRINCE *sits with his head in his hands, then wearily lays his head on the table and sleeps. The* HEADWAITER *softens the volume of the* SINGER *with a gesture. The* WAITERS *clear away the tables and chairs. The* CLOAKROOM ATTENDANT *emerges from her lair carrying a selection of extremely mundane coats and caps, which the* WAITERS *put on over their costumes. They all steal out softly, as the* SINGER *concludes. The* HEADWAITER, *after a last, proprietary look round, follows them. At his table in the shadows the* PRINCE *sleeps on, his head on his arms.*

SCENE II

Another section of the park. AMANDA *runs through the trees. Worn out with grief and exhaustion, she sinks onto the ground, at first in tears, then in uneasy sleep. Slowly, dawn creeps into the sky—a dawn of rose-pink and gray. There is the sound of a shot far away. Then another, closer. The* DUCHESS *and* HECTOR *appear in antiquated hunting costume, armed with shotguns. They are followed by a* GILLIE, *who carries spare guns and empty game bags.*

Gillie. Your shot, Lord Hector.

HECTOR *fires.*

Hector [annoyed]. Missed!
Gillie. Your shot, Your Grace.

The DUCHESS *fires.*

Duchess [delighted]. Missed! I am always delighted when I miss a bird. I love to see them in flight—they are so graceful, so carefree, so confident. I can never understand why, on certain arbitrary dates, we have to start pumping lead into the poor things. [*Suddenly she sees something white lying on the ground and screams.*] Heavens! What's that white thing? Did you hit something Hector?

Hector. I . . . I don't think so.

Gillie [*inspecting* AMANDA]. It's the young lady who is visiting Your Grace.

Duchess. Oh, my God. Is she hurt?

Gillie. No. She's asleep, Your Grace.

Duchess [*going to* AMANDA]. Asleep, and hurt too. Her face is still covered with tears.

AMANDA *wakes, and gives a little cry when she sees the* DUCHESS.

Amanda. Oh! Oh, it's you, madame! No, please don't speak to me. . . . I don't want to see anybody . . . I just want to get away from here as fast as I can.

Duchess [*motioning the others to go*]. Get away, child? Why?

Amanda. She's too strong for me, madame. . . . I laugh at her, and I think I'm stronger than she is . . . but I'm not. She's too strong for me. . . .

Duchess. She is very strong, child, but she is no stronger than you. Remember that she has one enormous disadvantage for any young woman. She is dead.

Amanda. She wouldn't even let him hold her hand. But his hands aren't really hard . . . they are simple, strong hands, made for loving . . . if only he would listen to what his hands tell him . . . but he won't. So you see, I must go away, because she's stronger than I am.

Duchess. You are twenty years old, you are alive and in love. There is nobody in the whole world stronger than you are this morning. Look around you, instead of brooding over last night's miseries . . . look. It's morning now.

And sure enough the light has brightened and the scene is transformed as the DUCHESS *speaks.*

The sun is already trembling on the brink of dawn. Everything living stirs and opens at his touch, the crocuses, the young reluctant beech leaves, and the shutters of honest folk. Oh, and the smells! The first early morning smells! The smell of the earth, the smell of wet grass, and the smell of new-made coffee, which is the incense we offer at Aurora's shrine.

And indeed we see a little inn in the distance at which the LANDLORD *has opened his shutters and is already brewing coffee. Later he brings out the little trees in tubs and the tables onto the terrace.*

And look . . . you can see the first colors of the day . . . vibrant green and tender pink. Soon you will hear the buzzing of the first bee, and feel the first tingle of warmth from the sun. Léocadia may have had the witchery of the night on her side . . . but you are twenty, and alive, and in love. Look up at the sun, and laugh! All the strength of the morning is yours.

The DUCHESS *disappears, discreetly. The sun suddenly comes out with a triumphant burst of music.* AMANDA *stretches her arms and laughs up into the sunshine. The music ends with her happy laughter. She goes over to the inn, where the* LANDLORD *has just finished arranging the terrace. The trees recede as the little inn moves into the foreground.*

Amanda. Landlord! [*The* LANDLORD *takes no notice. Louder.*] Landlord!

Still no response. AMANDA *picks up a stone and beats a tattoo on a tabletop. He looks at her, and then goes to see whether she has damaged the polished surface of his table, which he dusts angrily.*

Is this the Chime of Bells? [*The* LANDLORD *silently points to the inn sign.*] Thank you. Are you dumb?

Landlord. Yes.

Amanda [*not batting an eyelid, she smiles*]. Don't you find it an awful nuisance, being dumb?

Landlord [*half-conquered by her smile, answers, still sulkily*]. Oh, I manage.

Amanda. Have you been dumb for a long time?

Landlord. Thirty-seven years.

Amanda. Don't you do anything for it?

Landlord. I gargle.

Amanda. Gargle? Do you really?

Landlord [*wiping his tables*]. No, not really. But then I'm not really dumb. My gargles are a Green Devil and a

Skyrocket with every meal. Four a day. No more. I have to watch myself. My grandfather died of drink.

Amanda. Why wouldn't you talk to me before?

Landlord. Can't be too careful. I didn't know you—never spoke to you before.

Amanda. And now?

Landlord. Well, I've spoken to you now, haven't I? I know you. [*Pause.*] I sometimes take one in the morning, mind, if I'm pressed, in spite of my grandfather. Not often, but sometimes.

Amanda. One what?

Landlord. Green Devil.

Amanda. What's a Green Devil?

Landlord. It's a Skyrocket with a touch of bitters.

Amanda. And what's a Skyrocket?

Landlord. Exactly the same as a Green Devil, but without the bitters. Shall I bring two Green Devils?

Amanda. All right—two Green Devils. But d'you think the memory of your grandfather would prevent you from drinking mine as well? I'm not a bit thirsty this morning.

Landlord. Normally it would. But when a lady asks me —well, I'm prepared to stretch a point. [*He goes into the inn, and returns with two glasses and a selection of bottles.*] You from Dinard?

Amanda. Yes.

Landlord. I suppose you wandered into the park by mistake?

Amanda. Yes.

Landlord. I always get stray people in the summer who think this is a real hotel. It gives me quite a nice little bit of business on the side.

Amanda. Isn't this a real hotel, then?

Landlord [*as he prepares his extravagant concoction*]. Dear me, no. It's quite a story . . . the owner of this estate is a prince—a real one, mind. And he's rebuilt in his park all the places he used to visit with his girl friend years ago. How's that for an eccentric, eh? They say he does it to remind himself of her . . . personally I think it's all part of the council's crazy building scheme. . . . Still, that's none of my business. I look the other way. [*He sits at a table with both drinks.*]

Amanda. And used they to meet each other there?

Landlord. Who?

Amanda. The Prince and his girl friend?

Landlord. So they tell me.

Amanda [*amazed*]. What d'you mean? Can't you remember?

Landlord [*embarking on the second drink*]. No, I can't, and I'll tell you why. When they told the proprietors of this inn they wanted to knock it down and rebuild it here, brick by brick—well, they'd been there seventeen years, see? They were planning to retire—got a little cottage by the sea. So they put me in to run the place.

Amanda. But what happens when the Prince comes? Suppose he asks you questions?

Landlord. Oh, they briefed me good and proper, don't you worry. I've got it all pat—how they arrived in a taxi, how they ordered lemonade . . . every detail, see? I couldn't tell it better if I'd been there and seen them for myself—and if ever I'm stuck, I make it up. But he never notices. Sometimes I wonder if he was there himself. [*He goes back into the inn, delighted by the sensation he has caused.*]

Amanda [*calling him back*]. Landlord! Landlord!

Landlord [*reappearing in the doorway*]. What is it now?

Amanda. I like you.

Landlord [*suspicious*]. Why?

Amanda. You'll never know how much you've done for me.

Landlord. I have? [*He looks at her, on his guard.*] It was you ordered the Green Devils, you know. Three hundred francs.

Amanda [*giving him the money*]. There. And thank you very much.

At that moment, the PRINCE *comes through the trees to the inn, his collar turned up, shivering in the fresh morning air. Suddenly he sees* AMANDA.

Prince. Are you still here?

Amanda. Yes, I'm still here.

Prince. You must forgive me for my rudeness last night.

Amanda. Don't let's talk about it.

Prince [*an echo*]. . . . No . . . don't let's talk about it. . . . [*He shivers.*]

Amanda. You're shivering.

Prince. I always feel a little cold first thing in the morning.

Amanda. Why don't you sit in the sun for a bit? It's quite warm already.

Prince [moves forward, and looks at the inn]. That's the inn where we went together . . . we sat here . . . inside. It was very cold that day.

Amanda. We'll sit here, shall we? It's so warm this morning.

Prince [coming back to earth as he bumps into a chair on the terrace]. Yes . . . forgive me . . . yes, if you like. . . . I . . . I tripped over a chair . . . clumsy of me . . . I'm afraid I'm only half awake. . . .

Amanda. Don't you ever get up early?

Prince. I generally go to bed at dawn. But I'm afraid I dozed off in the night club . . . and now I hardly know whether I'm late to bed or early to rise. *[He shivers.]* How terribly cold it is.

Amanda. Honestly, it's quite warm . . . listen to the bees . . . they wouldn't be buzzing like that if it was cold, now would they?

Prince [ironic]. I suppose it's impossible for the bees to make a mistake. *[He sees that* AMANDA *is smiling.]* What are you smiling at?

Amanda. I thought you looked terrible last night. But you look even worse this morning.

Prince [still shivering]. I do not look terrible.

The LANDLORD *comes out, surprised. He approaches the* PRINCE.

Landlord. Good morning, sir. Am I to serve the lemonade here instead of . . . ?

Amanda. We don't want lemonade. Bring two cups of coffee, good and hot. The gentleman is very cold.

Landlord [thunderstruck]. Coffee! Oh, well. I only suggested lemonade because it always has been lemonade, every day for two years. If you'd rather have coffee, you shall have coffee. It's none of my business.

Amanda [calling after him]. Big cups, with rolls and butter!

Landlord [past surprise]. Big cups . . . with rolls and butter. *[He goes, muttering.]* Wouldn't have believed it.

Amanda. You don't mind if we have breakfast together?

Prince. No, I don't mind. *[He shoos away an inquisitive bee.]* Another of the brutes. . . .

Amanda. Oh, don't hurt him!

Prince. I suppose it would amuse you to see me eaten alive?

Amanda. He won't eat you!

Prince. Are you sure?

Amanda. Positive!

Prince. You know him.

Amanda. Very well.

Prince. You seem very much at home in the morning.

Amanda. And it's very nice to have you with me . . . allow me to introduce you, Prince Albert . . . the trees . . . the sun . . . the bees. . . .

Prince [*looks at her, murmuring*]. You are quite terrifying.

Amanda. Really?

Prince. You are like a tiny pink and white ogre.

The LANDLORD *brings out coffee in big blue cups and a plate of rolls.*

Landlord. Two big cups of coffee. Rolls and butter. [*He puts them on the table.*] Are you sure you wouldn't like me to bring the lemonade as well, sir?

Amanda. No!

Landlord. No, she says. I don't know what the place is coming to. . . .

He goes in again, grumbling. The PRINCE *watches* AMANDA, *who is buttering a piece of roll.*

Prince. Do you really propose to eat all that?

Amanda. I certainly do. And it's no good looking at me like that. I'm not ashamed of myself. I'm hungry.

Prince. A tiny pink and white ogre, serene and sure of herself, without a trace of tears or shame. You frighten me. Who are you?

Amanda. Just a girl in a white dress buttering a roll in the sunshine.

Prince. Didn't I meet you the other evening in the park beside the obelisk?

Amanda. Yes. The next day we met again in your aunt's house, and then we hired a boat and rowed up the river almost as far as Dinard. Then yesterday evening, we went to the Blue Danube. And now it's morning. And we are having breakfast at the Chime of Bells—the little inn you wanted to show me. Oh, it's a nice place in the morning sun!

Prince [*a cry*]. But this is the last day!

Amanda [*calm*]. The last? What do you mean? It's the third day—and it's only just beginning.

Prince. But what about this evening?

Amanda. This evening? We'll go wherever you like.

Prince. And tomorrow morning?

Amanda. We'll have breakfast together, just like this morning, and it will be the beginning of our fourth day.

Prince [*moving away*]. No!

Amanda. Oh, please wake up from your horrible dream, you've known me for three days just as you knew her . . . and you're in love with me.

Prince. I do not love you!

Amanda. If you didn't love me you wouldn't deny it so vehemently. [*Going to him.*] Touch me—please touch me. Everything will suddenly be so simple. . . .

Prince. If I touched you, Amanda, I think I would love you. . . . [*Turns away.*] I don't want to love you. . . .

Amanda. If you don't love me, I shall have to go away. [*He looks at her quickly. Suddenly something dawns on her.*] But when I have gone, you will remember me, even more than you remember her. [*Going to him.*] Your hands and your heart will remember me.

Prince [*calling, in spite of himself*]. Léocadia. . . .

Amanda [*implacable*]. You will remember me. . . .

Prince [*finally, softly*]. Yes, I will remember you. . . .

Amanda. Put your two hands on my shoulders. . . .

Prince [*turns to her*]. Amanda. . . . [*He would still argue with her.*]

Amanda [*softly*]. My darling Albert. . . .

Prince. Amanda. . . .

Pause. Suddenly the PRINCE *puts his hands on* AMANDA'S *shoulders, and stands quite still. She closes her eyes.*

Amanda [*whispering*]. Why don't you say anything? Now I am afraid. . . .

Prince [*a strange, wondering voice*]. But it is so simple . . . and so real . . . and so safe. . . .

Suddenly he embraces her passionately. The LANDLORD *emerges from the inn, discovers them and closes the blinds of the little terrace tactfully on them. The inn recedes. We hear two shots. A bird falls from the sky. The* DUCHESS *and* HECTOR *come in, guns at the trail. We*

have retreated in time a few minutes. The GILLIE *runs
ahead of them and begins to examine the bird.*

Duchess. It was you. I know it was you.

Hector. It couldn't have been me!

Duchess. You're such a clumsy oaf, I knew you'd have
to go and kill a bird sooner or later.

Hector. I distinctly saw you taking aim! I'm prepared
to swear it in a court of law!

Duchess. Really, Hector, you don't imagine I'd brief my
lawyers just to make you admit you'd shot a heron.

Gillie. It's not a heron, Your Grace—nor even a fla-
mingo. It's an outlandish sort of bird you don't often see
in these parts. Funny sort of creature. Its feathers are much
too long, they get caught up in the branches when it tries
to fly, and its feet are so arched it can't perch anywhere.
You can see it miles away, with that tuft of bright-colored
feathers on its head . . . and as for the noise it makes
. . . well, you heard that ridiculous squawk when Your
Grace fired that shot.

Hector. You see? It was you. Germain corroborates me.

Duchess. Very well, it was I. Now are you satisfied? [*To
the* GILLIE.] We don't need you any more, Germain. You
can go—and take the bird with you.

Gillie. What shall I do with it, Your Grace? It's not
even any good for eating.

Duchess. Bury it.

Gillie. Very good, Your Grace. [*He touches his cap, and
is about to go when the* DUCHESS *stops him.*]

Duchess. Germain. . . .

Gillie. Your Grace?

Duchess [*very tender*]. Bury it in my rose garden.

The GILLIE *touches his cap, and goes. Pause.* HECTOR
turns and looks off into the woods.

Duchess. What are you looking at, Hector?

Hector. It's Albert with that pretty girl at the Chime
of Bells. He's eating breakfast.

Duchess [*with immense satisfaction*]. Ah!

Hector. You know . . . I like that girl . . . not a bit
like Léocadia, really. . . .

Duchess [*picking up a feather that had fallen from the
bird*]. Léocadia. Poor Léocadia. She bid for immortality by
strangling herself with her own scarf . . . and now we

have killed her again, and in a way that would have hurt
her most . . . we have killed her memory.

Hector [*desperately bold*]. D'you know something? I'm
. . . I'm not sorry we've killed her.

Duchess. You're not?

Hector. Well, look how she got hold of Albert and
buried him in the past.

Duchess [*gently*]. No, Hector. The past buried him in
the past—as it does all of us. Albert is no different from
any of the rest of us. When you're forty, half of you belongs to the past . . . and when you are seventy, nearly
all of you. . . .

Hector. But Albert's only twenty-eight.

Duchess. He was always a precocious boy.

Hector. I don't belong to the past, what am I?

Duchess. A little backward. . . .

Hector [*hurt*]. Thank you. [*He turns away from her,
and looks off into the woods again.*] Good heavens! He's
kissing her. . . .

Duchess. Long live Amanda! [*Puts feather down.*] But
all the same . . . however useless, however frivolous and
fundamentally unjust that poor, silly, orchidaceous creature
may have been, surely nobody can blame us for pitying
her now . . . and shedding a tear for her. . . .

Hector. What? What was that?

Duchess. I was not talking to you, Hector. [*She looks
up at the sky.*] I was talking to Gaston. . . .

*She gets up briskly, she stops and looks off at the inn. Then
she goes, followed by* HECTOR, *at a jog trot as*——

The Curtain Falls.

ARDÈLE

Translated from ARDÈLE OU LA MARGUÉRITE *by*

LUCIENNE HILL

CHARACTERS

THE GENERAL
HIS WIFE
THE COUNT, *his brother-in-law*
THE COUNTESS, *his sister*
VILLARDIEU, *the Countess' lover*
NICHOLAS, *the General's second son*
NATHALIE, *his daughter-in-law*
TOTO, *his youngest son, aged ten*
MARIE-CHRISTINE, *the Countess' daughter,
    also aged ten*
ADA, *the chambermaid, mistress of the
    General*
ARDÈLE (*who is never seen*)
THE HUNCHBACK (*who never speaks*)

TIME: 1912 or thereabouts

ACT ONE

The hall of a country house. Two flights of stairs lead up to either end of a gallery running the length of the set, with a number of doors leading off it.

Morning. The scene is empty. A shrill voice is heard calling "Leon! Leon!" The GENERAL, *wearing a red dressing gown, bursts out of one of the rooms on to the gallery and makes hurriedly for another door.*

GENERAL [*shouting through the half-open door*]. Here I am, my love! . . . no, no, my angel. No, my dove, no. I did go away for a minute or two, yes, but only to my study. I had some work to finish. . . . What—last night? But I didn't leave your side. I got up for a few seconds to get some air, that's all—my asthma was bad again. . . . No, no, my love, not for more than an hour—only for a few seconds—truly. But you see, when you are half asleep, you lose all sense of time. I've explained that to you scores of times, now, haven't I? Go back to sleep, my love. It is still very early. I am busy getting everything ready for our guests. . . . Yes, my angel, I'll be back very soon.

He closes his wife's door, goes back to the room he left a moment before, and opens the door. ADA, *the chambermaid, is standing in the doorway. The* GENERAL *takes her in his arms and covers her with kisses.*

You warm, ravishing creature! You're like a ripe, juicy peach—wonderful—wonderful! You smell of hot rolls and honey and fruit cake and everything that's good!

Ada [*stands unmoved in the* GENERAL's *avid embrace*]. Breakfast is served in the study, sir.

General [*caressing her*]. How alive you are! Alive and warm and strong and firm on those two sturdy legs of yours. Ah, all's well with the world this fine morning! Life goes on all round me. Everything's fine. And you, you little fool, you don't give a damn, do you? You simply wait for the old boy to have done. That's all right, too. Everything's all right. Later on, when you are doing the

133

youngster's room, hang the bedding out to air and I'll come up. I've bought you what you wanted.

Enter NATHALIE *from a room on the gallery. The* GENERAL *releases the maid, who has remained unmoved throughout, and whispers hurriedly:*

Off with you!

ADA *disappears into one of the rooms without a glance at* NATHALIE. *The* GENERAL *and his daughter-in-law stand facing each other for a moment in silence.*

[*His voice shaking a little.*] Do I sicken you, Nathalie?
  Nathalie [*quietly*]. Yes.

She starts to come downstairs. The GENERAL *hesitates for a moment, then follows her down and stops her on the stairs.*

General. You are twenty years old, Nathalie. You are fine and unswerving and loyal, and I am a worthless old wretch.
  Nathalie. Yes.
  General. You brought a breath of fresh air into this great, gloomy house when you married my son. That first evening in the big drawing room, when you touched the piano that had been silent for so long, you were so young, and so lovely, that I thought I might learn, for your sake, to grow old. I saw myself, white-haired warrior of a hundred battles, the self-appointed protector of a clear-eyed little daughter-in-law. It was a fine role for me in the evening of my life. I had everything for it—memories of past glory, fine snowy whiskers, and a young man's heart beating under my faded medal ribbons. How sweet life was on that first Sunday. There you were in your white dress—as I walked to church with you on my arm. I prayed to God that day that I might never give you cause to despise me. Ah, but then that was a Sunday, and I daresay the Lord was very busy. I don't suppose he heard me.
  Nathalie. Evidently not.
  General. I should have given Him a hand, of course—one is always apt to let God do it all—but there, it was too much for me. I have learned from sad experience that I've seldom had the power to carry out my good intentions.
  Nathalie. Why justify yourself to me? I am only your son's wife, and you are free.

The voice is heard from above, calling "Leon! Leon!"

General. Do you hear that? I'm free, am I, with that mad creature upstairs calling me from her sickbed every ten minutes for the last ten years? Life is long and hard and made up of minutes, Nathalie—you have not had to learn that yet—and every one too precious to waste in futile hopes and vain regrets.

Nathalie. It was for love of you that your wife went mad. Young as I am, I know already the price one pays for love. That matchless treasure she gave you, what have you done with it?

General [simply]. I have borne it. There is so much you don't know, Nathalie. You married my eldest son without love—no, don't turn away—I am an old fool but I am not blind—and so you dream of love, like the little girl that you are. Oh, love is real enough; you will find it someday, but it has one archenemy—and that is life. You may have noticed that the poor, for all their eternal complaining, have in the final reckoning less trouble with their pennies and halfpennies than the rich with their millions. Either way, each one of us is so alone, that I wonder, when all's said, if one isn't better off without the burden of another's love.

The cry of "Leon! Leon!" is heard, farther off it seems.

[In answer to Nathalie's *inquiring look.]* No, this time it's the peacock in the grounds calling to its mate. By a curious whim of fate, every unquiet creature in this household shrieks my name. But the peacock's unrest lasts for a season only—come the autumn and my name will continue to echo in this place, until the day when she or I gives up the fight and dies. Dream away, Nathalie, yours is the age for dreams. But there's your love for you—that piercing shriek every ten minutes to control my movements. The taste for freedom must indeed be strongly shackled in the hearts of men!

The cry again, "Leon! Leon!"

Still the peacock.

Nathalie. Go up to her, all the same.

General. I will. I have done so every time for ten years now. I am sanguine, but devoted nonetheless. Don't think too badly of me, Nathalie. That girl is my freedom. It takes a certain courage and a certain greatness even to be truly base.

Nathalie. It is not for me to judge you.

General. And yet I feel you are in some way my appointed judge. The Lord knows why.

Again the cry, "Leon! Leon!"

This time it is she. Her voice is just a shade shriller than the peacock's. [*He goes up the stairs.*] You may well stand there, like my embodied conscience, gazing at me with those great eyes full of wordless condemnation—I am not beaten yet. I don't say you won't win in the end. But before these crossed swords on my shoulder kept me safely at H.Q., I learned during my thirty-two campaigns in the field to go down fighting. And after all, you are terrifying, yes, but not so formidable as a full battalion of Arabs, convinced that Allah's waiting for them on the other side. It will be a splendid fight all the same—a struggle to the death between a hoary old lecher and a silent girl. [*He gives a short laugh, and shouts down over the banisters.*] Granted my wife is an angel. She is dying for love of me, and I am untrue to her—agreed. I was madly in love with her too, you know, once. But angels don't stay young, and you wake up one fine morning to find an old angel in curlers beside you on the pillow. If God had intended love to last forever, I am sure He would have seen to it that Beauty kept her lustrous eyes forever, too. In behaving as I do, I have the impression that I am in some dimly apprehended way fulfilling His divine intention.

The cry of "Leon! Leon!" is heard again.

[*Enters his wife's room and says calmly.*] Here I am, my love. I was talking to Nathalie.

NATHALIE *stands for a moment in silence, then crosses the hall and goes out into the garden. The* MAID *appears in a doorway laden with brooms and dusters.* TOTO *comes running out of another room and hurls himself on her yelping.*

Toto. You juicy peach! You big fruit cake! You hot roll and honey!

Ada. Master Toto! Master Toto! Stop it! Give over! I'll tell your father!

Toto. Go on, then—tell him. He'll give me sixpence

to keep my mouth shut. You're going to hang my sheets out of the window, aren't you? I know—that's the signal. And then Father will come up, and then you'll lock yourselves in. Oh, you juicy peach! You ripe banana! That's what Daddy does, isn't it? Oh, you're wonderful, you're wonderful!

Ada. Master Toto! You ought to be ashamed! Let me go! [*She strikes him.*] Little swine!

Toto [*thrusts his hands in his pockets and glares at her with silent venom*]. You wait till I grow up. [*He shakes his fist at her suddenly like the ten-year-old little man that he is.*] Wait till this house belongs to me. Just you wait till I'm grown up and I feel like it too!

ADA *shrugs and enters the bedroom.* TOTO *pulls a face at her and slides down the banisters. At the bottom of the stairs he strikes an attitude and declaims in the grand manner:*

"Toto—I forbid you to slide down the banisters. You are wearing out the seat of your trousers, and you will hurt yourself!"

He goes towards the pantry, yelling the "Marseillaise" and kicking the furniture in his way.

General [*coming out on to the gallery*]. Toto! That's enough!

Toto. What do you mean—that's enough! That's the "Marseillaise!"

General [*defeated*]. All right! All right!

He goes back into the room and bangs the door. TOTO, *beside himself with contempt, kicks another unoffending stick of furniture as he goes.*

Enter the COUNT *and* COUNTESS, *and* VILLARDIEU *in motoring costumes. Nothing must distinguish the* COUNT *from* VILLARDIEU—*same mustaches, same high collars, same monocles, same air of distinction, and probably same club. Perhaps, if anything, the color of their caps differs slightly, but that is a subtlety.*

Countess. Not a soul. This house has always been lamentably badly run.

Count. Since your sister-in-law's illness, my dear, that is fairly understandable, surely?

Countess. Before Emily's illness things were no different. The poor woman spent her time brooding over my brother like a lovesick hen, and the servants already had the bit between their teeth. Take off your things, Villardieu, I am exhausted. I am sure you must have been doing thirty.

Villardieu. Thirty-five.

Countess. Very rash.

Villardieu. I must say I feel a twinge of conscience at allowing myself to be brought here uninvited. If, as the General's telegram seemed to suggest, you have been summoned here for a family conference, my presence——

Count [without a trace of bitterness]. You are one of the family, Villardieu.

Countess. Gaston, I beg of you, spare us your wit so early in the day. And Villardieu, for Heaven's sake, don't take umbrage over nothing at all. [*To the* COUNT.] Why don't you try to find someone? Our idea of driving straight here from the Casino seemed wildly amusing at four o'clock this morning—there's always something heroic about the dawn—but now, at eleven, I am increasingly aware that I haven't slept. I must look a hundred.

Count [gallantly]. You are as fresh as a rose! [VILLARDIEU *gives him a baleful look. The* COUNT *turns to him.*] I took the words out of your mouth, my dear fellow? Forgive me. [*He rises.*] I will see about our rooms. I imagine that the General, simple old soldier that he is, will have prepared a double room for Lilian and myself. If so, my heartfelt apologies, Villardieu. [*He bows graciously and goes out.*]

Villardieu. Did you hear that!

Countess. He is intolerable.

Villardieu. He appears to be singularly lacking in tact. He is only your husband, after all.

Countess. His nerves are on edge. Things are not going too well with his little seamstress. I must confess I should like to meet the girl. She is as ugly as sin, from all accounts.

Villardieu. How do you know?

Countess. Alissa saw them in Rumpelmeyer's having tea. The creature was getting into serious difficulties with a meringue! Gaston blushed like a beetroot when he saw Alissa. I am not especially malicious, but I hope she makes him suffer.

Villardieu. You are very interested in him all of a sudden?

Countess. She is young, pretty, maybe. Do you think he is really in love with her?

Villardieu. I am supremely uninterested either way.

Countess. She is tubercular, you know. Alissa says she coughs incessantly. A very common little thing, I believe. Her eyes are quite large, but I am told she squints.

Villardieu. Too bad.

Countess. Hector. This studied unconcern of yours bores me. It's hopelessly unfashionable. The English stiff upper lip went out years ago. You don't mean to tell me that it is a matter of complete indifference to you if the husband of your mistress gets himself talked about all over town with a slut?

Villardieu. I wish it were a matter of complete indifference to you. Really, Lilian, I sometimes wonder whether you do not still care for that man. Last night at the Casino you smiled at him across the roulette table the entire evening.

Countess. He was losing at every turn. I was laughing at him.

Villardieu. I am not blind. There was a suspicion of sympathy in your every smile. There are certain things, Lilian, which I will not tolerate!

Countess. No scenes this morning, please. I am far too exhausted.

Villardieu. In Heaven's name, Lilian, why this jealousy, why this exaggerated interest in the man? You might at least have the decency to hide your feelings. Everyone has noticed it. The day before yesterday, at Lady Harding's ball, you danced with him twice. It puts me in a very embarrassing position. At one time you took his hand, in full view of everyone.

Countess. Only in fun, as I might have taken anyone's.

Villardieu. There are certain things which a respectable woman simply does not do—even in fun. It is not just because the man is your husband. I am broad-minded, I hope, but there are some things I will categorically not allow.

Countess. Your vanity is beyond belief.

Villardieu. My self-respect, if you please. Our relationship is publicly recognized, as you well know. Besides, I am unhappy.

During the scene VILLARDIEU *has been pacing up and down the hall.*

Countess. Your way of suffering makes me giddy. Sit down.

Villardieu. If you go on like this you will drive me to something desperate. As a matter of fact, on the way here I had an uncontrollable impulse to accelerate to forty, and put an end to it all.

Countess. What happens at forty?

Villardieu [*soberly*]. The engine gets out of control.

Countess. Hector, have you forgotten Marie-Christine? You know very well that if I refused to go with you to Venice, if I insisted on remaining with my husband, it was solely because I was determined that my daughter should know nothing of all this. Am I to stifle even my maternal instincts, Villardieu?

Villardieu. I have accepted everything for the sake of your child, Lilian: our infrequent meetings, this hateful farce of our triangular life together. All I ask is that you behave with a modicum of decency.

Enter the COUNT *and* NATHALIE, *carrying a bunch of wild flowers.*

Count. There is a spell on this house. I met a fairy in the garden who tells me she has the power to open doors.

Nathalie. Good morning, Lilian. I am sorry. No one heard the car.

Count. How odd. It's noisy enough.

Villardieu. It is the latest De Dion. What do you expect with a thirty horsepower car—chamber music?

Count. I meant no offense, Villardieu, believe me. Besides, speaking purely for myself, of course, I love noise. It stimulates me.

Countess [*kissing her*]. Nathalie, my dear, I am delighted to see you again. How well you look! And how is your husband?

Nathalie. Very well. He is in China.

Count. There's a man who knows how to live.

Countess. May I introduce the Marquis of Villardieu, a very great friend of ours?

Count. Our very best friend. [*To* VILLARDIEU, *who is glaring at him.*] I am quite serious.

Nathalie. Isn't Marie-Christine with you?

Countess. We drove straight here from the Casino at four o'clock this morning. She is coming by train later, with her governess.

Nathalie. Excuse me. I will go up and tell them that you are here. [*She goes.*]

Countess. She is delightful, isn't she? She married my profligate waster of a nephew suddenly, on impulse. I have often wondered why. She is not in love with him. Of that I'm quite sure.

Count. I daresay that will simplify things for them quite a bit later on.

Villardieu. My dear Count, our position, yours and mine, is a delicate one. Please try to bear it in mind.

Count. Oh, I will indeed.

Villardieu. You made an unfortunate remark just now, if you remember.

Count. But dammit, man, if you weren't my best friend, why should we go everywhere together, you and I, like Siamese twins?

Countess. For the last time, Gaston, I forbid you to make a matter of such gravity the subject for your wit.

Count. What else can I do with it? Take it to heart?

Countess. You are incapable of suffering, I know that, but you might at least have the good taste to simulate, if only out of courtesy, what you do not feel.

Count. The three of us are floundering in such a whirl-pool of confused emotions, my dear, that if we have to simulate those we do not feel to boot, we run a serious risk of going under.

Countess. Try not to be facetious to begin with. That might help.

Villardieu [*darkly*]. Either way, there are some things I definitely will not tolerate.

The GENERAL *appears with* NATHALIE *on the stairs.*

General. Forgive me, Lilian. I was with Emily. I was not expecting you so early.

Countess. We came by motor car. How is she?

General. Just the same. Good morning, Gaston, how are you?

Count. Very well, sir—and you? Still hale, I see.

General. Like an old tree. I blossom every spring. It's a fine show, but the trunk, alas, is hollow.

Count. Ah! You will bury us all.

General. Maybe—but I'd like to have done that while I was still young.

Countess. Leon, let me introduce a great friend of ours, Hector de Villardieu. He has been spending the summer with us at Trouville, and I brought him along. I hope you don't mind. My brother, General Saintpé.

General [*slightly surprised*]. Delighted, sir.

Villardieu. Your servant, sir. I had the honor, sir, of serving under your command as a lieutenant in the Fortieth Horse, in North Africa.

General [*vaguely*]. Um? —Don't remember you?

Villardieu. I was posted in '98, a few months before you relinquished command of the unit.

General. Ah, that accounts for it. You were with Bourdaine, then?

Villardieu. Yes, sir.

General. Can't say I congratulate you. Deplorable commander. No foresight. It was I got him the sack, you know. Ah, I should have stayed a colonel. Those were the days! Plenty of men, plenty of horses, plenty of Arabs to fire on, and not a woman within a hundred miles!

The cry of "Leon! Leon!" *is heard at that moment.*

[*Turns to his sister and says in an undertone.*] What the devil did you bring that lout here for?

Countess. I'll tell you later. Does she still call for you all the time?

General. More than ever. Shall I tell him?

Countess [*meaningly*]. I have no secrets from Hector.

General [*looks at her, then understands*]. Ah, yes, I see. I had heard talk of a Cuban diplomat. Anyhow, at your age I suppose you begin to know what you're about.

Countess. Thank you!

The cry is heard again.

Villardieu. You have a peacock, General?

General [*simply*]. No, sir. That is my wife.

Villardieu [*horrified*]. Oh, I do beg your pardon!

General. It seems we are to have no secrets from you. Right, I will begin with my own. She calls me like that regularly every ten minutes. You'll get used to it. Otherwise, the house and grounds are very pleasant.

Again the cry.

[*Going up.*] Coming! [*Turning to* VILLARDIEU.] I am delighted to have made your acquaintance, my dear sir. Delighted. We must have a chat about the Fortieth Horse. Hell's bells, man, but those were the days!

Countess. But, Leon, your telegram! You call us here posthaste, and you have not even told us why.

General. It's about Ardèle. What a business. Nathalie, tell them, will you? I must go and pacify Emily. I'll come straight down again.

Countess. What is it? What is the matter? Is Ardèle ill? Where is she?

The voice calls again, "Leon! Leon!"

General [*opens the door and goes in, saying*]. Here I am, my love. I wasn't far away. [*Exit.*]

Countess. Well, Nathalie, what is all this mystery?

Nathalie [*embarrassed*]. Well, Aunt Lilian, it's about Aunt Ardèle—you see——

Countess. Just call me Lilian, will you? Aunt Lilian sounds ludicrous.

Nathalie. It is about Aunt Ardèle—Lilian.

Countess [*to* VILLARDIEU]. This is my elder sister, the one I told you about—do you remember?

Villardieu. Oh, yes, the one who is—er——

Countess [*cutting him short*]. Yes.

Villardieu. Sad. Very sad.

Countess. What is?

Villardieu. Well, her being—er—really, I think I ought to leave.

Countess. Don't be silly. Sit down. Nathalie, you may speak quite freely in front of M. de Villardieu. He is our greatest friend.

Nathalie [*hesitating*]. Well, you see—this is extremely embarrassing—I——

Count [*forgotten in his corner*]. Is it all right if I stay?

Countess. Gaston, you are seldom funny. Do your best not to be objectionable. Now, Nathalie, will you please explain. If my sister is not ill, what in the world can have happened for Leon to summon me here by telegraph?

Nathalie. I know it is silly, but I am really very embarrassed. I would much rather the General told you himself.

The GENERAL *appears on the landing.*

General. Have you told them?

Countess. Not yet. Nathalie can't stop blushing. Leon, we have just driven for seven whole hours at breakneck speed in an open coffin on wheels. I sincerely hope this is not your idea of a practical joke. For the last time, what is all this about?

General [*solemnly*]. I have summoned you here for a family conference.

Villardieu [*rising*]. Do you wish me to go?

Countess. Hector—sit down. A family conference? About Ardèle, who is my senior by three whole years? In God's name, why?

General. When I say a family conference, I mean in fact the immediate family circle only. I have not thought fit to call up the reserves for such a painful, and indeed such a confidential, matter.

At this VILLARDIEU *looks at the* COUNTESS *and half rises.*
She waves him back to his seat.

You, however, are her sister. Gaston is, after all, my brother-in-law——

Count. Villardieu is my friend.

General [*ignores the interruption*]. Nathalie, her niece by marriage. I have also asked Nicholas, who is a grown man now, to attend.

Nathalie [*rises, panic-stricken by these words*]. Nicholas is coming here? I—I mean, I didn't know you had written to him.

General. I don't imagine he will come. In the two years he has been at Saint Cyr, it has not pleased him to spend a single day's leave here. But I wrote all the same. As Ardèle's nephew, he may be affected by the scandal later on. It is only right that he should have his say.

Countess. Scandal? What scandal? Leon, you have talked in riddles long enough. Explain yourself.

Villardieu [*rising*]. I feel the General is ill at ease. This is a very difficult position for me. If you will excuse me, I would prefer to go.

Countess [*pushing him back in his seat*]. Hector, once and for all, will you sit down and keep quiet. I have already told you, Leon, you may speak quite freely in front of M. de Villardieu. Gaston, please tell him so too, will you?

Count. You may speak quite freely, sir. Villardieu is my other self. No offense, my dear fellow.

General. As you wish. I am an army man. I don't want to play hide-and-seek with you all. Now then, does he know she is a hunchback?

Countess. Leon! Yes, I have explained to him as an intimate friend that my sister has in fact a slight deformity.

General. Rubbish! She's a hunchback. And what's more, she is forty-f——

Countess [*interrupting*]. Leon!

General. Anyway, she is three years older than you are. [*He explains to* VILLARDIEU.] An old maid, you know, romantically inclined, of course—with one consuming passion—the piano. That is just to give you a rough idea. In any case, you are bound to see her in the flesh sooner or later—that is, if you stay here for any length of time.

Countess. Does she know we are here?

General. Not yet.

Countess. She will be down to lunch, won't she? Where is she now?

General. In her room.

Countess. At eleven o'clock in the morning? But what about the flowers?

General. I have locked her in. Here is the key.

Countess. Locked her in? But why?

General [*looking at* VILLARDIEU]. You are sure you want to stay? Right. I think she has a lover.

Countess. A lover! You must be dreaming.

General. I wish I were. I have been pinching myself black and blue for the last three days. When I see a pin, I prick myself with it; when I light a cigar, I hold the match to my fingers just to make sure. But it's no good, I am not dreaming.

Countess. But Ardèle is a cripple, she is old—that is to say—she must be past the age to—er—not of course that age has anything to do with it—but in her position! In her state of health! Why, even as a girl Ardèle never entertained any hopes of marriage. She knew very well that no one—this sounds brutal, I know—but although she was in fact quite pretty, no man could ever have brought himself to——

General [*cutting in*]. But that's just it. Someone has, I tell you!

Countess. Do you mean that someone has asked for Ardèle's hand in marriage, and she has been foolish enough to take this proposal seriously?

General. Proposal fiddlesticks! Your sister has fallen in love with a man and has made up her mind to run off with him. Pray God she isn't his mistress yet. It's our last hope.

Countess. Leon, how can you! Ardèle, with her religion, her high moral principles—Ardèle could never do such a thing! Ardèle is a saint, Leon, a saint.

General. Maybe, but now the saint wants to get married.

Countess. But to whom?

General. You remember me telling you that Toto wasn't getting on too well with his Latin?

Countess. I don't see the connection.

General. You soon will. As you know, Emily, ill as she is, cannot bear the thought of sending him to boarding school. Since with the vicar he never got beyond the first declension, and when I took a hand we invariably came to blows, I decided to get him a tutor.

Countess. I always said you would have to pay the price for peace and quiet.

General [*with a dry laugh*]. Peace and quiet, as you say! But let me finish. The Vaudreuil put me on to someone— a wonderful chap who brought up their eldest son. With them seven years—a fount of knowledge—the soul of honor—and so on and so on. So I send for him. And what do I see? You'll never guess—a hunchback! Not that his hump worried me, mind you—I've got used to humps by now. The fellow looks competent, respectable, intelligent, so I engage him. I do, however, take the precaution of warning Ardèle. One never knows, the hypersensitivity of the deformed, you know. Not at all. They get along very well. They find they have a mutual passion for music, and so every night in the big drawing room, there they sit, hump to hump at the piano, singing duets! The man has, to give him his due, a rather good voice. Now music bores me, but I say to myself, if it amuses Ardèle, and if Toto gets on all right with his Latin, then everything is fine. Everything was more than fine—it was wonderful. From piano playing they graduate to botany. First they plant an herb garden, then they start collecting butterflies. Picture them, if you can, prancing about together in the meadows, brandishing butterfly nets! This idyllic state of affairs lasts for six months. Then one fine morning, what do I see? Ardèle saunters down to breakfast with paint on her face! "What's this?" I say, "what's this?" You know me, I launch straight into the attack—I bring up all my big guns—I get her well and truly with her back to the wall— and, presto! she bursts into tears and confesses that she is in love with the hunchback!

Countess. But this is dreadful! I hope you gave her to understand that she——

General. I tried, of course, but there was positively no way of making her see reason. Wait till you see her. I never knew a woman so changed. She's twenty years younger, she's bright, sparkling, alive! She even gives me the impression that her back has grown straight.

Countess. What about him?

General. I sent for him. He's a very unassuming sort of fellow, with no background to speak of, and I said to myself "I'll bombard the bounder!" So I deck myself out in full-dress uniform—medals, baton, the full regalia— and I wait for him, rigid to attention behind my desk, the Iron Duke to the life. He comes into the room, white-faced and quaking, and I attack. I accuse him of intrigue, of seduction—I felt a bit of a fool with your sister forty-odd years old—but no matter—I was magnificent. And in all fairness, I am bound to admit that he acquitted himself pretty well, too. He said he quite understood that there was no question of his marrying into the family, that he expected nothing, but that he couldn't help his feelings, he was in love with Ardèle, and that no power on earth would make him deny his love.

Countess. But surely you pointed out to him how grotesque——

General. He maintains with a certain amount of logic that he is a man despite his hump; and as Ardèle has one too, you can see that I hadn't a leg to stand on. I sent him packing, that's all I could do. He refused the month's salary to which he was entitled and installed himself at the local inn, where he is now—and there you are.

Countess. And Ardèle?

General. That night I caught her trying to get out to join him, so I locked her in.

A *silence.* VILLARDIEU, *increasingly embarrassed, rises.*

Villardieu. A very painful business. I really think it would be better if I——

As no one takes the least notice of his discreet attempt to leave, he resumes his seat.

Count [*lights cigar and says calmly*]. Will their children be born with humps, do you suppose?

Countess. Gaston, you are revolting! The mere idea of such a marriage is unthinkable. Imagine the scandal!

Count. How do you propose to stop it? Ardèle has money of her own, she is of age, amply so, in fact. What do you suggest—solitary confinement?

Countess [*rises*]. I will talk to her. Give me the key.

General. She has bolted the door on her side. She won't let you in. I forgot to mention that she has refused all the trays I have sent up to her. She has eaten nothing for three days.

He lights a cigar and holds the lighted match to his finger once again, to no avail. He crosses to VILLARDIEU *and taps him smartly on the shoulder.*

Those were the days, eh—in the good old Fortieth Horse!

Villardieu [*startled, jumps automatically to attention*]. Yes, sir!

General. Easy! Lord, I'm worn out.

He goes to the sofa and lies down. Meanwhile the COUNT-ESS *has gone upstairs and knocked at* ARDÈLE's *door.*

Countess. Ardèle! Ardèle darling. Little sister. Are you listening? It's Lilian. Leon asked me to come. I must talk to you. Ardèle, open the door. Open the door at once. Ardèle!

COUNTESS *waits a moment, and then turns away discouraged.*

General. Lock the door!

She does so, comes down the stairs, returns the key and sits down. A painful silence. VILLARDIEU *is still undecided whether or not to leave.*

Countess. Well, Gaston, have you nothing to say?

Count [*quietly*]. What could I say to any purpose? We agreed long ago, my dear, that love is a law unto itself.

Countess. Gaston, have you no moral sense at all? What can these two deformed creatures possibly know of love? Besides, there are other things to consider. What of the world? Think of the scandal!

Count. The world accepts other—irregularities, as you well know, my dear. It even finds them rather charming. It will find this one distasteful and grotesque—that's all. There will be a slight variation in the world's opinion this time, and one more scandal for it to enjoy.

Enter the MAID.

Ada. Lunch is served, sir.

General. Oh, yes, I forgot to tell you. We lunch at midday. [*To the* MAID.] Delay it a little, will you, and show M. Villardieu to the blue room. I have put you and Gaston in the big south room, as usual, Lilian. We will try to sort out this business and talk to Ardèle after lunch.

The company rises and makes for the various rooms. The COUNT *takes the* GENERAL *aside.*

Count. Is this the only telephone in the house?

General. There is an extension in the library. Why?

Count. Well, it's like this. There has been, as you may know, a certain rearrangement in my married life.

General. I gathered so.

Count. Appearances are kept up, of course.

General. Ah, that's the main thing.

Count. Only I have a girl friend, you know, a delightful little thing—and I took the liberty of arranging for her to stay at the inn in the village during our stay here. I would like to telephone to her in private. She is a little nervy just now and I am rather worried about her. Yes, it's the real thing this time, my dear fellow. The child adores me, and as I cannot give her a great deal of time, I am afraid she is not very happy. The other day she tried to kill herself by taking an overdose of laudanum.

General. The whole thing sounds enchanting!

Count. Yes, but a little harrowing, nonetheless. At my age, you know, it is almost too much to be given all.

General. Clown! What is she like?

Count. She is a dressmaker—gay, witty, affectionate, adorable——

General. How old is she?

Count. Twenty-two, with enormous dark eyes, a tender, untried heart——

General. And am I to be allowed to see this little prisoner of yours?

Count. Of course. We will all have lunch together in the village. It's strange. When I broke with Lilian, I was ready for a lighthearted, casual affair, and before I knew, where I was, I found myself head over heels in love. I saw her walking down the Rue de la Paix one day in the pouring rain, and I offered her my umbrella——

They are going off to the library when the cry "Leon! Leon!" is heard above.

General [hesitates a moment, then shrugs]. Hell, I won't go. I'll say I thought it was the peacock. Yes, you were saying—your umbrella?

They go into the library. The stage is empty for a moment. In the distance a train whistle is heard. Then the puffing of a local train. NICHOLAS, *in the uniform of an army cadet, enters carrying a suitcase. He is faintly surprised at finding nobody in. He puts down his suitcase and takes off his cap.* NATHALIE *appears on the gallery, and stops dead on seeing him.*

Nathalie. So you came.

Nicholas. Yes. [*A pause.*] I took the short cut from the station across the wood. I stopped for a moment by the millstream, where a shirt had been left out to bleach on the stones just as before. Then I jumped over the breach in the old wall, by the big walnut tree, and I walked up the hill where the beehives are. I don't know how long bees live, but I felt somehow that they remembered me. Everything is the same in this house. In two years nothing has changed. Not even you.

Nathalie [softly]. Not even I.

Nicholas. Your skirts are only a very little longer than they were.

Nathalie. You are a man now.

Nicholas. You see, it only needed time.

Nathalie. Yes.

They stand gazing at each other, silently.

Nicholas. Nathalie, why did you marry my brother?

She stands motionless, without answering.

ACT TWO

When the lights go up again, the dining room doors are open, and the guests can be seen at table, having finished lunch. The Count *is speaking on the telephone, glancing nervously from time to time in the direction of the dining room.*

Count. Now you are not being fair, my little pet. I swear I can't speak any louder . . . because there are people here . . . no, no, my lambkin, I'm not neglecting you. I am here on a very important matter, my sweet, you know that. I'll come to see you the moment it's settled. . . . But of course I'll have the time, I'll make the time. . . . No, my angel, not for a little while yet . . . in an hour, perhaps. . . . I *do* love you. . . . No, no, please! Please don't hang up! . . . Don't . . . hang up!

He puts down the receiver with a sigh, and goes back into the dining room, passing the two children on their way out into the hall.

Marie-Christine. Why did they excuse us from table, do you think?

Toto. Didn't you see? They want to talk about—things. They were trying all during lunch, and just when it got interesting one of them looked at us and started to cough.

Marie-Christine. What did they want to talk about?

Toto. Oh, things, nasty things.

Marie-Christine. What nasty things?

Toto. Love stuff. They'll start talking now we've gone, I expect. We'll go and listen, if you like. I know just the place—come on!

Marie-Christine. No, I don't want to. I'd rather dress up in their clothes. I know, let's play at scenes—let's dress up and be married and have a scene!

The General's wife screams from upstairs: "Leon! Leon!"

Marie-Christine. What's that? It sounds like a bird.

Toto. A bird! That's Mummy calling Daddy. She calls him like that every ten minutes.

Marie-Christine. Why?

Toto. To find out where he is.

Marie-Christine. Why?

Toto. Because she's afraid he might be with the maid. Look out!

ADA *enters, carrying the coffee.*

[*Angelic.*] Well, Marie-Christine, what would you like to do—play croquet? Or would you rather come out onto the terrace and feed the carp?

Ada. If you are going to the pond, Master Toto, take care you don't fall in.

Toto. Oh, yes, Ada.

Ada. You'll be nice to your little cousin, won't you?

Toto. Oh, yes, Ada, of course I will. We're going to play mothers and fathers.

Exeunt children. ADA *arranges the coffee cups on a low table. Enter the* GENERAL *hurriedly.*

General. Where are the children?

Ada. Out on the terrace.

General. Who was the man in the kitchen with you just now?

Ada. The plumber. He's come to mend the waste pipe on the second floor.

General. What's happened to Cotard?

Ada. That's his mate. Cotard says he's too old to come all that way on his bicycle.

General. Well, his mate's too young. I shall send to town for a plumber.

Ada. What if he's too young, too?

General. Then water can squirt day and night from every pipe in the house! What was he saying to make you giggle like that? I could hear you every time the pantry door opened.

Ada [*giggling*]. Oh, things. You know what men are. Whenever they see a girl they start fooling.

General [*an old man suddenly*]. Ada.

Ada. Yes?

General. Be true to me, Ada. I love you. [*His gaze falters as she looks at him.*] Well, I—I need you. I know you don't love me, but I'll give you anything you want. I feel so alone, so helpless, in this house. Without you, without your warmth, without your body close by me every night I'm lost, I'm like a child. [*He looks at her.*] What are you laughing at, you little fool? Am I as amusing as the plumber's mate?

VILLARDIEU *enters.*

Yes, that's right. Bring in the brandy, will you, Ada?

Ada. Yes, sir.

She goes. The GENERAL *offers* VILLARDIEU *a cigar, takes one himself and lights it. He holds the match to his finger hoping against hope; and murmurs dejectedly:*

General. No, no good. [*In answer to* VILLARDIEU'S *astonished stare.*] Facts are facts, after all. I am not dreaming. Tell me, do you ever think back on the old days?

Villardieu. Sometimes, yes.

General. You are not happy either, are you? And yet Lilian is a charming woman—a little mad, of course, but charming. She has been getting steadily younger for the last ten years—I can't think how she does it. Well, now, what's wrong?

Villardieu. If you don't mind, sir, I would really rather not——

General. Come, come, the way things are at the moment, the least we can do is be honest with one another. What is it, why are you not happy?

Villardieu. I am jealous.

General. Jealous, begad! Of a plumber's mate, eh?

Villardieu [*shocked*]. I—I beg your pardon?

General. Nothing. An idle fancy. It would have been a fascinating coincidence.

Villardieu. I have reason to believe that the Countess is still in love with her husband.

General. I wouldn't put it past her.

Villardieu. It is all very well to move with the times: I am a broad-minded enough man myself, God knows—but I do insist on a certain clarity, a certain precision in my personal relationships. Do you know that I practically control their life together?

General. Do you really?

Villardieu. Oh, yes. I am always there. I never sleep at home now. I never have a single meal at my club. Fortunately my income is large enough to enable me to devote all my energies to the matter in hand. I have my own room, of course, on account of Marie-Christine and the servants, and as the walls are as thin as paper and every whisper can be heard all over the house, it is quite out of the question for me to go to Lilian, or for her to come to me. I spend my nights watching the Count's door. I have a very strong suspicion that they are meeting in secret.

General. A highly uncomfortable state of affairs, to say the least. So you and Lilian—er—Devil take it, man, you can tell me!

Villardieu. Never. Or very seldom. As Lilian is jealous of the Count and will go to any lengths to prevent him from meeting his little piece, she sees to it that he does not leave her side all day. Shopping, art exhibitions, tea parties, the three of us do the rounds together—and at night, while I watch her door, she watches his. Of the three of us, the Count alone might stand a chance of sleeping—I say might, because his girl friend, whom he can never get away to see, leads him one devil of a dance, and I am convinced that he doesn't sleep a wink either.

General. At least it is all very moral, even if it isn't much fun.

Enter the COUNT *and* COUNTESS, *followed by* NICHOLAS *and* NATHALIE.

Countess. Well, Leon, are we going to have a talk with Ardèle now?

General. The difficulty is to get her to come out. [*He gives her the key.*] Will you have a try?

Countess. She has already refused to listen to me.

General. Try again. I can't. She has a grudge against me. If you think it might help, you may tell her if you like that in your opinion I went too far in locking her in.

The COUNTESS *takes the key and goes up the stairs.*

Villardieu. I think perhaps it would be better if——

No one pays the slightest attention to him and he sits down again. The COUNT *lights a cigar, and settles himself in comfort.*

Count. I think she's plucky, Aunt Ardèle. Three days without food! The trout was excellent, General. [*To* NICHOLAS *and* NATHALIE, *who are sitting beside him.*] Have you ever tried a hunger strike?

Nathalie. No, never.

Count. What about you?

Nicholas. No.

Count. I did once. I held out till the cheese, and at that point it struck me that I was being very silly and that a man must live, after all.

General. Exactly. Don't you agree, Nathalie?

Nathalie. Yes, yes of course.

General. Nicholas, take that stupid look off your face. I sent for you because this scandal may affect you too one day. You are very young, but pay attention and try to form an opinion of your own. It will be called upon when we come to make a decision by and by.

The COUNTESS *has unlocked the door. She listens for a moment.*

Countess. Ardèle, it's Lilian. We are all here, Gaston, Nathalie, and even Nicholas, who has been granted special leave to come and see you.

Count. Tell her Villardieu is here too. It'll please him.

Countess [*ignoring the interruption*]. We want to say that we are disgusted by Leon's inhuman treatment of you——

General. Don't overdo it. She'll think herself a martyr.

Countess. ——and we would like to talk it over with you. Won't you open the door and let us in? Or come down yourself and join us in the drawing room? What did you say? [*To the assembled company.*] She says her mind is made up. She flatly refuses to open the door, and wants to be left alone to die.

General. Left alone to die! To die of love and despair, I suppose! My God, I have been desperate to the point of death a good half-dozen times myself, but did I die? Not on your life! [*To the* COUNT.] Did you?

Count. No, I survived.

General [*rising*]. A door is locked? Right! Break it down! One crowbar, three volunteers—— You, you and you!

Countess. Leon, keep calm! You will achieve nothing that way. Ardèle, little sister, Leon has told me the whole story and my heart goes out to you. I would like to talk to you about it. I am younger than you are, but I know so much more about life. Will you let me give you some advice? [*She listens a moment, then straightens, tight-lipped with fury.*] Ardèle, how dare you!

General. What did she say?

Countess. Something extremely unpleasant. Do as you please, Leon. I wash my hands of it.

General. But tell us what she said, for Heaven's sake! If we are going to spend our time insulting each other, we will never get anywhere.

Countess. My private life is no concern of anyone, least of all my family. And incidentally, I wonder how she could possibly know. It gives me a charming idea of your conversation together when I am not here. How dare you discuss me and my affairs? Have I ever presumed to criticize you? On the countless occasions when I surprised you cuddling the chambermaids, did I ever fail to turn a blind eye?

General. Chambermaids? What chambermaids? Nicholas, leave the room! Oh, all right, as you were. It's too late, anyhow, and it isn't my fault if your aunt's gone out of her mind. Death and damnation, Lilian, I'll have you know I do exactly as I please!

Countess. Well, my lad, and so do I!

Count [*coolly*]. And so does Aunt Ardèle. Really, you astonish me. Why do you deny her the very rights you claim for yourselves?

Countess. Gaston, try not to be more ingenuous than you can help. You know perfectly well it is simply a question of avoiding a scandal.

Count. Nonsense. You must give the world somthing to get its teeth into now and again.

Countess. Besides, let's be realistic about this. Despite her age, Ardèle must be considered an irresponsible child. What can she possibly know of love?

Count [*calmly*]. Of love as you or I know it, as the General or Nathalie or Villardieu know it, nothing, I grant you. But of love as Ardèle knows it why, everything, surely? And perhaps Ardèle has the answer. That may indeed be love, who knows?

Countess. You are being flippant as usual, and talking arrant nonsense into the bargain.

The cry of "Leon! Leon!" *is heard again from above.*

Countess. Was that the peacock?

General. No. It's Emily. Coming! [*He goes upstairs, and shouts down to them from the gallery.*] For ten years I have remained within earshot of that voice. I too could have grasped life with both hands and enjoyed it. A cuddle with my chambermaids—that is all life holds for me. So let no one dare reproach me for it now! [*He opens the door and says in a different voice.*] Here I am, Emily. Yes, everyone is here. We are chatting. . . . Oh, of this, that and the other. Why don't you have a little sleep? [*He closes the door.*] I give you ten minutes to make up your minds. After that, I'll have that door down!

Count. And then?

General. If she refuses to eat, I'll cram her. Like a goose.

Count. And then?

General. Then she'll eat her meals, she'll play her piano, and she'll forget her hunchback. All correct—attention—dismiss!

Count. And if things don't go according to plan? If she is genuinely in the final stages of despair? If this love of hers, which appears so grotesque to you, were indeed her sole reason for living now, what then? It is very trying I know, but you see, General, hidden away beneath her hump, Aunt Ardèle has a soul.

General. Maybe, maybe. In theory, the blockheads they sent me as recruits in Morocco had souls too, but if I had allowed for that, do you imagine I should ever have got them to form fours? The great thing is to know what one wants. [*Barking.*] Isn't that so, Lieutenant?

Villardieu [*startled to attention*]. Yes, sir!

Count. Stand easy!

VILLARDIEU *throws away his cigar in fury and goes to the window.*

First of all, we are in France, the war in Morocco is over and won, and Aunt Ardèle is not a recruit. And as for you, General, that's a fine speech for a barrack square, but I know you, you don't believe a word of it. Would you like me to speak to her? I have a feeling that I might manage better than the lot of you.

General. As you please, old chap, but I'm none too hopeful.

The COUNT *goes upstairs and stands at* ARDÈLE'S *door.*

Count. Aunt Ardèle. It's Gaston. You are unhappy, Aunt Ardèle, and I am not very happy either. Would it bore you very much if we chatted a little, you and I, on the subject of happiness?

Countess. A promising beginning!

Count. I am doing my best. [*He listens, and then*

smiles.] Thank you, Aunt Ardèle. I am very glad to know you are fond of me. I, too, am very fond of you——

General. They're swearing undying love now. She'll get the idea that every man jack is crazy for her in a minute. That will be gay.

Count. No, no Aunt Ardèle, that is not true. You are not old. You have proved it.

Countess. Of course, she is not old at forty-f—— Anyhow, her age has nothing to do with it.

Count. Aunt Ardèle, you have all your life before you, and life is full of humble little joys for every day. Your music, your flowers, your water colors, were those things not lovely too? [*He listens.*] No, no, they are worth far more than you imagine. We expect too much always—life is made up of pennies and halfpennies, and there's a fortune to be had for those who can collect them. Only we despise them and we wait for life to settle our account with a golden sovereign. And we stay poor, with all that treasure scattered everywhere around us. Aunt Ardèle, golden sovereigns are very rare. [*He turns to the others.*] I have very little stomach for all this platitudinous nonsense. I'm just trying to be helpful. [*He listens.*] What was that, Aunt Ardèle? I didn't quite catch—— [*He listens.*]

General. Well, what is she saying, man?

Count. She says with remarkable good sense that having found a golden sovereign it is supremely foolish to let it slip through one's fingers.

General. Talk to her about her duty. That sometimes does the trick. Tell her that I too have seen golden sovereigns slip past me one by one, and that all the same I stayed.

Count. Aunt Ardèle, I have been asked to talk to you about your duty. Now there are one or two of us here who consider ourselves free, and whose lives are in certain measure the object of scandal.

Countess. Gaston, are you mad? We are not discussing ourselves at the moment.

Count [*speaking through the door*]. Well now, if we don't behave absolutely well, it is because there remains deep down inside of us all a faint little notion of duty in the midst of our confusion which prevents us from behaving downright badly.

General. He's getting muddled. Once and for all, let me break down that door!

Count. I speak for myself as well as the rest. [*He listens.*]
That is very sweet of you, Aunt Ardèle, but I am unhappy
all the same, and even your good opinion of me does not
make it easier to bear.

Countess. You are not, I hope, making this an occasion
for self-pity.

Count [*covers his ear with his hand*]. A little quieter
there, please. Hullo! Hullo! Don't ring off. What is that
you say? Leon revolts you?

General. Ha, that's good! That's very good! She is in
love with a hunchback, and it's me she finds revolting!

Count. Leon revolts you, my dear, because he has stayed
by Emily's side all these years and gets along as best he
can. It is always, alas, our decent feelings which prompt
us to our evil deeds. Had he cared less for her, he would
have put her away ten years ago, and he would not incur
your censure now. Nothing simpler. And for Lilian and
Villardieu and myself it is the same. Our nice scruples
have brought us where we are.

Countess. Gaston, we are discussing Ardèle and a hunchback, not myself and not Villardieu!

Villardieu [*leaping up the stairs*]. I warn you. This
business has nothing whatever to do with me, and I will
not allow my private life to be involved.

Count. But mine?

Villardieu. That is your affair.

Count [*kindly*]. But, my dear chap, your private life, my
private life, where's the difference? [*He bends down to
listen.*] No, Aunt Ardèle, I was talking to Villardieu, a
very great friend of Lilian's and mine. That's it. You have
understood perfectly. Am I unhappy? No, not exactly.
You are only a novice, Aunt Ardèle. Wait a bit. This great
capacity for pain blunts itself you know, in time. Now,
had I lost Lilian the very first year of my marriage——

Countess. Gaston, have you no shame? For the last
time, we are discussing Ardèle's case now, not our own.

Count. But my poor dear Lili, they are one and the
same.

Villardieu. What do you mean, your poor dear Lili?
How dare you, sir?

Count. Keep calm, my dear fellow. You are right, Lilian,
it is not your case, nor mine, nor Villardieu's, nor the
General's we are discussing now. It is Love itself which is
on trial. Aunt Ardèle has the demon of love hidden in her

hump like a malignant spirit, stark love exploding in her twisted form, under her wrinkled skin. And we, who since we can remember have played blindman's buff with Love, come suddenly face to face with him at last. What a meeting!

Countess [*in a strange voice*]. Does he frighten you, Gaston?

Count. Lilian, I loved you once. Fifteen years ago when I took you from your father's house to be my bride, I too came face to face with love, and I was not afraid. It is when you catch a glimpse of him obliquely or from behind, or as he draws away that he is terrible.

Countess. And your latest love, your great love with the pinpricked fingers, does that frighten you too?

Count. My feelings are too worn for me to fear them now, but when I see her eyes as they gaze into mine, then yes, I am afraid.

Countess. You surely don't imagine that she loves you, do you? The girl is making a fool of you, my poor Gaston. Everyone knows that.

Count. May everyone be right. May there be no more love, anywhere, save in the hump of Aunt Ardèle, and may we suffer less, the lot of us. It's like a children's game, you see. You pass the lighted match from hand to hand, and you either burn your own fingers, or else get rid of the match in time and watch the others burn theirs. And either way it isn't very pretty.

General. But can we never love and be loved gently, without hurting one another? Dear God, can we not leave others and ourselves in peace for once?

Count. In peace? Tell us about war, General. Soldiers have always had puerile notions about peace.

General. But I am serious. I want to know. Agreed my wife went mad for love of me. She is in hell, I grant you. But is that my fault? I do what I can for her, but I'd like to be able to live a little too—without floods of tears and everlasting reproaches and daggers at my throat! Is it so much to ask? Surely there must be a way?

Count. We have been looking for it a long time now.

General. But, good God, some have found it, haven't they? The world is full of happy people. When I can get away for ten minutes or so I watch them sometimes: in the streets, in cafés, greeting their friends, all smiles, taking their women by the waist—devil take it, they are alive!

They're men and women, ordering their drinks, discussing at leisure whether to go on to a theater or go back home to bed. And I sit in my corner and watch them like a bewildered old fool, wondering whether to go over to them and ask for the formula.

Count. They could not possibly tell you it, General. They think themselves immortal lovers; but the formula, nevertheless, is very simple.

General. You, do you know it?

Count. Yes. They are not in love. There is very little love in this world, which is the reason it still keeps on turning more or less. Emily's diseased love is unbearable to you, but if you yourself did not love your wife, or at least had never loved her, if there were nothing left in you of the young subaltern in spectacles who thought to build his life with her, you too would be sitting quietly in a café with another at this moment. You too would be a man.

General. But Emily need not have gone so far. She needn't have gone mad, dammit!

Count. Don't fool yourself—it was the least she could do. Otherwise it would mean she gave you very little in the first place. Love served you in full measure, for one night or for ten years, and now you have to foot the bill. You pay by installments, but Love is generous. You are given plenty of time—sometimes all your life—in which to pay.

General. But why—why this frenzy to tear oneself limb from limb as if one harbored a personal grudge against oneself? Why not try to limit the damage?

Count. This is war, General. You are in favor of humane warfare, is that it? Prohibition of barbs on the bayonet? International control of the design of the bullet, so that it makes a nice clean little hole when it kills you? No, the thing once started, all means are equally good. Each is out for the other's skin, that's all.

Countess. Your cynicism is overdone, Gaston. In your efforts to dazzle us your reasoning has gone awry. You know very well that love is, above all, the gift of oneself.

Villardieu [*who has been forgotten, cries suddenly*]. Exactly!

Count. Poor old Villardieu, so you believe that too? I'll tear myself to shreds, I'll kill myself for the Beloved! Of course. Just so long as the Beloved is the projected ideal of my own self, just so long as he or she is my thing, my property, my self. It is so good to escape from one's immense and awful solitude. On one's own, one simply would not dare. But to give your all to this other being which is you—oh, the sweet summer rain on a parched and arid heart! Until the day when, by chance, by a whim, the other becomes another, no more. Then, of course, you cut your losses. What have you got to give another in this world? Why, that would be philanthropy. It wouldn't then be love.

General. Something tells me we are going astray. Let's get back to Ardèle, or else help me break down the door!

Count. Ardèle? But we never left her. Aunt Ardèle is Love. If we can dissuade her from giving all of herself to her hunchback, then perhaps we can all of us be saved. Villardieu, you are in love with my wife; you, General, are in love with life. In your case, Lilian, it's more simple— you are at the stage now when one almost admits it to oneself—you are in love with love. Ever since you began to feel yourself grow old, you became afraid of not recognizing yourself sufficiently in my eyes, and you set out to find others, at whatever cost, in which to study your own image. It is not of me you need be jealous, Villardieu. It is of her. It is with herself she will be false to you too, someday.

Countess. You have gone beyond the bounds of cynicism now. Be quiet, or I shall leave the room!

Villardieu. Lilian, have I your permission to keep him quiet by force if need be? [*He seizes the* Count *by the lapels.*] Count, if you are not a coward, you will give me satisfaction for this! Spare me the necessity of provoking you!

Count. All right, all right, old chap, you'll take a pot at me and I'll take a pot at you, but it won't solve anything. [*He turns back to the door.*] Hullo? I'm sorry, Aunt Ardèle, we were cut off. What's that? You only live once, you say? Not quite so loud, please, I can't hear you very well. You have waited, you say, forty years and more for this joy which lifts you out of yourself? Go ahead, Aunt Ardèle, come out of yourself, throw your bonnet over the windmill, snap your fingers at the world, since either way you will one day have to go back alone into your hump to die. May I correct you, however, on one small point. Thank God one only lives once. It is amply sufficient. [*He moves away from the door, very tired suddenly.*] I have had enough. Your turn now to consult the oracle. Eternal truths bore me a little. What's more, I can hear myself assuming a pathetic tone of voice which I find distasteful to a degree. Come now, who will try? Is there an enthusiast among you to convert Aunt Ardèle?

Nicholas. I will! [*He runs wildly up the stairs and bangs with both fists on the door.*] Aunt Ardèle! It's Nicholas. Stand firm! Laugh at the world! Laugh at what they are pleased to call scandal! Love whom you want to love, and don't listen to them! If they didn't tell you you were deformed and too old, they'd say you were too young, and either way they'd do their level best to spoil your happiness!

Nathalie [*who has leaped up the stairs to him*]. Nicholas, you're mad. I forbid you, I absolutely forbid you to speak, you hear?

Nicholas. You have no right any more to forbid me anything since you married my brother. Can you forbid me to say that I loved you, that you loved me, that they forced us to ruin our lives forever, just as they are trying to force her now, and always for the same old reasons—because it's either too soon or too late? Yes, I will tell them! I'll tell them all! That's the only reason I came back!

General. This is the last straw! We only needed this little tale to round off the family saga! Nicholas, go up to your room! What we did, we did for the best, because we felt it to be our duty.

Count. That's it! Up to your rooms! Let us lock ourselves in like Aunt Ardèle, all of us! That's the best we can do—not see each other any more!

Nicholas. Aunt Ardèle, before they stop me, are you listening? You must go on loving, do you hear? Loving in spite of them all, in spite of everyone and everything! Loving with all your heart and all your strength so that you will never, never be like them!

General [*struggling with him*]. Nicholas, that's enough! Come away from this door at once! [*He succeeds in dragging him away.*] What stops me giving you a good hiding I don't know.

Nicholas [*quietly*]. But I do, Father. It's shame.

General [*defeated, mutters*]. What have I to be ashamed of? Striving to set a bit of order into chaos, doing as little harm as I possibly can, trying to live a little before I have to die?

The voice cries "Leon! Leon!" and almost immediately the peacock cries from the garden, "Leon! Leon!"

[*Exploding.*] God Almighty! Hers and the peacock's together! Hell, I've had enough!

In the midst of the cries and the GENERAL'S *shouting,* ADA *is heard.*

Ada [*off*]. Master Toto! Miss Marie-Christine! Stop it!

Enter ADA, *trying to separate the two children, who are fighting savagely.*

General [*at the top of his voice*]. What the devil is going on? Can one never have a little peace in this place?

Countess [*seeing her hat on the child's head*]. Marie-Christine! My hat!

Count [*calmly*]. Don't make such a fuss. Toto has mine.

Ada. I can't separate them, sir. They're fighting like cat and dog. [*The children are eventually separated.*]

Toto [*yelling*]. We're not fighting like cats and dogs! You don't understand. We're married! We're playing at scenes!

General. Scenes? What scenes do you think you're playing at, kicking and screaming like a couple of wildcats?

Toto. Love scenes!

General. All right! Now off with you both at once to the kitchen, do you hear me? And if I catch you touching those clothes again I'll knock the living daylights out of you!

ADA *drags the children away. The telephone rings. The* GENERAL *answers it irritably.*

Yes, what is it now? What? Who? Oh, yes, hold the line will you? Gaston, for you.

Count. Could I take it in the library?

General. Not now that I have answered it. You'd be cut off.

Count [*takes the receiver*]. What does it matter anyway? Here goes!

General. Yes, here goes! Who cares? I have had about as much as I can stand!

Again the voice calling "Leon! Leon!"

[*Exasperated, answers without moving.*] Yes, I'm here.

Count [*on the telephone*]. But monkey darling, but my little dove, my lambkin, I swear——

Countess. If you knew how silly you sound with your Lilliputian menagerie. Everyone is listening.

Count. But my angel, I love you, I swear I love you! Don't, please don't! Don't do that—I implore you! Josette! ——[*He puts down the receiver hurriedly.*] She has rung off! General, can you let me have a carriage immediately?

General. I'll have one harnessed. But why?

Count. She has just taken an overdose of laudanum. She did it once before. I must go to her at once.

Countess. Gaston, don't be so absurd. You surely don't imagine the girl cares for you enough to want to kill herself?

Count. Enough to pretend to, at any rate. And one of these days she may well fail to bungle it. The carriage will take too long. Villardieu, I have never asked a favor of you —but I think you owe me one at least. I must give her an emetic within fifteen minutes. Drive me there in your De Dion.

Villardieu. Very well, with Lilian's permission. But afterwards I insist that we settle our private account.

Count. Yes, yes, of course.

Countess [*as they go*]. You are pathetic, my poor Gaston. Make haste to your lambkin. My heart bleeds for you.

Count [*pausing in the doorway*]. And mine, Lilian, bleeds for you. Fortunately we are laughable, all of us, otherwise the whole business would be sad indeed!

He goes, followed by VILLARDIEU. *The* COUNTESS *shrugs and examines her face in a mirror, smoothing out her wrinkles.*

Countess. Oh, how stupid it all is! If only it did not age one so! I must lie down. I am utterly exhausted. [*She goes to her room.*]

The voice is heard again.

General [*tonelessly*]. Coming!

He climbs heavily upstairs to his wife's room. NATHALIE *and* NICHOLAS *are left alone. They have not taken their eyes from each other since the outburst.*

Nicholas. We must break our silence now, Nathalie.

Nathalie. You mean we may never break it now, ever.

Nicholas. No. Tonight, when they are all asleep, I will come down as I used to long ago. I will wait for you in the hideout we had when it rained, under the stairs, and you will come down to me.

Nathalie [*in a whisper*]. No.

Nicholas. Yes. You say no, but you are trembling, Nathalie. You love me, you know it—and my brother is a thief and I despise him. You will come down.

ACT THREE

SCENE: *the same.*

A faint light appears. It is night. For a few moments nothing can be heard but the rain falling in torrents outside. Then a shadowy figure is seen moving across the stage. Suddenly it stops and disappears behind some hangings. TOTO appears on the gallery in his nightgown. He listens for a moment at his father's door and vanishes. The figure comes out from his hiding place. It is NICHOLAS. He watches the hall door for a moment, astonished at his little brother's extraordinary behavior, then hides in a corner under the stairs where there is a small divan. TOTO comes back, laden with hats, walking sticks, furs and coats, and tiptoes back to his room. NICHOLAS watches him go, fascinated, and then lights a cigarette. In the light of the cigarette, he can be seen to smile at TOTO's activities. A clock strikes eleven or twelve, one cannot be quite sure which. The outline of a man appears in the garden. It is the COUNT, who has returned wet through, his trousers turned up; he is wearing a raincoat, a straw boater, and carries an umbrella. He feels for the light switch, and a dim light comes from a bronze Cupid at the foot of the stairs. NICHOLAS has put out his cigarette and withdrawn into the shadows. The COUNT puts down his umbrella and starts up the stairs on tiptoe without seeing NICHOLAS. As he reaches the gallery, the COUNTESS comes out of her room in her dressing gown.

COUNTESS [*in a low voice*]. So you're back!

Count. Yes.

Countess. You're in a terrible state!

Count. It is raining very heavily, and I lost my way coming back.

Countess. You will catch your death of cold!

Count. No such luck, my dear. [*He makes a move to go.*]

Countess. Well?

Count. What do you care? She is out of danger.

Countess. And—comforted?

Count. That is another story, and one which cannot possibly interest you. With your permission, I will sleep on the sofa in the library. [*He is about to go a second time when the* COUNTESS *stops him.*]

Countess. Gaston, I am jealous of your little seamstress and intolerant of your relationship with her, I know, but it hurts me to see you suffer.

Count. I too am unhappy when I hurt you. But the child is in love with me now. She has nothing to do with our private quarrel, and however disproportionate it may appear to you, her suffering is more than I can bear. It is because of your selfish jealousy and your intolerable demands that she took that poison tonight.

Countess. What nonsense. She took very great care to warn you in good time.

Count. I daresay, but it is very unpleasant nonetheless to go through all that pain, and vomit at the end of it. We have never taken that risk, remember, you or I. I would like never to hurt anyone again, ever. Good night, Lilian.

Countess. Gaston, had you noticed that we had virtually stopped speaking to each other? I have felt for so long the need of a quiet talk with you.

Count. This is hardly the place for it. Villardieu sleeps at the end of the gallery.

Countess. Come in here.

Count [*genuinely shocked*]. At this time of night, with you in your night attire? If he were to find us together, there would be the devil of a fuss. No, no. It's quite impossible.

Countess. I simply must have a long talk alone with you soon. When we get back to Paris, we must arrange to meet in some quiet little teashop somewhere.

Count. My dear, you know you will never be able to get away. Besides, there is no such thing as a quiet little teashop. One invariably runs into someone or other. Don't think of it, Lilian, it's far too risky.

Countess. Well then, on the way home, say at Trouville. Take a closed cab and wait for me at the station. I will wear a thick veil and get away to meet you somehow.

Count. We'll look a guilty pair if we are caught.

Countess. You are my husband, after all!

Count. After all. Ah, yes, there's the tragedy. No, Lilian, you are playing with fire, my dear. Think of Marie-Christine. You have no right to risk a scandal. The pattern of your life is traced now. Be reasonable. Go back to your room. —Look out!

VILLARDIEU *has opened his door suddenly. He stands on the threshold in his dressing gown. The* COUNTESS *gives a startled cry and runs back into her room.*

Villardieu. I see. So my suspicions are confirmed.

Count [*smiling*]. Of course not. Go back to sleep. I am going to spend the night on the library sofa.

Villardieu. And our duel? Are you still willing?

Count [*kindly*]. If you like.

He goes. VILLARDIEU *goes back into his room and the house is again quiet. Then* ADA *comes out of the servants' quarters in her nightgown with her dressing gown slung over her shoulders, and carrying a candlestick. She goes up the stairs in her bare feet, carrying her shoes, and enters the General's study. Almost immediately the* GENERAL *leaves his wife's room and follows* ADA. *Again silence. A clock strikes the quarter.* NATHALIE, *fully dressed, appears on the gallery, listens for a moment, and then goes downstairs to join* NICHOLAS.

Nathalie. They were coming and going every few minutes until just now; I dared not come down.

Nicholas [*in a whisper*]. But you are here—at last.

Nathalie. Yes, my darling.

Nicholas. It is still two years ago. You are spending your holidays here as you do every summer. We have until October to be happy, and one day—one day you'll see— I'll be a man.

Nathalie. You are a man.

Nicholas. And you are my brother's wife.

Nathalie. Don't say any more. Hold me close to you. Listen! The rain has stopped. All of a sudden it is so quiet that I can hear your heart. I'm afraid. It would be terrible if they were to come down.

Nicholas. Ada has gone up to Father. Gaston is sleeping in the library. They have other things to do but think of us.

Nathalie. They are ugly, all of them. And as I came down to you, I felt ugly too.

Nicholas. No.

Nathalie. Yes. I am in your arms again, just as I used to be, but I am listening for the slightest sound like a guilty fugitive. I am afraid, like your father with that girl up there, that someone will suddenly call my name.

Nicholas. Maxim is in China. He is enjoying himself at this very moment with some little yellow whore out there. He's not the kind to waste a night—not he.

Nathalie. Don't talk about him any more.

Nicholas. The thief! With his big man's hands and his confident smile and his captain's uniform! How the girls ogled him always—how they blushed when he swaggered over to them at dances! "Really, you haven't the first idea, Nicky, old chap! Take them by storm! Sweep them off their feet!" The thief!

Nathalie. Don't let it hurt you any more, my darling. Rest. Lay your head on my lap and rest.

Nicholas. He has touched you.

Nathalie. Hush. Be quiet.

A silence.

Nicholas [*asks, like a child*]. Why did you marry him, Nathalie?

Nathalie. I had refused all the others. You were so young, shut up in your college, and my aunt could no longer afford to keep me. Her daily complaints, her everlasting little book in which she accounted for my every penny, my threadbare gloves, my made-over dresses, my meager portions at meals—I paid for all that by my humiliating servitude. I read all her pious books to her, I got up in the middle of the night for her hot water bottles and her poultices for as long as I could bear it—ill-fed, shabbily dressed, but grateful, mark you. I stood it all for just so long as I did not realize my spirit was about to die. Until one day she hurled abuse at me for a basin of spilled milk and I saw then that if I waited a few more years the girl you would find when you were at last grown up would no longer be myself. It was then your brother noticed me, I often wonder why, and I chose him rather than another so as not to lose you altogether.

Nicholas [*holding her closer*]. But I am grown up at last, and I waited for you. The others laughed at me, but I waited. Even when I heard of your marriage, I still waited, because I knew this night would come. Maxim had you among a hundred other women, but I have never touched any other one but you.

Nathalie. Nicholas, let me go.

Nicholas. It's not because they wrote your two names in a register and an absent-minded priest mumbled a string of words over your bent heads that that made you his wife.

Nathalie. No. But because I accepted him. And those two words "I will," which were no doubt just words for him, bound me forever to myself and my own choice. I love you, Nicholas, and only you, but I will never be yours. Let me go. I must go back.

She has risen. NICHOLAS *takes her in his arms and holds her to him.*

Nicholas. No.

Nathalie. I order you to let me go. I implore you—let me go.

Nicholas. No, it has been so long—but it has come at last after a thousand wasted days. We are even, Maxim! We are both men now. And if I have to kill him to get you back, then kill him I will!

He kisses her. She frees herself quickly and takes his head in her hands.

Nathalie. Nicholas, my dear, my little Nicholas. You are even younger now since you have grown so strong. It is impossible, my darling, believe me, it's impossible.

Nicholas. Why? Because he took you first, and without love?

Nathalie. No, my dearest, no.

Nicholas [*crying out*]. Then why?

Nathalie [*startled, covers his mouth with her hand*]. I could never, never tell you. Quiet! Look! [*She draws him violently into the shadows.*]

Nicholas. What is it?

Nathalie. There is a man outside in the garden.

Nicholas. There can't be. Gaston is back. Father and Villardieu are upstairs.

Nathalie. Hush! He's uncertain. He is moving from tree to tree like a thief.

Nicholas. You're dreaming. There are no thieves in these parts.

Nathalie. It is someone who knows the house. He can't possibly see the rockery, yet he's gone right round it. He's making straight for the terrace. I think he's waving to someone.

Nicholas. But to whom? He's coming this way. He's coming in! Let me fetch my gun——

Nathalie. No. Stay where you are. Quiet, now I think I know who it is. —My God! it's horrible! It's he!

Nicholas. Who?

Nathalie. The hunchback!

The hesitant figure of a man, misshapen, wrapped in a big hooded cloak, is seen coming in through the French windows. He peers cautiously round the deserted room and goes up the stairs, one at a time, listening all the while. As he reaches the gallery, Aunt Ardèle's door opens wide and the hunchback disappears into the room.

[*In a murmur.*] He came prowling around the house like the mangy dogs after Sally when she is shut indoors. She signaled to him from her window—she knew they had forgotten to lock her door again, and she let him in. Oh, it's too hideous! No, don't touch me!

Nicholas. But why?

Nathalie. Those two upstairs, they are touching each other, they are in each other's arms! Oh, how hideous love is!

Nicholas. Nathalie, that's blasphemy! Their love is hideous, yes, but not ours.

Nathalie. There is no difference. Our love of long ago was as deep and pure as a summer's morning. But now, if we loved each other furtively, in secret, it would be ugly and horrible like theirs. Go away from here, Nicholas, quickly—leave this place, and don't come back save with another wife one day!

Nicholas. Nathalie, you're mad! We are young and fine and strong, you and I, and we have been in love since we were children. What do the others matter, clowns and buffoons who know nothing? Forget them. We alone in this house have the right to be in love.

Nathalie. Not any more. Let me go. Don't hold me in your arms—please—please! [*She rubs her face.*] Oh, how I wish you hadn't kissed me!

Nicholas. Nathalie, darling, it's I—I am here—Nicholas —I am yours and you are mine since always, and nothing is ugly between us!

NICHOLAS *goes to take her in his arms, but she backs away from him.*

Nathalie [*wildly*]. No!

Nicholas [*bewildered and helpless*]. When we held each other close outside on the lawn in the dark, long ago when we were small, you swore you would be mine.

Nathalie [*cries*]. Not any more! Not yours as well!

Nicholas. What—did you say?

Nathalie [*softly*]. We are not children any more. I didn't want to tell you, but perhaps it's better that you should know. My heart is full of you, my darling, and Maxim fills me with loathing, but when he took me on that first night, I, who thought I should die of hatred and contempt —I moaned with delight in his arms; my head thrown back, my eyes wild, I abandoned myself to my body's pleasure and I forgot you until morning.

Nicholas [*with a mad cry*]. Nathalie!

Nathalie. The next morning I wanted to kill myself from sheer disgust. But I didn't kill myself and I waited humbly for the night to come again. And I've been waiting ever since. That's all. I've told you now.

At this moment, the cry is heard above, "Leon! Leon! Leon!" incessantly now and shriller than ever. The door of the General's wife's room opens violently and she comes out a disheveled, terrifying figure in nightgown and bed jacket, clutching a woolen shawl round her shoulders. She moves to the top of the stairs and screeches into the silence.

General's Wife. Leon! Leon! Leon! Leon!

NICHOLAS *and* NATHALIE *remain transfixed. The* COUNT *rushes from the library, the* COUNTESS *and* VILLARDIEU *from their rooms.*

Countess [*shrieking*]. Emily!

The GENERAL *appears at last, struggling into his dressing gown.* ADA *will come out behind him a little later, her hair flowing, clad in her long, close-fitting nightgown.*

General. What the blazes is all the row about? Emily! Get back into bed at once.

Emily [*screaming and struggling and hanging onto the banisters*]. I won't go back to my room! They are in there, next door; I heard them. I felt them. I feel everything, always. For ten years I've watched. For ten years I've listened from my bed. Even if I'm asleep when you get up, the moment you go with that girl I am awake!

General [*blustering*]. What girl? What are you talking about? Why don't you go back to bed?

Emily. I can tell to the very minute. I can tell when the dog goes to the farmyard to find the bitch—I can tell when they bring the bull to the village, when the beasts join one another in the woods, under the ground, in the fields, in the trees! Do you think I sleep all night long? I watch for them, listen to them, feel them all!

General. Emily! Go back!

Just then the peacock cries "Leon! Leon!"

Emily [*fighting him off*]. No, I won't go back! There's the peacock calling too out there, and the weasels and the badgers and the foxes in the clearing, and the insects, all the millions of insects anywhere in the silence of the night! Every living thing trembling—quivering with lust and torturing me. I can even tell when the flowers lift their heads and open their petals obscenely in the dawn! You are horrible all of you, horrible, you and your loving! Stop them, I say! Stop them both! I am not mad. I know there's no stopping the beasts of the earth. But you, at least, stop calling to each other like cats all round me! Those two next door! Stop them before I scream!

General. But stop whom, in heaven's name? Emily, go back to bed! Ada, get her sleeping draught.

Emily. I don't want my sleeping draught. They are in there! They are in there together! Make them stop! Make them stop!

General. No, Emily, don't be silly. That's Ardèle's room. She is alone.

Emily. No, she is not alone! I can hear, I can see, the two of them!

General. What the hell are you talking about? [*He rushes to Ardèle's door.*] Ardèle! Open the door at once! Emily is having a fit. Open the door this minute or I'll break it down. Ardèle—do you hear?

Emily [*in a hysterical torrent of words through the* GENERAL'S *speech*]. That is what sent me mad—feeling you all around me, all of you! Feeling you [*to the* GENERAL] with your eyes, your nose, your hands lusting after all the women you ever saw! All, all of them. Those you made me entertain, those who passed you in the street, those who rubbed against you in the theater, the ones whose pictures you gloated over in the papers, and since the ones you could see with your two eyes weren't enough —all those you imagined, all those you created in your dreams! You would be talking to me—I'd have managed to get you alone in my room with no one to look at but me, but then your eyes, as they gazed into mine, would be making love with an unknown woman somewhere else! The whole world swarmed with women, women with hats and fans and smiles and sweet words and teasing glances, and always there like ripe fruit asking to be plucked. And all around, the smell, the heady smell of women everywhere! I watched for them so much and for so long that I learned to recognize the ones you wanted, to smell them out as you did—even before you sometimes, to feel even what you felt, to desire them, to make love with them myself, like you!

General. Now, Emily, that's enough. I have spent my life at your bedside, and you know it. You're wandering. Go back to bed. Go to sleep. It's very late.

Emily [*chanting as the* GENERAL *propels her back to her room*]. All—all of them! Madame Lietar, the Pocholle sisters, Gilberte Swann, that Malibran woman, and Odette Donnadieu, Clara Pompon, the dancer at the Grand Theatre in Bordeaux, the canteen waitress in Morocco, and every single inmate of the students' hostel on the Boulevard Raspail!

General [*pushing her to her room and protesting at each new name*]. No, no—what are you talking about? Go back to bed.

Emily. Yes! Yes! All of them! I have never had a moment's peace. Even those I would never have believed possible. Women in books who have been dead a hundred years, the little girl on Prizegiving Day, the Sister Superior on the day Marie-Louise took the veil, and the day—the day of the Tattoo—when you rushed forward to kiss the hand of the President's wife!

General. No, no. That's ludicrous. The President had beckoned me himself. You're dreaming. Come along now.

Emily [*now a drooping, pathetic creature, murmurs as she is led to her room*]. I know—I know everything. I'm watching—watching——

As the door is reached, two shots ring out close by. Everyone stops dead, but the madwoman, who appears not to have heard, continues her wailing chant.

I'm watching! I'm watching! I'm watching!

General. My God! What's that? See to her, will you? This time I am breaking down that door!

The COUNT, *the* GENERAL *and* VILLARDIEU *throw themselves against the door, puffing and blowing and getting into one another's way. They make a ridiculous, wholly ineffectual trio. This must also be a clown act, despite the anguish of the situation. Finally,* VILLARDIEU *pushes them aside, takes a run at the door and breaks it in, falling with it. The* GENERAL *steps over him into the room.* VILLARDIEU *gets to his feet, rubbing his shoulder. There is a pause. The* GENERAL *comes out again and says quietly.*

The fools. They've killed themselves. Run for a doctor, someone. I think Ardèle's still breathing.

VILLARDIEU *runs out. The* COUNT *and the* COUNTESS *follow the* GENERAL *back into the room. Below,* NICHOLAS *and* NATHALIE, *who have not moved all this time, stand looking at each other.*

Nathalie [*softly*]. You see, we don't even have to kill ourselves now. These two who were made for the world's laughter, they have done it for us. Good-by, Nicholas. Never think of me again. Never think of love again, ever.

NATHALIE *goes quickly up to her room.* NICHOLAS *stays a moment motionless, then goes out into the garden. A door opens and* TOTO's *head appears. Seeing the coast is clear, he and* MARIE-CHRISTINE *come out of the room. They are dressed up. Over their nightgowns they have hung themselves with scarves, feather boas, furs, top hats and overcoats.* TOTO *has even made himself a false mus-*

tache, heaven knows with what. They look all of a sudden like two grotesque little dwarfs strutting down the stairs, striking poses and making ridiculous melodramatic gestures. A spotlight is trained onto the darkened stage.

Toto [*rolling his "r's" to make it really passionate*]. My dearest!

Marie-Christine. My beloved one.

Toto. My darling wife, I adore you!

Marie-Christine. I adore you too, my dear little darling husband!

Toto. Not as much as I adore you, my dearest love!

Marie-Christine. Yes I do, my dearest love, a hundred times more!

Toto. No. No you don't!

Marie-Christine. Oh, yes I do! I do!

Toto. You don't! You don't! Because if you loved me less, one day I'd kill you!

Marie-Christine. No, my dearest darling, I'd kill you first!

Toto. No, you wouldn't. I would!

Marie-Christine. No, you wouldn't. I would!

They face each other, stamping their feet and shouting.

Toto. I'd kill you first!

Marie-Christine. No, I would!

Toto [*seizing and shaking her*]. No, I would, you silly little fool. I tell you it's me that loves you most!

Marie-Christine. No it isn't, it's me. It's me that loves you most! [*She struggles to get free of him.*] You horrid beast! You nasty pig! You dirty black spider!

They fall to the ground, biting and scratching, shedding their finery, their hats flying. The curtain falls as Toto, *yelling, rains blows on his cousin.*

Toto. I'll show you who loves you most, you little half-wit! I tell you it's me who loves you most, you nasty pie-faced little horror, you beastly crawly caterpillar, etc., etc., etc.

The Curtain Is Down.

MADEMOISELLE COLOMBE

Adapted by

LOUIS KRONENBERGER

CHARACTERS
(*In order of appearance*)

COLOMBE
JULIEN
MME. GEORGES
MME. ALEXANDRA
CHIROPODIST
MANICURIST
HAIRDRESSER
GOURETTE
EDOUARD
DESCHAMPS
POET-MINE-OWN
GAULOIS
DANCERS
STAGEHAND

PLACE: A *theatre in* PARIS

ACT ONE

SCENE I: *Sometime around* 1900
SCENE II: *A few days later*

ACT TWO

SCENE I: *About three months later*
SCENE II: *Three hours after Scene I*
EPILOGUE: *Two years earlier than Scene II*

ACT ONE

SCENE I

SCENE—*The corridor flanking the dressing rooms, with one whole side of Mme. Alexandra's dressing room exposed, and at one end the door to her inner retiring room. The corridor is badly lighted; the dressing room is still dark.*

AT RISE: COLOMBE *is seated and* JULIEN *pacing back and forth. They seem to be waiting for something. The dresser,*
MME. GEORGES, *comes in carrying a chair.*

MME. GEORGES. Sit down, Mr. Julien. You'll probably have to wait a while.

Julien [*at some distance*]. Thanks, Georgie—but I just told you I'd rather stand.

Mme. Georges. My oldest boy had to stand, too. Now he's got varicose veins. I always have to sit and it's just the opposite—my rear end hurts.

Julien. Oh, go bury your rear end. I wish the old girl would hurry up.

Mme. Georges [*to* COLOMBE]. It starts with an itch in the feet, then it goes into the legs, then it gets you in the back. . . .

Julien [*shouting to* COLOMBE]. For God's sake, tell her you're not interested. If you don't, she'll show you over her whole body.

Mme. Georges. Thirty years I've been a dresser, Mrs. Julien, always sitting around waiting for the play to end.

Colombe. But you don't *have* to sit.

Mme. Georges. Yes I do. My phlebitis.

Julien. The hell with your phlebitis. Find out if the old girl's on stage.

Mme. Georges [*shaking her head*]. Uh-uhm. She always goes to her dressing room before she rehearses. A fine way to refer to your mother.

Julien. Stop lecturing me.

Mme. Georges. Listen to him. My oldest all over again. I will say, my third one, the one who died of t.b., he was easy to bring up—always spitting quietly in his corner. [*To* COLOMBE.] How old is *your* baby?

Colombe. Just a year.

Mme. Georges. Are his movements regular?

Julien [*grabbing her in exasperation by the arm*]. Georgie, if you don't shut up, I'll break your neck.

Mme. Georges [*quite unruffled*]. Men, Mrs. Julien. I've known him since he was so high.

Julien. Uhm. That's how long I've been hearing all this.

Mme. Georges. He was a *nice* little boy. Used to ask for caramels. Didn't you?

Julien [*letting her go and walking off*]. If you say so.

Mme. Georges [*to* JULIEN]. You didn't have strong lungs either.

Julien. They're much stronger now. The caramels cured me.

Mme. Georges [*sudden thought*]. I hope the baby doesn't cough?

Julien. Georgie, my son doesn't cough, my wife doesn't cough, [*indicating himself*] none of us cough. Go on [*indicating downstairs*], see if she hasn't come.

Mme. Georges [*impervious*]. My fourth son, the one in the Foreign Legion, developed a sort of dog bark.

Julien. Georgie, you *sure* they're rehearsing today? I've got to see her.

Mme. Georges. Gets married without a word, waits two years, and then calmly strolls in just before a rehearsal. [*To* JULIEN.] Don't worry, you'll see her—and hear from her, too. You and your mother have never gotten along. Not like Mr. Edouard; he knows how to handle her.

Julien. What's she playing in now?

Mme. Georges. *The Goddess of Love.* A play with five changes. Why can't she do *Athalie* again—a classic, and she only has to change once.

Julien. Georgie, it's damn near three o'clock. Be a good girl, go down and see if the others haven't come.

Mme. Georges [*exiting as though her aches and pains were pieces of heavy luggage*]. Two flights of stairs: have you any idea how many times I go up and down every day? [*Exit.*]

Julien. *The Goddess of Love.* One of her *femme fatale* roles. That's bad.

Colombe. Why?

Julien. The only times I've made even a dent on her

were when she was cast as a mother. The theatre's sure
something!

Colombe. You make too much of everything .

Julien. Do I? [*Eruptively.*] When I was four, the Mater
sent me to live with a blacksmith twenty miles outside
Paris. For months she never came near me. Just as I was
half dead from cold and hunger, Poet-Mine-Own brought
her the script of *The Sins of the Mother.* In the first act
she abandons her baby on the steps of a church—snowing
outside, singing within. In the fifth act she's stabbed with
remorse for 91 lines. I once counted them. After the dress
rehearsal, she got into a carriage with two friends and a
photographer to see the poor little kid it broke her heart
to have to board out. Imagine the publicity: Mme. Alexandra, the nation's greatest emotional actress, who every
night abandons her baby in the theatre, photographed in
real life with a little four-year-old she adores. Except that
the four-year-old was such a mass of skin and bones, and so
scabby with dirt, they couldn't photograph him. The
next night Mommy had all Paris drenched in tears. The
rumor had spread that with her own child at death's door,
she'd insisted on going on. The play was a smash. At least
I got *something* out of it—she sent me to live in Switzerland like a human being.

Colombe. My poor Julien. I never realized. . . .

Julien. I've never run down [*with a sarcastic inflection*]
literature since. Thanks to Poet-Mine-Own's throbbing
verses, I'm well enough today to serve in the army.

Colombe. Is Poet-Mine-Own . . . ?

Julien. Yes. Robinet. He calls Mommy "Madame Inspiration" and she calls him "Poet-Mine-Own." You'll
get used to it!

Colombe [*after a brief pause*]. Do you think she'll do
anything for us?

Julien. Not if she can help it. But I don't see how she
can—a soldier son and his gallant little wife. She'll have
to do something.

Colombe. It's not nice to talk that way.

Julien. I know. Don't you think I'd like the word
"mother" to stand for something . . . good?

Colombe. Why is she so fond of your brother?

Julien. To begin with, Edouard's jockey father was the
one real love of her life. She still sends him money.

Edouard learned fast how to get on in the world—he'd hang around the theatre getting hugged and kissed, a little angel sucking a lollipop. I remind the old girl of my father —a moody army officer.

Colombe. Darling, you aren't always easy to live with, you know. Either you're yelling your head off about something or you refuse to open your mouth. Was your father that way, too?

Julien. Apparently he was considered impossible. So honest himself that he made everyone else squirm. And like a first-class misanthrope, he carefully fell in love with a woman who could only break his heart. He thought mother would make him sublimely happy. She did, for three weeks. Then she left him for the juvenile lead.

Colombe. And your father killed himself?

Julien. Yes.

Colombe. How ghastly!

Julien. Yes. Mother was terribly put out.

Colombe. Julien, she's still your mother. Don't you think if you tried a little harder . . . ?

Julien. No, my love, I don't.

Colombe. I'm afraid you're impossible, too.

Julien. "Impossible" is an unpatriotic word—don't you dare apply it to a prospective soldier of France.

Colombe. If you'd ask your mother, I'm sure with the people she knows you could be deferred.

Julien. No thanks. I hate it, but I'll go through with it.

Colombe. Just because you hate it? [*He smiles faintly.*] And what about me all that time?

Julien [*going to her, suddenly gentle*]. Darling, you're all I've got. It's going to be hell to leave you—but you wouldn't love me if I walked out on the job to stay with you.

Colombe. Are you crazy? Of course I'd love you.

Julien. Well, I can't. You might love me, but I'd only hate myself.

Colombe [*with a sigh*]. You make everything a problem.

MME. GEORGES *rushes in, talking loudly.*

Mme. Georges. She's here! She's downstairs, giving some students her autograph.

Julien. Haven't they unhitched her carriage horses and put themselves between the shafts? Aren't they imploring her to let 'em pull her through the streets?

Mme. Georges. If you're going to start in that way. . . . [*Sympathetically.*] Don't, Mr. Julien. When I see what your brother manages to get with a little flattery. . . .

Julien. Georgie, you just feel sorry for *yourself.* I'll handle me.

Mme. Georges [*after shaking her head at* COLOMBE]. Anyway, I'm going to let her know you're here. [*Exit.*]

Colombe [*going up to* JULIEN]. Darling, you know what we're here for. Please be nice. Think of the baby . . . and me.

Julien [*pricking his ears*]. Listen to that—just listen to that. It puffs, it pants, it wheezes, it yanks its damn carcass up step by step—who'd ever believe that on stage it's a young girl, it's youth itself—it doesn't even walk, it floats. That's my mother!

Colombe [*shouting in protest*]. Julien!

Julien. Stand at attention! Before you shall appear the goddess of love of the entire Third Republic. I know you go for love; you'll be impressed.

Colombe. Darling, I'm frightened.

Julien. Oh, it doesn't bite.

Colombe. Julien, it's you I'm frightened of.

MME. ALEXANDRA *appears, surrounded by* MME. GEORGES *and a collection of hairdressers, chiropodists, etc. Sweeps past* COLOMBE *and* JULIEN *without so much as a look, and bangs into her dressing room.*

Mme. Alexandra [*snappish*]. My son! Of course not. Tell him I don't care to see him. [*The dressing room door is shut.*]

Julien [*sits like a stone, aghast, till his mother disappears. Then bursts out*]. This is just a little too much! This time I'll show her!

Colombe [*trying to restrain him*]. My darling, calm down. You won't get anywhere by yelling.

Julien. Let me go. I feel like yelling. I'd choke if I didn't. Mother! [*He flings himself upon her dressing room, knocks at the inner dressing room door, which is locked. Rattles it.*] Mother! Let me in! Let me in, or I'll break the door down. [*Rattles on in vain.*] Mme. Alexandra, if you don't open the door, I'll smash all your imitation china, I'll rip up your fake Persian rugs. Let me in, or it'll cost you a damn sight more than anything I want from you.

The dressing room door opens a little. The CHIROPODIST
appears, clutching it firmly.

Chiropodist. Madame wishes to inform monsieur that
she can't see him. She has a rehearsal.

Julien [*through the half-open door*]. Mme. Alexandra,
I am calm. I am inconceivably, indescribably calm. But
this just happens to be something that I can't go into with
your chiropodist.

Mme. Alexandra [*from within*]. Tell him to get out
of my dressing room and wait in the corridor.

Julien [*teeth clenched, white with anger; suddenly*]. As
you wish, mummy dear. I'll wait in the corridor, mummy
dear. [*He goes out, slamming the door; turns red when he
sees* COLOMBE *trembling.*] Was I calm enough for you?

The CHIROPODIST *closes the door and waits there till* MME.
GEORGES *goes out and through the corridor to lock it
again—a sneaky, self-important bit of pantomime.*

Mme. Georges. You sure are making headway, Mr.
Julien. I begged you to behave.

Julien. Sorry. Frightfully sorry.

Mme. Georges. After all, it's you that wants the help—
you're the one that's got to make the effort.

Julien. Did I walk past *her*? Did I refuse to see *her*?

Mme. Georges [*after a second*]. How much do you
want? Maybe if she knew the amount. . . .

Julien. I have to serve my country. I want her to look
after my wife and child while I'm away.

Mme. Georges [*with a low whistle*]. Three years is a
long time.

Julien [*significantly*]. Yes.

During all this, MME ALEXANDRA *has changed into a
dressing gown. She sits on a kind of throne: the* CHIROPO-
DIST *takes her foot, the* MANICURIST *her hand, the* HAIR-
DRESSER *her head.* GOURETTE, *her secretary, stands waiting,
papers in hand. There is the sense of an ancient idol com-
panied by priests.*

Mme. Alexandra [*after a moment*]. Gourette!

Gourette [*advancing obsequiously*]. Yes, madame?

Mme. Alexandra. What's the mail?

Gourette. A bill for your *Goddess of Love* costumes. It's
the third one.

Mme. Alexandra. Really? What else?

Gourette. The stagehands want a raise.

Mme. Alexandra. They do? What else?

Gourette. The Consumptive Students Aid Society are having a benefit.

Mme. Alexandra. I've already given the students.

Gourette. These are consumptive students.

Mme. Alexandra. Are they students or are they consumptives?

Gourette. They say that Mme. Sarah Bernhardt sent them a statue she carved herself.

Mme. Alexandra. Tell them I'm not a sculptress, like Mme. Sarah Bernhardt—I merely act.

Gourette. Mme. Sarah Bernhardt's gift will get a lot of publicity.

Mme. Alexandra. Anything Mme. Sarah Bernhardt does gets a lot of publicity. Is it a big statue?

Gourette. If it's the one she exhibited at the last Salon, it's about this big.

Mme. Alexandra. Is that all? I'm amazed. [*Calls out.*] Georges!

Mme. Georges [*in the corridor, to* JULIEN]. She wants me. You stay here now—it'll work out all right. [*She goes into the dressing room with her passkey, closing the door behind her.*] Yes, madame?

Mme. Alexandra. What did you do with that great big bronze horror—that thing I never could get rid of?

Mme. Georges. The naked lady?

Mme. Alexandra. The naked lady's a Rodin! Give them a Rodin just because they've got consumption?

Mme. Georges. Oh—you don't mean the Skeleton?

Mme. Alexandra. Tha-a-at's it. Skeleton pulling someone after him.

Mme. Georges. It's called "Death and the Young Man." It's at home—in the attic.

Mme. Alexandra [*to* GOURETTE]. Send it with my very best wishes.

Gourette. But "Death and the Young Man"—for young men with consumption?

Mme. Alexandra. And why not? It's one of the *few* things that'll make them feel how well off they are.

Julien [*impatient*]. If she thinks she can keep **me** waiting all afternoon. . . .

Colombe Please, Julien, I beg of you.

Julien [*goes and knocks at the door*]. Mother!

The whole dressing room stops dead, waiting for MME.
ALEXANDRA'S *next move.*

Mme. Alexandra [*to* GOURETTE]. What else?

Julien [*knocking again*]. Mother!

Gourette. A young man from Rouen who's seen you
three times in *The Goddess of Love* and would die for you.

Mme. Alexandra. Good. Thank him. What else?

Julien [*knocking*]. Mother! Let me in.

The dressing room stops dead again.

Mme. Alexandra [*to* GOURETTE]. What else?

Gourette [*dead-pan*]. A line from Mr. Julien, that he's
coming here to see you today on very urgent business.

Mme. Alexandra. What else?

Julien [*kicking the door*]. Mother! I'll keep kicking the
door till you let me in.

Mme. Alexandra [*to* GOURETTE, *who has been listening,
with a faint smile, to* JULIEN]. Did you hear me? I asked,
what else?

Gourette [*the smile vanishing*]. The firemen, madame.

Mme. Alexandra. What can they want? There's no fire.

Gourette. Their annual benefit. . . .

Julien [*who has gone on kicking the door*]. Mother!
Mme. Alexandra! If you don't give a damn about me, think
of the beautiful paint on the door.

Colombe [*dragging him away*]. Julien, that's enough—
you're being dreadful!

Julien [*stops; looks at her; quietly*]. Oh—you think I'm
awful, too? All right, I'll stop. [*Goes and sits down.*]

Mme. Alexandra. What else?

Gourette. What shall I do about the firemen?

Mme. Alexandra. Oh—send them all the flowers that
came yesterday.

Gourette. Flowers, to firemen?

Mme. Alexandra. Certainly.

Gourette. But they're really rather faded.

Mme. Alexandra. They can water them. Watering things
is their specialty. [*Gets up.*] That's enough for now. I'm
tired. I'm going to get ready for rehearsal.

Gourette. As you wish, madame.

Exits: MME. GEORGES *goes to open the door for him with
her passkey, motions to* JULIEN *and* COLOMBE *to wait*

quietly. MME. ALEXANDRA *goes into her inner dressing room followed by her staff;* MME. GEORGES *quickly rejoins her. Alone in the corridor with* JULIEN *and* COLOMBE, GOURETTE *changes his tone.*

Gourette. The bitch!

Julien [*looking at him*]. Yes.

Gourette [*coming closer*]. It's been like that every day for ten years. "Yes, Mme. Alexandra." "Quite, Mme. Alexandra." "Oh, at once, Mme. Alexandra." [*Suddenly, after a cowardly glance at the closed dressing room door.*] God damn your stinking soul, Mme. Alexandra! . . . When will I be able to say it to her face?

Julien. Any time you care to. You're a free agent.

Gourette. You can say that; you're her son. Mama's boy can act up now and then. But mama's secretary: he either says nothing or he says, "Indeed yes, Mme. Alexandra"— and with a smile, too. That's part of the contract. Sometimes, if I don't guess right off exactly what she wants, know how she tells me? Heaves a statuette at my face. By now, I've learned to duck—but even then, I have to keep on smiling. What temperament!—she *couldn't* be anything but a genius. We admire her, God how we admire her, God how sick we are of admiring her. It's a privilege to serve her—it has to be, it's such a damn lousy living.

Julien. Why do you stay?

Gourette. Because I need my . . . two meals a day. They're all I do need, with everything else I have to swallow. "Why do I stay?" Why do you suppose I stay? Why do you come? . . . If just once I had the guts to. . . .

Julien. Get out of here. You're disgusting.

Gourette. Yes, I know. I'm disgusting, I'm nauseating, I'm a worm, I'm anything you care to call me. But don't worry—someday the worm will turn. Run along now, kiss mommy like a good boy. We all have our pride, we all have our principles, we all can be pushed just so far— only next thing you know, we're bowing right down to the ground.

He exits with a nasty laugh. JULIEN *remains standing, distraught.*

Julien [*suddenly*]. I'm sick—let's get out of here.

At this moment EDOUARD *appears, walking rapidly toward the dressing room. Stops, amazed, in front of* JULIEN.

Edouard. My God—Julien! Where'd you come from? [*Notices* COLOMBE.] And who's the young lady?

Julien. My wife. My brother Edouard.

Edouard. Oh, of course: I'd forgotten. . . . Where in God's name have you two been—two years and not even a postcard. Were you in America?

Julien. I was in Belleville, giving piano lessons. And Belleville's not exactly a music center.

Edouard. And now you've come to kiss and make up—— [*Smiles.*] Want help?

Julien. No thanks. We're leaving.

Edouard. Come on, let me have a shot at it. I'll make it easy for you.

Julien. Thanks; you're very kind, but we're leaving.

Edouard. Need anything? I'm flat myself, from the horses. But [*indicating the dressing room*] help is at hand —a mere matter of minutes. Hold on, don't move.

Julien. No. We were in the neighborhood, so we thought we'd call. Madame's not at home. Don't worry, it doesn't matter. And it was nice to see you. [*Tries to stop* COLOMBE *from going to* EDOUARD.]

Colombe. Don't listen to Julien, monsieur. He's so . . . proud. He did come to try to see your mother.

Julien [*trying to shut her up*]. Quit it, Colombe.

Colombe. We have a little baby, and Julien's about to go in the army. We came to ask his mother to look after us while he's gone.

Edouard [*incredulous*]. You didn't ask to be deferred?

Julien. No. I leave for camp tomorrow.

Edouard. And this child stays behind, flat broke and with a baby in her arms? That's what you're here to explain?

Colombe. Exactly, monsieur. And because his mother couldn't see us right away, he insists on leaving.

Edouard. I must say, you haven't changed any. [*To* COLOMBE.] He's going to make you extremely unhappy, my child.

Colombe. I love him, monsieur.

Edouard. I'm sure you do. We all love him. But that needn't stop us from thinking that life isn't quite the torture chamber he makes it. And if I hadn't come along, he was going to march off straight to camp and save France? First of all, my hero, we're going to get you deferred.

Colombe. Julien, you see!

Julien. No, thank you. I don't want to be deferred.

Edouard. Of course not! You prefer "left, right, left" with sixty pounds of assorted lead and iron on your back. I don't blame you—it sounds fascinating. And what fun for this charming young lady—she can be all alone in Belleville, washing diapers or trying to find the money for the baby's milk. One can be a patriot, you know, without making one's wife join the bread line! Please, wait five minutes—let me see what I can do. [*Goes into the dressing room, enters the inner retiring room without knocking, calls out gaily.*] Mother darling, I bid you good day!

JULIEN *doesn't move.* COLOMBE, *with an admiring look at the departing* EDOUARD, *comes closer to* JULIEN.

Colombe. My, he's nice. See, I was right to tell him about us.

Julien. Yes. [*Suddenly, in a different voice.*] Colombe— listen to me. After tomorrow, you'll be alone here—and life's not quite everything you think it is.

Colombe. I know, my darling.

Julien. It can be very tough. It has nothing to do with the pretty speeches people make.

Colombe. I know. You've told me before.

Julien. Now you'll find out for yourself. All the things that impress you about [*slight gesture toward dressing room*] . . . these people, are just for show.

Colombe. Yes, Julien.

Julien. I know how good your intentions are: but you're still just a child, you can't know what goes with their idea of a good time—or what comes after.

Colombe [*laughing a little*]. I ought to be scared to death?

Julien. There's nothing to laugh at. Yes, you ought to be scared to death.

Colombe. Darling, I'll really try to be, if that pleases you. But is "their idea of a good time" really so awful?

Julien. Yes.

Colombe. Things like someone telling me I'm beautiful and wanting to buy me flowers?

Julien. Yes.

Colombe. But what can be the harm if I say "thank you" for the flowers, and that's the end of it? It doesn't mean a thing—it's you I love.

Julien. I know. But it's not going to be simple. I'll be way off somewhere—if you really love me. . . .

Colombe. Darling, I do love you—no one but you.

Julien. You don't know how I want to believe you. Are you listening?—you're not looking at me.

Colombe. I'm not looking at you, but I'm listening—very hard.

Julien [*his seriousness slightly comic*]. If you love me as you say you do, you'll forget about such things.

Colombe [*with a tender little smile: incredulously*]. No pretty things or corsages—or even compliments? I can't look around in shops at all the beautiful clothes I can't afford?

Julien [*unhappily*]. No, baby.

Colombe. But I don't want you to buy them for me. I just want to look at them. What harm can it do to look at them?

Julien. I don't even want you to look at them.

Colombe. You're asking something awfully difficult.

Julien. Everything good is difficult.

Colombe. I'd know what you meant if you said I mustn't let anyone else buy them for me; but. . . .

Julien. No, Colombe. Try to see what I mean. You're my wife: when you married me, you were willing to get along with what I could give you; you were willing—weren't you?—to be poor.

Colombe. Yes.

Julien. I warned you what it would mean—babies keeping us awake at night, your hands all red from washing dishes. You didn't have to agree to it—and yet you did.

Colombe. I did because I loved you.

Julien. I know. But it's not enough to love me. I won't be here. Promise as the two of us did. . . .

Colombe. You mean before that awful mayor with his breakfast in his beard? That time doesn't count.

Julien. Then promise, as we promised the priest.

Colombe. All right, I promise. Now are you happy?

Julien. Cross your heart.

Colombe. Cross my heart. But it's not because I promise, silly—it's because I love you.

Julien. No. Don't you see: that's not it. Tomorrow maybe you won't love me. I want it to be because we chose each other, because we've become part of each other.

Colombe [half mystified, half hurt]. Then it doesn't even matter that I love you?

Julien. Of course it matters, but I mean something more. Look. Please. I could have known somebody else, you could have known somebody else, and loved him for his looks or something. That kind of love we can feel for lots of people, because we're young and need love. You're something different. Other people are hard or mean, and the ones that aren't bastards are blockheads. Ever since I was a little kid all they've done is hurt me. I hate them.

Colombe. You don't go out of your way to make friends yourself.

Julien. Not that kind of friends. I've built a better world of my own. A world that means you, and that little monkey that just grins at us, before he really lets us know what he's like.

Colombe. He's your son, whatever he's like. If he's not everything you want when he grows up, won't you love him anyhow?

Julien [with a fierce sincerity]. No.

Colombe. Then you only love us for our good points: if I lied or stole or something, you wouldn't love me?

Julien. I don't know.

Colombe. Do you think that means a *thing?* You've got to love me faults and all.

Julien. You've only got a few little girl's faults.

Colombe. And if someday I had a great many big girl's faults—bad faults—then you wouldn't love me? And you think that's love?

Julien. Yes.

Colombe. Yes—you do. But that's not how I want to be loved. I want you to love me as a woman, not as a little girl.

Julien [smiling; beaten]. All right, when I get out of the army, I promise I'll love you that way. We'll throw the most god-awful scenes, we'll stage the most terrific reconciliations. But while I'm away, darling, do what I ask: keep away from these people. [*Suddenly, at once comic and touching.*] Be the way I like you to be.

Colombe [still a little irritated]. I always am—you should know that.

Julien [*hesitates: then bursts out*]. He'll be back! Another thing, Colombe—don't start seeing much of Edouard.

Colombe. But he's so nice.

Julien [*savagely*]. You mustn't just because he's so nice. If you love me, you won't—because I'm not nice.

Colombe. Is that something to brag about? It's nice to be nice.

Julien. No!

Colombe [*with a comic little sigh*]. Darling, how complicated you make everything! How careful I keep having to be. And it's really so simple—people are nice, if you're nice to them.

Edouard [*coming back, shouts*]. Still there, you lovebirds? [*Comes into the corridor, looking pleased.*] One for our side, children! She refuses to see the undutiful son but is all agog to meet his wife. Incidentally—what name shall I say?

Colombe [*like a schoolgirl*]. Colombe, monsieur.

Edouard. I *like* it—but what *is* it?

Colombe. A saint's name.

Edouard. That's too bad. But I'm sure she wasn't a . . . terribly saintly saint. Took Thursdays off, or something. [*To* JULIEN.] Sonny, stay put for just five minutes: if Ma sees you now, she'll hit the ceiling. First let's have her warm up to Colombe, then you come on in the second act. You know the scene: the son all humility, the mother all forgiveness. One thing, though—I haven't told her she's a grandma. At her age it could be very dangerous. One of these days we'll have a doctor and nurse in attendance and break the news. How's it all sound?—or is it too much for your Puritan soul?

Julien [*mumbling*]. Thank you, Edouard—you're being very good.

Edouard. No—I'm not good; you know very well I'm not. But I like your wife and you *are* my brother. We have to show a little family feeling once in a while. Come along, Colombe; and stop calling me "monsieur." Try Edouard. [*They go into dressing room:* COLOMBE *gazes about in admiration.*] Quite something, isn't it? Ma does know how to give things an air. Of course everything's studiously false. Sit down on this pouf that's doing its damnedest to look like Louis XV, and wait for me. I'll go catch the tiger. Buck up——

He goes into the other dressing room. COLOMBE *and*
JULIEN *are each alone, with a wall between them.*

Julien [*suddenly*]. Colombe!
Colombe. Yes?
Julien. You promised!
Colombe [*a little impatiently*]. Yes, Julien. Please!

DESCHAMPS, ALEXANDRA's *codirector in the theatre, and*
POET-MINE-OWN *enter the far end of the corridor. They
are a matched pair of top hats, frock coats, high collars,
mustaches and canes.*

Deschamps. Perfect!
Mine-Own. You *really* think so?
Deschamps. It's inspired.
Mine-Own [*fatuously*]. I must admit, I think it's quite
a good new scene.
Deschamps. Poet-Mine-Own, the last act'll be a sensa-
tion. [*Walks in front of* JULIEN.] *Pardon,* monsieur. [*Rec-
ognizes him.*] Why, it's Julien. What are you doing here?
Julien. Waiting for my mother.
Deschamps [*a little uneasy*]. She knows you're here?
Julien. Edouard's passed on the news.
Deschamps. Please, no fireworks just before rehearsal.
We open on the 22nd—every minute counts. Ask Robinet.
[*Notices* POET-MINE-OWN's *bristling air.*] You're not going
to greet each other?
Mine-Own [*icily*]. I'm waiting.
Deschamps. For what?
Mine-Own. An apology.
Deschamps. Apology for what?
Mine-Own [*indicating* JULIEN]. Monsieur knows very
well for what.
Deschamps [*recollecting*]. Oh—the kick in the pants!
You mean that's still awaiting settlement?
Mine-Own. Decidedly.
Deschamps. Julien, say you're sorry. You two can't keep
on like this. Ten to one you don't even remember what
you came to blows over.
Julien. I remember perfectly.
Deschamps. You sure have changed! Robinet, *you* show
some sense. After all, a kick in the pants isn't like a slap
in the face. A kick in the pants is no stain on the honor.

Mine-Own [*primly*]. The *seat* of the pants.

Deschamps [*at a loss*]. Was it? Well, maybe the seat of the pants does cast a bit of a stain on the honor. Julien, you've gotta make the first move.

Julien. If I move anything, it'll be my foot. And if it's my foot, I can't guarantee *where* it will move.

Deschamps. You're really impossible. Come along, Robinet. [*Enters the dressing room, pulling* ROBINET— *who glares at* JULIEN *and shows by the way he walks that he fears another kick—after him. Noticing* COLOMBE.] Hello.

Mine-Own [*putting on his monocle; in happy surprise*]. Mademoiselle.

Deschamps. You're waiting for Mme. Alexandra?

Colombe. Yes, monsieur.

Mine-Own [*flitting about* COLOMBE, *murmuring to* DESCHAMPS *loud enough for* COLOMBE *to hear*]. Exquisite, isn't she—absolutely exquisite. [*Aloud.*] Haven't we met before, mademoiselle?

Colombe [*rather embarrassed*]. Yes, monsieur—two years ago, at the theatre.

Mine-Own [*suddenly remembering*]. I remember now! Then you're here with——[*Indicates* JULIEN.]

Colombe. Yes, monsieur. I'm his wife.

Mine-Own [*in a "you'll-need-them" tone of voice*]. My very best wishes.

Deschamps [*who has been at the dressing room door*]. You there, Mme. Alexandra? Poet-Mine-Own is here with the new scene—it's terrific.

Mine-Own [*simpering with false modesty*]. Deschamps goes too far. But I do think you're going to like it.

Mme. Alexandra [*bursting in with her retinue*]. Where's my wonderful new scene? And the little girl—very nice. Good afternoon, my dear. Mine-Own!

Mine-Own. Madame Inspiration! [*They fall into each other's arms.*]

Mme. Alexandra. My great, great man. When I think what a darling he is, besides being a genius. I hope you slept well?

Mine-Own. I couldn't sleep. Your play!

Mme. Alexandra. Oh, my play—my wonderful new scene. The Muses have drained my sweet poet. A chair, someone—a chair for Poet-Mine-Own. [*The staff scurry about for an armchair for each of them. She stops them*

with a gesture.] None for me—not today. Just a footstool
—to sit at a great man's feet.

Mine-Own [*getting up*]. No, no: I won't allow it!

Mme. Alexandra. What a darling. Like fresh bread. I
must kiss him again. [*They kiss again.*] Wonderful poet!

Mine-Own. Glorious artist!

Mme. Alexandra [*suddenly detaching herself: down to
earth*]. Well then—two chairs. [*They sit down: she looks
at* COLOMBE.] Why, she's a dream! Of course her hair's all
wrong. I'm listening, Poet-Mine-Own.

Mine-Own [*who has pulled a script from his pocket*].
This is after the big scene—when Leonore has decided to
die.

Mme. Alexandra. I see it all. She lies there, already pale
as death. Her dress is draped about her in gigantic folds—
about twenty-five yards of material.

Mine-Own. I'll begin: "Moon, dear! Cold planet, lifeless
as my heart. . . ."

Mme. Alexandra. God, how beautiful! Achingly beautiful! . . . "Cold planet, lifeless as my heart!" I know just
how to read it. I can give it everything. [*While talking,
she never stops looking at herself in the mirror. Suddenly,
in a different voice.*] Lucien, you ass!

Hairdresser [*hurrying toward her*]. Mme. Alexandra?

Mme. Alexandra. Just what are you trying to do to me?
I look like a poodle. And what on earth are these curls?
Will you please do something about it immediately! Then
I want you to go to work on this young lady. Mine-Own,
I'm listening.

Mine-Own.

"Moon, dear! Cold planet, lifeless as my heart,
   Wouldst of my woes I make for thee a chart?"

Mme. Alexandra. I like that better.

Mine-Own [*disconcerted*]. You don't like the first line?

Mme. Alexandra. I mean my curls. It's very beautiful,
Poet-Mine-Own—very classical.

Mine-Own.

"Wouldst of my woes I make for thee a chart?
   Of the loved one betrayed, the loving one bereft,
   Tears for the thief, curses on the theft?"

Mme. Alexandra. . . . "curses on the theft." [*Medi-
tates.*] Quite!

Mine-Own.

"My love has the midnight, mortuary scent

Of lilies drugged with sleep. Ah, once-content,
Now bitterly unhappy heart, decide. . . ."

Mme. Alexandra. Genius, sheer genius! You see, Lucien,
you've got to quiet down my curls. And with the young
lady—turn around, dear, in the light—hair very high on
the forehead, very low on the neck. Skin like velvet and
she keeps it hidden. And who found you that mortifying
dress?

Colombe. Julien, madame.

Mme. Alexandra. That authority! Go on, Mine-Own,
I'm listening: "Happily unbitter heart, decide!" "It's already engraved on my memory. [*To* COLOMBE.] Darling,
let me help you, you won't recognize yourself. Georgie,
give me my jewel box.

Mine-Own [*continuing while* MME. ALEXANDRA *is busy
with* COLOMBE].

"Now bitterly unhappy heart, decide
To be Life's widow—or be Lethe's bride."

Mme. Alexandra [*getting up and patting him*]. Like
. . . alabaster, dear poet. Edouard, you do have taste.
. . . Where did you find this pretty child?

Edouard. No one would recognize her. Mother, you're
a magician.

Mme. Alexandra [*working on* COLOMBE]. Why don't
you use jewelry, you little idiot—it's so right for you.

Colombe. I don't have any.

Mme. Alexandra. I didn't either, at your age, but I used
to buy things in junk shops—artificial, but better than
nothing.

Colombe. Julien dislikes artificial jewelry.

Mme. Alexandra. Don't mention that name to me.
When people get too grand for fake stuff, they should
be in a position to buy real. Mine-Own, it's just shattering!
But there's something I want to ask—you know who this
child is?

Mine-Own [*rather coldly*]. Yes.

Mme. Alexandra. It's the wife Julien's saddled me with.
He's joining the colors. After all the Bastille Days when
I've recited the "Marseillaise," you know they'd gladly get
him deferred. But monsieur doesn't wish to be deferred.
Monsieur is mad for military life, like his father before
him. Of course he leaves his wife in Paris without a sou.
She's got to have a job. Mine-Own, as long as you're doing
this scene over, you could drop in something for this

child. Nothing really—four or five lines, somebody who comes to console Léonore—an earth-spirit—or a sister-in-law.

Deschamps [*suddenly exploding*]. O-o-oh no! A new part that the management'll have to pay for! Not today, thank you.

Mme. Alexandra [*a thundercloud*]. Will you kindly shut up? Who are you, may I inquire?

Deschamps. I just happen to be codirector here—in charge of money matters, as I recall. Besides you're more than able to look after your own family without me. You get half the take as it is.

Mme. Alexandra. Swine—utter swine! Make him leave —I can't bear having him near me.

Deschamps. We're in production. A cast of 32, and a million costumes. We won't make our expenses as it is: it's out of the question to write in another part just because [*almost apoplectic*] . . . blood is—tighter than water. . . .

Mme. Alexandra. All you think of is money. You sicken me. Night after night, I wear myself to the bone, I drag out my guts for your sake.

Deschamps [*still raging*]. When you do it free of charge I'll be delighted to thank you.

Mme. Alexandra. Ho, ho, will you? [*Suddenly wrapping herself in her dignity.*] Well—I've a sick headache coming on—I can't rehearse today.

Deschamps [*alarmed*]. Mme. Alexandra! We open the 22nd!

Mme. Alexandra. Then we won't open the 22nd.

Deschamps. But we can't possibly postpone. Your present show won't have a leading man after the 20th—you know he's going into something else.

Mme. Alexandra. We can play it without him.

Deschamps. No, we can't. Even with him, nobody comes. [*Mastering himself.*] Mme. Alexandra, it's four o'clock. The cast has been waiting downstairs to rehearse since half past two. We've got to open on the 22nd. [MME. ALEXANDRA *merely stares.*] Go down and rehearse —I'll do something about the girl.

Mme. Alexandra [*inexorably*]. Seven francs a performance—matinees, double.

Deschamps. For four lines?

Mme. Alexandra. All right, she'll speak twelve lines. You filthy tradesman, I can't think why we put up with you.

Deschamps [*licked*]. All right, seven francs—even if she's invisible! Only go downstairs now and rehearse!

Mme. Alexandra [*turning toward* Poet-Mine-Own]. It's a treasure of a scene.

Mine-Own. But I'd barely started to read it.

Mme. Alexandra. That doesn't matter—I've guessed the rest. Dear friend, you will throw in a few lines for this child—she can run through them at the end of the rehearsal. Georgie, try to find her a dress; she can't go down there looking like this.

Deschamps [*groaning*]. Please, Mme. Alexandra—they've been waiting since half past two!

Mme. Alexandra [*inspecting herself in front of her cheval glass*]. Edouard, you've got a good eye—see that she looks all right.

Edouard. Yes, Mater. [*To* Colombe.] Come along, miss.

Deschamps [*shouting at* Colombe, *who doesn't move*]. Do as you're told: go try that dress on.

He goes out, slamming the door; passes Julien *in the corridor without even seeing him.*

Mme. Alexandra [*in front of her mirror*]. How ducky! Now I don't look a bit like a poodle. I look like a seal.

Hairdresser [*rushing toward her*]. But Mme. Alexandra. . . .

Mme. Alexandra. You deserve to be killed, but I haven't got time now. Poet-Mine-Own, Master Poet! Your scene is torrential. Only, know what I'd do if I were you?

Mine-Own [*uneasily*]. No, dear friend.

Mme. Alexandra. I'd cut out the first six lines.

Mine-Own. But I only read you eight.

Mme. Alexandra. Exactly. I'd start with the seventh: "My bitterly unhappy heart, decide. . . ." It's so much more . . . instinctive that way.

Mine-Own [*in despair*]. But the lilies. . . .

Mme. Alexandra [*exiting the while*]. Don't let that worry you. I'll have real ones standing about in tall vases. That's better, you know: always show, when you can, rather than tell.

Mine-Own. But. . . .

Stunned, he exits after her. They go right past Julien. Mme. Alexandra *either doesn't see him or doesn't want to.* Mme. Georges *then comes out and trots over to* Julien.

Mme. Georges. It's all fixed. Mme. Alexandra was very nice—made M. Deschamps put her in the show. Mr. Edouard helped tremendously, too.

Julien [*raising his head; stammering*]. They're p-putting her in the show?

Mme. Georges. Yes. M. Mine-Own is writing her a part, and she'll get seven francs a performance. You needn't worry now about going away.

Julien [*suddenly*]. And who's going to look after the baby?

Mme. Georges. Oh, at his age they do nothing but sleep.

Julien [*fed up*]. Georgie, leave me alone. [*Indicating dressing room.*] There's no one there now, I can go in?

Mme. Georges. Mr. Edouard's picking her out a dress— they want her to rehearse this afternoon already. [*Shuffling off: mumbling.*] She'll get double for matinees.

Edouard [*coming out, calling back*]. Till tonight, princess? [*Bumps into* Julien *in the doorway.*] Have a look in. You won't recognize your wife. Georgie tell you it's all set? Gotta run now: will I see you later?

Julien. I doubt it.

Edouard. The best of luck then, general. And don't worry about Colombe—we'll look after her.

He goes out. Julien *goes into the dressing room and stops.* Colombe *appears in a charming dress, unimaginably altered. She rushes to the mirror without even looking at him, and squeals with pleasure.*

Colombe. Julien! Don't you know me?

Julien. Yes. At least I know your voice.

Colombe [*in front of the mirror*]. You can't imagine what a show they put on! They all talk at once, then they all shriek at once, then they fall into one another's arms. Julien, they're putting me in the new show. I've got lines, I'm getting a costume. And it's nothing in the dim future —I start right in this afternoon. [*Keeps looking at herself.*] It's me—can you believe it, Julien?

Julien [*who has closed his eyes and doesn't move. In a dull flat voice*]. I don't know what to believe, Colombe.

Colombe *stares at herself in the mirror, no longer aware that he is there. Smiles at herself, murmurs in ecstasy.*

Colombe. It's me. It *is* me.

JULIEN *turns round and looks at her.*
Curtain.

SCENE II

SCENE—*A badly lighted empty stage. A tree, a table with chairs on top of it, one or two other props. Mid-stage, a work lamp throws a skimpy light: far back, dressed up and leaning on a parasol, stands* MME. ALEXANDRA, *who barks toward the wings.*

MME. ALEXANDRA. Well?

Sceneshifter [from offstage]. No one yet, Mme. Alexandra. They probably thought the rehearsal was for 2:30 —the way it usually is.

Mme. Alexandra [in her noble, grand-mannered enunciation]. Crepp! [*Starts roaring and raging up and down the stage, like a caged lion.*] The whoors, the 10-franc whoors. The 6-franc markdowns. The 4-franc has-beens. To keep me waiting! And they want a rrraise! I'll give them a rrraise! [*A shadow appears timidly between two flats. It is* COLOMBE *in her debut dress. She doesn't dare approach* MME. ALEXANDRA, *who, shouting "whoors" for the last time, turns and sees her. Her attitude changes as her voice does—she leans, in high-romantic style, against her parasol.*] Oh—it's you, dear child. I was dreaming.

Colombe. I'm a little early, Mme. Alexandra—the rehearsal's not till 2:30.

Mme. Alexandra. I know. But I like to come before the rest do, and be alone on the stage with the great ones who played here once, and are no more. I dream, I slip out of myself, I murmur an immortal phrase or two . . . and then it's rehearsal time, and I tuck the past away.

Colombe. I'm terribly sorry to have interrupted you, Mme. Alexandra. I'll go back to the dressing room.

Mme. Alexandra. Oh, it's just as well—I've dreamed all I dare for one day. [*Suddenly.*] You play cards?

Colombe. No, Mme. Alexandra.

Mme. Alexandra. That's too bad, we could have had a little game while we're waiting for those lice. I'll tell your fortune instead. [*They take the chairs off the table, and sit in them.*] Here, cut the cards. [COLOMBE *cuts,* MME.

ALEXANDRA *starts laying them out.*] 1, 2, 3, 4, 5—a club.
That's good. Uhm. . . . Still better. There's a blond
young man and a nice trip somewhere. Hhm—the blond
young man again.

Colombe. But Julien's dark.

Mme. Alexandra. Julien?—you don't suppose people
have their fortunes told to hear about their husbands?
[*Lays out more cards.*] 1, 2, 3, 4, 5—the king of hearts
and ten of clubs together. You're going to marry a very
important man with scads of money.

Colombe. But I'm already married.

Mme. Alexandra. That's no way to talk! I've been married eight times. Let me congratulate you, my dear.

Colombe. Eight times! *Real* marriages?

Mme. Alexandra. Why, I should think so—do I look
half-witted? In my position, I *always* married my lovers—
I even married one of them twice. Boulin—the sugar
Boulin. First after his mother died, and then after his
father.

Colombe. To comfort him?

Mme. Alexandra. Good God, no! To help him get going
with his millions.

Colombe. Were you happy with him?

Mme. Alexandra [*looking at cards*]. The king of diamonds—another very important man for you. [*Resuming.*]
Happy with a husband who refused to bathe? When he
died, I married his son by his first wife—a nice, clean-cut
boy. But the son died in my arms and what was left went
back to his mother. Unfortunately, I couldn't marry her.
And she knew nothing about how to handle money and
died richer than any of them.

Colombe. Are there really people so rich they can buy
anything they want?

Mme. Alexandra. No, that's the funny part. Poor Boulin
—the father—would have given anything to be witty.
Couldn't. He tried—all day long, wherever he went. "How
do you do-do-do?" he'd say. Or "Remember me to your
children—if they are yours." . . . [*Shrugs.*] No: with all
his money, he couldn't get what he wanted.

Colombe. Then what do most rich people do with their
money?

Mme. Alexandra. They hang on to it. [*Sees* GOURETTE
come in; screams at him.] Oh, it's you, you clown! Is it
time for rehearsal?

Gourette. No, Mme. Alexandra: rehearsal's at 2:30.

Mme. Alexandra. I'm aware of that.

Gourette. The concierge told me you were here, madame. I was in my office, working on your statement for *Le Matin.*

Mme. Alexandra. Oh, Just what am I stating?

Gourette. Your opinion of love.

Mme. Alexandra. They bore me! Do I ask them for *their* opinions?

Gourette. The editor just phoned; says that Mme. Sarah Bernhardt gave them a most vivid statement.

Mme. Alexandra [*growling*]. I daresay.

Gourette. He said it was very personal. What it came down to was, she didn't believe there *was* any such thing.

Mme. Alexandra. Then say that *I* do—that I do with all my heart.

Gourette. That's just what I was going to say, Mme. Alexandra. May I read it to you: "This tumult that has always overwhelmed us women, this imperious surge. . . ."

Mme. Alexandra [*interrupting angrily*]. You damn fool —do you want to make a laughingstock of me?

Cries to POET-MINE-OWN *who has just come in.*

My other self! My second voice! Rescue me from this demented oaf. *Le Matin* wants to know what I think of love.

Mine-Own [*kissing her hands*]. What! They ask God what He thinks of God—they ask the sun its opinion of light? Simply tell them that you *are* love.

Mme. Alexandra. I can't tell them that myself. My good right hand, find me a seemly sentence or two.

Mine-Own. Certainly. [*Starts.*]

Always I have given, and you have given back.

Always you shall give, and I will give to you. . . .

Mme. Alexandra [*interrupting*]. Not poetry, my poet, not poetry! They know I don't write poetry.

Mine-Own. Uhm. Perhaps a *pensée*—an epigram.

Mme. Alexandra. That's it. A nice epigram.

Mine-Own [*to* GOURETTE]. Take this down. "For real love to flower, we must first root out of us the black weeds of passion."

Gourette. A little slower, please.

Mme. Alexandra. Mine-Own, what are you telling us? Love *is* passion. My God!

Mine-Own. Yes, it. . . .

Mme. Alexandra. I was driven mad by love, I drove others mad. Think of Alfonse Sableur flinging himself, in top hat and tails, into the lion cage at the circus. For me! [*In a lyrical actressy tone.*] How that man loved me! He would die for me—he would kill for me. [*To* COLOMBE.] You're a woman—you'll understand. You love someone else, so to this man you say no—you've no choice. Suddenly there's a terrific roar around you—this . . . friend has got to his feet, has leaped from the box, has bounded into the cage among the lions. The crowds are in a tumult, but no more than your heart, for all at once you understand. You cry out: "Alfonse, I love you. Come back. I am yours." Too late!

Colombe. They tore him to pieces?

Mme. Alexandra. No. He got out. But then I didn't love him any more. He should have taken me right there among the lions—but he let the chance slip through his fingers.

Mine-Own. How beautiful! How womanly! [*To* GOURETTE.] Don't lose a word of it. —And then, dear lady?

Mme. Alexandra. We left the circus in silence, my husband and I.

Mine-Own. And Alfonse?

Mme. Alexandra. He rushed off to Monte Carlo and lost four million francs on zero the very first night.

Colombe. And then put a bullet through his brain?

Mme. Alexandra. Not exactly. He married a Rothschild.

Mine-Own. Miriam?

Mme. Alexandra. No, Hannah. The flat one.

Colombe. It's like something you read in books, Mme. Alexandra. What must one be to be loved like that?

Mme. Alexandra. Just a woman. I was soul and sex, dreaming and waking. Alfonse—and there were many like him—realized that to hold me the ordinary bourgeois attentions were not enough. He really worked at it, he made an effort. One day, when I had no appetite whatever—I used to put my glove on my plate, actually I was trying to reduce—Alfonse, frantic that I wouldn't eat anything, made the waiter at Maxim's bring him a raw rat—and consumed it in front of me.

Mine-Own. How mad! How male!

Colombe. And then you managed to eat a little something?

Mme. Alexandra. Eat a little something? After that, I

couldn't eat for weeks—ugh! My dear, it's the perfect way
to diet. [*Laughing.*] The best part was, Maxim's tacked
50 francs on the bill for the rat.

Mine-Own. Speaking of rats, I just saw our broker. Do
you have any Wagons-Lits stock?

Mme. Alexandra. Yes. He advised me to buy it.

Mine-Own. Well, he just advised me to sell it. It's due
to drop. He says to put the money into . . . it's a secret,
but if we could go to your dressing room, I could hint. . . .
[*She looks at him as she starts to leave the stage.*] There's
a real killing to be made in . . . [*lowers his voice*] South
American copper.

Gourette [*just as they are exiting*]. Mme. Alexandra,
how shall I end your statement about love?

Mme. Alexandra. What a time to bring up that nonsense again. See me after rehearsal.

Exits with MINE-OWN.

Gourette. Yes, of course. And after rehearsal——
[*Mimics.*] "Can't you see how drained out I am?" And
then tomorrow, when they run Réjane's opinion of
love. . . .

Mme. Georges [*who has tiptoed in*]. You might as well
go back to your office. They're on the subject of their in-
vestments—we'll be lucky if the rehearsal starts by four.

Gourette [*muttering*]. Why the hell should I worry?
[*Exits.*]

Mme. Georges. We all have money problems, don't we,
Mrs. Julien? The public doesn't know. My neighbors all
envy me—"What a life you lead, Mme. Georges." You
like it?

Colombe [*lost in reverie*]. Oh, yes.

Mme. Georges. You wouldn't rather be home with your
husband and child?

Colombe [*suddenly exclaiming*]. No!

Mme. Georges [*looks at her, shrugs, prepares to exit*].
Well, I've got to press madame's goddess robe. Beautiful,
but 95 pleats. Oh, here's our leading man.

She exits. GAULOIS *makes an imposing entrance: felt hat,
flower in buttonhole, stick.*

Gaulois. Good afternoon, my sweet. You the first?

Colombe. Mme. Alexandra's here.

Gaulois. Our star on time? What next? I was hoping for a few minutes with you. How're things coming?

Colombe. Mme. Alexandra says I'm doing all right.

Gaulois. Your progress is amazing—an awkward moment here and there, but, really, amazing. You must come to my place after rehearsal sometime, we'll go over your part.

Colombe. You mean it, M. Gaulois?

Gaulois. A spot of sherry, a dab of pâté—we'll chat. I've a cute little place—Moroccan. [*Comes closer.*] I'm mad about you. I can't sleep any more.

Colombe. You ought to sleep.

Gaulois. I can't. I keep seeing you in front of the fire on my tiger-skin rug. I moan all night long like a condemned man. I drink and drink to forget, and I only remember. You're always there and I can never quite touch you. Sometimes toward dawn I drop off exhausted—my valet finds me stretched out by the cold hearth.

Colombe [*dazzled*]. You have a valet?

Gaulois. A Moroccan.

Colombe. He must be handsome.

Gaulois. He has a scimitar at his belt. He stands waiting with folded arms, then serves you without a word.

Colombe. He's a mute?

Gaulois. When he should be, like all good Moroccans —and good valets. So come see for yourself. I'll put on Moroccan dress, too—a great white cloak that I got of an Arab chief. I'll squat in the corner to contemplate you.

Colombe. You can contemplate me here, M. Gaulois.

Gaulois. No, no. I've been waiting for you all my life.

Colombe. Really?

Gaulois. Always. And you've been waiting for me—I know you have. Has anyone else ever loved you like a condemned man?

Colombe. No.

Gaulois. Then you've never *known* love. You've never known yourself.

Colombe. But I hardly know *you*, M. Gaulois.

Gaulois. You know I love you.

Colombe. Julien loves me too.

Gaulois. No doubt. But how? Would Julien roll on the ground for you?

Colombe. No. [*Suddenly.*] Would you eat a raw rat, just to give me an appetite?

Gaulois [*completely thrown off*]. A raw rat? Why a raw rat?

Colombe. I just wondered.

Enter DESCHAMPS.

Deschamps. Ah, Gaulois. Good afternoon.

Gaulois. Good afternoon.

Deschamps. You know, there's a costume rehearsal this afternoon. Alexandra's already dressed.

Gaulois [*looking glumly at him and seeing through him*]. Well, then, Colombe, we'd better get dressed too.

Deschamps [*countering*]. She has plenty of time; she doesn't come on till the last act. [*To* COLOMBE.] There's something in your contract I'd like to talk over with you.

Gaulois. Oh, of course, the contract! All right, see you later. [*Exits.*]

Deschamps. Come to my office for a minute after rehearsal. A spot of sherry, a dab of pâté, and we'll sign our little paper. I know I made a fuss the other day—but that was just for effect. Don't worry, you shall have your seven francs. Would you like some of it in advance?

Colombe. Oh—could I?

Deschamps. Come in after rehearsal—and you needn't say anything to Mme. Alexandra; she counts her pennies, you know. I'm an easy mark.

Colombe. Thank you, M. Deschamps. You're very kind.

Deschamps. Not with everybody. Not with everybody. Tell me—this is really your best dress?

Colombe. Yes.

Deschamps. We can't have that! I know just the dressmaker who could make you just the thing—a little suit, maybe in that walnut color they're showing.

Colombe. Uhm—but wouldn't you think a little fur cape with a hat to match? I saw one on the Rue de Rivoli this morning.

Deschamps [*taken aback*]. Oh! Well, perhaps trimmed with fur.

Colombe. Only what can I buy on seven francs a day?

Deschamps [*softly*]. We'll work it out, between the two of us.

Colombe. You're terribly kind, M. Deschamps.

Deschamps. I really am, you know, in spite of my reputation.

Enter Poet-Mine-Own.

Mine-Own. Where's my little, where's my little, where's my little nymph?

Deschamps [*frigidly*]. Right here. With me.

Mine-Own. You know, Deschamps, I can't get her out of my mind. Last night I wrote eight more lines for her.

Colombe. For me?

Mine-Own. All for you. I couldn't sleep a wink, thinking of you.

Colombe. You, too? Nobody around here is able to sleep.

Deschamps. Robinet, you know how long the play is. You can't make it longer.

Mine-Own. My dear Deschamps, this child is going to be a sensation. I could give her a ten-minute monologue and the audience'd eat it up.

Deschamps. Of course: she's wonderful. But she doesn't come on till the last scene, when the women are putting on their gloves.

Mine-Own. For once, leave it to me. I'll work with her on her part. After the rehearsal, Colombe, you come to my apartment for a spot of sherry, and then we'll go to work.

Deschamps. She's tied up after the rehearsal.

Mine-Own. That's too bad; this comes first. We open the 22nd—this child has to work, Deschamps!

Deschamps. She's also got to sign her contract.

Mine-Own. That takes days, doesn't it? Go get it, and she'll sign it now.

Deschamps. It's being drawn up now.

Mine-Own. You're supposedly the businessman and you make the poet talk business. The play opens the 22nd, and this child's part can make or break it.

Edouard [*who has come in and overheard; smiling*]. I've the solution for all of you. Since Colombe can't perform stark naked—much as we regret the fact—and there's just time enough, after rehearsal, to order her a dress, I'll take over. Her date will be with the dressmaker. [*Smiling at them both.*] That is, if you *really* want to open on the 22nd.

Deschamps. All right, maybe that's the best idea. See you all later. [*Exits.*]

Mine-Own. The theatre is a great institution, when everything else comes ahead of the script.

Edouard [*still smiling*]. Mine-Own, Mother's looking for you.

Mine-Own [*unwilling to leave*]. I just this minute left her.

Edouard. Since then, she's been deep in thought—and decided the new scene is too long.

Mine-Own. Too long? Why all she's done is cut it.

Edouard. After deep thought, she only likes the very last line.

Mine-Own. Only one line! And what, pray, is only one line to rhyme with?

Edouard. I can't tell you yet—I haven't had time to work it out.

Mine-Own. This is too much. Who wrote this play?

Edouard. Dozens of people say you did.

Mine-Own [*like a madman*]. I'll take it off the boards. She—she can have the last line, but we'll see who has the last word! [*Exits.*]

Colombe. This is awful. What'll they do?

Edouard. Nothing whatever. This is the theatre—while they're rehearsing a drama, they're also staging a comedy. [*Changing his tone.*] The important thing is that I rescued you from those two old goats. [*Looks at her.*] Or do you find them fun?

Colombe. I do in a way. They sniff, and circle round me, and roll their eyes, and say they can't sleep at night.

Edouard. Who can't sleep at night?

Colombe. M. Gaulois and M. Poet-Mine-Own.

Edouard. Deschamps can?

Colombe. Yes, Deschamps can. But he wants to give me an advance on my salary. And a little walnut-colored suit.

Edouard. And what decision have you reached?

Colombe. The suit might be very attractive.

Edouard. Come, come, my sweet. Don't look so inno-cent. I mean, which benefactor?

Colombe. There's only one. The others only offer their insomnia and a little sherry.

Edouard. It's just as well I'm here to stand guard over honor.

Colombe. What honor?

Edouard. The family's. I'd hate to have to slap all three faces—I don't mind getting killed so much, but to have to get up three times at 5 A.M.!

Colombe. You're the one with the evil thoughts: they only want to help me with my part.

Edouard. They do? That's the best they could think up?

Colombe. Didn't you think up the same thing? Didn't I go to your place?

Edouard. Yes, but for the sake of your career. To prove it, I didn't even offer you sherry.

Colombe. I noticed.

Edouard. Just the script—read standing up in the dining room. It's not that I'm a moralist—but sipping sherry side by side on a divan: I don't think I could handle that.

Colombe. I'm afraid I don't understand.

Edouard. You don't? Well, then, my sweet: when I have fun, I have fun; and when I guard the family honor, I guard the family honor.

Colombe. Since we're going to order my dress this evening and I can't come to your place, couldn't we rehearse my part now instead of talking foolishness?

Edouard. Of course. [*Reaching in his pocket.*] Here's my script: I'm never parted from it.

Colombe. I'm sure this bores you to death.

Edouard. Frightfully.

Colombe. I can always ask M. Gaulois—it might not bore him.

Edouard. No, perhaps it wouldn't. So *I'd* better suffer. Let's do the end first: it wasn't right yesterday.

He sits—she crosses toward him.

Colombe. "And if I were to tell you I loved you?"

Edouard. "I wouldn't believe it."

Colombe. "And if I were to tell you I'm sick at heart?"

Edouard. "With eyes like yours?"

Colombe. "What do you know of my eyes—when you never look at them?"

Edouard [*getting up and taking her in his arms*]. "Never?"

Colombe [*lets him look at her, then turns bashfully away*]. "Not so hard, monsieur—you make me blush."

Edouard. "You thought to play at love, and now are caught in its snare. You yearn, as much as I, for the kiss I'm about to take."

Colombe [*letting her head fall on his shoulder*]. "Yes, baron."

Edouard [*looking at her for a moment over his shoulder, then sighing in another tone*]. The baron—kisses you.

Colombe [*without moving*]. Was it any better than yesterday?

Edouard. Yes, my angel. You little devil, where did you learn all this?

Colombe. I just speak the way I feel.

Edouard. Do you do it so well by imagining you're with Julien?

Colombe. Julien would never talk to me like that.

Edouard. Gaulois?

Colombe. No.

Edouard. But you still think that you're yourself—Colombe?

Colombe. Yes. A Colombe who loves the baron.

Edouard. And when we do the farewell scene, you'll feel terribly unhappy?

Colombe. Not really. Though I'll really want to cry.

Edouard. Has Julien ever made you cry?

Colombe. Yes, sometimes.

Edouard. And when you cry, while you're acting, it's those tears you think of?

Colombe. No. It's not the same.

Edouard. But you really cry?

Colombe. I cry, but I'm not really sad—deep down.

Edouard. But when you cry with Julien—you're really sad, deep down?

Colombe. Yes—that's real life.

Edouard. You're sure you've never cried with him *without* being really sad, deep down?

Colombe. Why do you ask that?

Edouard. For my own good. I just can't believe that anyone who cries so heartbreakingly whenever she feels like it, wouldn't sometimes decide that she feels like it.

Colombe. You mean I'm a liar?

Edouard. What a horrible word! But women do have their own patented way of telling the truth: only backwoods idealists like Julien wouldn't know that.

Colombe. I don't like you to speak that way of Julien.

Edouard. Why?

Colombe. He's a real man.

Edouard. I know—and women love real men. They need them for the kind of game they play. With bad eggs like me, they know that kind of thing won't work. But it can still be fun.

Colombe. Fun?

Edouard. With people like me. You can drop the mask and relax. It must be terribly wearing to always have to be a womanly woman.

Colombe [*breaks out laughing*]. Edouard, you really *are* a bad egg.

Edouard [*moving away*]. Of course! Well, shall we do the scene once more before the high priests of art take over the stage?

Colombe. If you want. [*Places herself.*] Suppose M. Gaulois discovers me in your arms?

Edouard. I'm sure he would know we were only rehearsing a scene.

Colombe. "And if I were to tell you I loved you?"

Edouard. "I wouldn't believe it."

Colombe. "And if I were to tell you I'm sick at heart?"

Edouard. "With eyes like yours?"

Colombe. "What do you know of my eyes—when you never look at them?"

Edouard. "Never?" [*Gets up, takes her in his arms: suddenly murmurs.*] You wicked little devil. [*Lets her go; says with a childlike softness that cuts under his man-of-the-world air.*] Even so, we mustn't hurt Julien!

They stand against each other without daring to look each other's way.

Curtain.

ACT TWO

SCENE I

Scene—*The dressing room corridor, as in Act One, Scene I, but seen from the reverse side with* Colombe's *dressing room exposed, and the door to* Mme. Alexandra's *opening on the corridor.* Mme. Georges *is in a chair:* Julien, *in uniform, paces back and forth; opens* Colombe's *dressing room door.*

Julien. Is this hers?

Mme. Georges. Yes.

Julien [*closing the door*]. There was no one at the house.

Mme. Georges. To come back like this without a word! We didn't expect you, Mr. Julien.

Julien. We suddenly got a 24-hour pass because there's a new general.

Mme. Georges. Is the new one nicer?

Julien. They're all alike.

Mme. Georges. Now don't act the way you usually do. Tip your hat when you pass him.

Julien. And be led out and shot? She didn't even go home for dinner!

Mme. Georges. You know the theatre—her time's not her own.

Julien. There was a woman at the house—someone she pays to watch the baby.

Mme. Georges. She's a very good mother—spends her last sou on the baby. You know she got a raise?

Julien. A raise? [*Quickly.*] Oh yes, I know!

Mme. Georges. Ten francs a day now. And a bigger part. I s'pose she's written you all the news here. . . .

Julien. She wrote that. . . .

Mme. Georges [*breaking in*]. *Eve and the Serpent* was a flop. M. Poet-Mine-Own and Mme. Alexandra swore and cursed at each other—I don't know where people in their circle learn such language. Well, then they made up and now they have a hit—*The Realm of Passion*—the dresses take ten minutes to hook up.

Julien. And she comes on late?

Mme. Georges. No, she's on at the start—she'll be here any minute. Unless Mr. Edouard took her to dinner and brings her back in a cab.

Julien. Edouard takes her to dinner?

Mme. Georges. Sometimes. So does M. Gaulois. That's very unusual for a leading man. But he couldn't be nicer.

Julien. I see.

Mme. Georges. A little thing like that who's all alone, everyone feels sorry for her.

Julien. I can believe it.

Enter GOURETTE.

Gourette [*shouting*]. Curtain in ten minutes!

Mme. Georges [*exiting*]. No! Madame's not here—and neither is Mrs. Julien.

Gourette. That's not my lookout—I've enough to worry

about. [*Shouts.*] Curtain in ten minutes! [*Sees* JULIEN; *changes his tone.*] Ah, Mr. Julien! This is a surprise—you managed to get off?

Julien. As you see.

Gourette. Army life's getting to be quite a snap. Not like in my day. You were panting for a little theatre atmosphere?

Julien. Yes. [*After a second.*] I got your letter.

Gourette [*half blushing, half sneering*]. So soon?

Julien. Last night. Thanks for writing.

Gourette. I thought you'd want to be up on the latest stage gossip.

Julien. Yes. Got five minutes to go out for a drink?

Gourette. No; it's too close to curtain time. And I have to dress—I have to fill in, somebody got sick.

Julien [*seizing him by the arm*]. Then let's go in here— I'll only be a minute.

Gourette. I know. But I ought to warn you, it's her dressing room.

They go into COLOMBE's *dressing room. A voice calls "Georgie!"*

Mme. Georges [*re-emerging*]. Yes, M. Gaulois?

GAULOIS *appears at the entrance to his dressing room in a Moroccan robe and his underwear, putting on make-up.*

Gaulois. Would you get me my shirt? Has our little one come?

Mme. Georges. Not yet. But I've a surprise—Mr. Julien has.

Gaulois. No!

Mme. Georges. I told him how nice you've been about his missus.

She closes the door. In COLOMBE's *dressing room,* JULIEN *has been listening to them: now he grabs* GOURETTE *by the collar.*

Julien. Who is it?

Gourette. That's *it!* It'd be fine if we knew right off— but that's the tough part about having an unfaithful wife: who's she unfaithful with?

Julien. Tell me or I'll beat your brains out.

Gourette. You're all alike—"I'll strangle you"; "I'll murder you." The sure sign of the beginner! It's not that simple, you know. It's a real part, it's one of the established roles—the romantic lover, the heavy father, the deceived husband. You've got to learn the lines, you've got to know the cues. It's an art, a very great art, and it takes time.

Julien [*taking him by the throat*]. God damn you, cut that out—tell me, or I'll kill you.

Gourette. That'd be fine training: you wouldn't even get to be an understudy. I know: you want to prove your virility. It's useless. Stop choking me, Mr. Julien—it's not me, you can be sure of that. I'm too ugly.

Julien [*letting him go, taking hold of himself*]. Why did you write to me?

Gourette. Because I like you—and because it made you a . . . colleague. . . .

Julien. You don't know who it is?

Gourette. No.

Julien. Who's she been going out with?

Gourette. Ah, now we're getting somewhere. That's sound: a good cuckold should be methodical. I can only help in small ways, you know—I'm merely the confidant. The brilliant hunches, the inspired detective work will have to come from you. There are four candidates.

Julien [*with a start*]. Four?

Gourette. Four *possibilities*, that is; I didn't mean four certainties. Edouard, Gaulois, Poet-Mine-Own, and our master of the revels, M. Deschamps. A lovable group, aren't they? I think you can skip the hairdresser—though he does do her hair an awful lot, and women go for him.

Julien. The man has a smell.

Gourette. The animal in him—which you shouldn't minimize; that could be part of his appeal. One of the first rules of your new profession is: don't go by what *you* feel, by any ideas *you* have in the matter. That's exactly why most cuckolds . . . flunk.

Julien. Five with the hairdresser!

Gourette. Don't be upset. I knew a captain who suspected his entire company. Think what a colonel would have to go through.

Julien. I'll strangle all five of them!

Gourette. Yes, you can—but it won't help. You won't get relief even if the guilty one's among them.

Julien. She'll be back any minute—I'll worm it out of her.

Gourette. You good little boys, how you all go about it. You'll never learn *anything* that way.

Julien [*groaning*]. But Colombe loves me.

Gourette. She may. But it won't help.

Julien. I left her, like an imbecile, with this stinking gang. She's just a baby.

Gourette. Uhm. The trouble with babies, we can't read their minds.

Julien. What should I do?

Gourette. Now you're starting to show promise. Begin by studying the classics in the field: it's going to be very strange at first, and you'll need help. In a minute she'll come in, she'll smile, she'll kiss you: watch out, it'll all seem terribly normal. But life gets very odd for the cuckold: strange coincidences start piling up as they never used to. The letters that don't come, or come too late. The phones that ring—and there's no one at the other end. The friends you haven't seen in years who stick like a leech for a whole afternoon: all the things in ordinary life that are kind of peculiar, that you can't quite dope out— they're suddenly crystal clear! Nothing will be mysterious. The alibis will be perfect—terrifyingly perfect. There was something hearteningly ambiguous about the old life: now there's an answer for everything. Only every answer will breed ten new questions. The gas man who rings the bell won't just be the gas man—he'll be a question. The song she's humming, the article she's reading—questions. The new color of her lipstick—a tremendous question. Life will be a long weaving snake dance of questions; and you yourself will become an eavesdropping, dresser-drawer-rummaging, sounds-in-her-sleep-pondering . . . question mark.

Julien. No! I'll ask her nothing.

Gourette. Oh, yes, you will! And when you're all finished, you'll have barely started. Now you'll begin on yourself— questioning yourself, doubting this, doubting that, finally deciding you invented it all. That day you will be the real thing—a *cordon bleu* among cuckolds. [*Listens.*] Here she comes! Make up your mind, Mr. Julien: either you want help and listen to me; or you can be your own lawyer and see what happens.

Julien. What shall I do?

Gourette. To begin with, hide. That's another rule: always hide.

Julien [*looking frantically around as the voices outside come nearer*]. Where?

Gourette [*opening a cupboard and pushing him inside*]. In a cupboard—headquarters for cuckolds! [*He has pushed him into the cupboard, now rushes out into the corridor; cries.*] On stage for Act One!

Mme. Alexandra [*rushing in, followed by her staff*]. Stop bellowing like that, you half-wit! The curtain'll go up when I'm ready. Are you doing Doussin's part again to-night?

Gourette. Yes, Mme. Alexandra.

Mme. Alexandra [*disappearing into her dressing room*]. That'll be a treat for the audience.

Colombe [*entering with a cry*]. Where is he? Where is he? [*Goes to her dressing room, sees no one, runs out.*] Georgie, Georgie! Where's Julien? [*Goes back, sees* JULIEN, *who has come out of the cupboard, throws herself into his arms.*] My darling! Where did you come from?

Julien. The cupboard.

Colombe. What were you doing in there?

Julien. Playing a little joke on you.

Colombe [*squeezing him tight*]. This is wonderful! It's been so long!

Julien [*gently*]. Longer than you can imagine.

Colombe. But you've been busy. All the things you had to learn, while your little friend here's been all alone, waiting for you. This is so nice. And how handsome you look in uniform: like a general.

Julien. Not yet—though there are rumors.

Colombe. Sit down, I'll bet you're tired. [*She sits on his knees.*] What's the most you have to march at one time?

Julien. Twenty-five kilometers.

Colombe. But they let you take a streetcar home?

Julien. No.

Colombe. And all the other things you have to do, your laundry and everything. I'll bet you don't have time to think of me.

Julien. Plenty of time.

Colombe. Of course you'd say so. But when you're not working and you're with the boys—it's a vacation, too. Good riddance to wives. If the girl back home is cold, she should take a hot-water bottle to bed.

Julien. How's the baby?

Colombe. Oh, he's fine. Do you like my little **walnut**-colored suit?

Julien. Uhm hmm—very nice. And I bet expensive.

Colombe. No, not a bit. I found a dressmaker who gives you a price and lets you pay so much a week. Anyhow, you know I'm quite a money-maker now. I'll be able to treat you once in a while—so you can have fun and treat the girls. We know all about you—think we didn't know why you refused to be deferred?

Julien. There are very few girls around camp, Colombe.

Colombe. There are enough. I'm sure you were unfaithful.

Julien. But I wasn't. [*In a natural tone.*] And you?

Colombe. Me? Darling, don't be silly: I wouldn't have even had time. I've got a pretty big part in the new play: I've had to work my head off. Are you going to come and applaud me? Knowing you're out front'll give me stage fright, but still—— Oh, baby, my big sweet baby, it's wonderful to have you back. And you look so well!

Julien. Do I?

Colombe [*kisses him, stands up*]. Being without you does have its good side, it makes it so wonderful to be together again. Will you forgive me if I dress? We ring up any minute. I'm late. [*She goes behind a screen. While she undresses, you see her naked arm throw a dress over the screen. Calling out.*] How long is your leave?

Julien. Twenty-four hours.

Colombe. Is that all? Couldn't you say you missed your train?

Julien. No.

Colombe. But darling, that's awful. I've been invited out after the show by some people who can do a tremendous lot for me—it would take too long to explain—and tomorrow I have to rehearse all afternoon.

Julien. It's very simple—you break your date.

Colombe. Oh, Julien, baby, I just can't—my whole future's involved.

Julien. So is mine. And a military future can be mighty brief.

Colombe. Don't talk that way. You'll nave other leaves, but I may never have another chance like this. These are very big people who could get me into the Folies-Bergères. They need somebody my type for a sketch in the next

revue. Don't worry, darling, I'll wear clothing—otherwise
I wouldn't even consider it.

Julien [*getting up, shouting suddenly*]. Stop talking
such slime. Colombe, you're coming home with me tonight.

Colombe [*after a silence*]. It's sure like old times.
You've just come back and you're screaming already!

Julien. Yes, I'm screaming—and I'll scream worse if I
have to. But I know this much: you're not going in for the
kind of thing you're talking about.

COLOMBE *appears in panties and corset from behind the
screen.*

Colombe [*innocently; hands across her breasts*]. What
are *you* talking about?

Julien. Stop playing dumb.

Colombe. But I'm not, baby; really I'm not.

GAULOIS *comes out of his dressing room, two-thirds
dressed, and knocks at* COLOMBE's *door.*

Gaulois. Are you there, my little monkey? I wanted
to tell you to watch your step. [*He half opens the door, sees*
JULIEN; COLOMBE *has run behind the screen.*] Oh, forgive
me.

Julien. Forgive *me.*

Gaulois. Enjoying your leave?

Julien. Immensely.

Gaulois. Good! You know the new scene?

Colombe. Yes, M. Gaulois.

Gaulois. Good! We're using it tonight. [*Goes back to
his dressing room.*]

Julien. Why does he call you his little monkey?

Colombe [*emerging*]. I don't know. He's got a nickname
for everybody. He's helped me a lot with my part.

Now DESCHAMPS *rushes around self-importantly; taps
discreetly on* COLOMBE's *door.*

Deschamps. Are you there, my little titmouse?

Julien. Now it's a titmouse.

Deschamps. I just wanted to tell you to watch your step.
[*Has opened the door—sees* JULIEN.] Oh!—sorry.

Julien. So sorry.

Deschamps. Awfully sorry. I wanted to tell your wife
something. Everything all right?

Julien. Everything's all right.

Deschamps. You look fine.

Julien. Thanks. That's what everyone says.

Deschamps [*to* COLOMBE *behind the screen*]. I wanted to tell you we're going up on time tonight! Don't be late. [*He trots off.*]

Julien. Little titmouse. From that scum. God, he's awful.

Colombe [*emerging*]. There you go. You have to see the worst in everything. They shouldn't think of me as a little monkey, they shouldn't think of me as a little titmouse: what *do* you want them to call me—"*Madame la duch-esse*"?

Julien. How could you make friends with such scum?

Colombe. I haven't made friends with them. I see them every day—I have to work with them. Nobody else is so disagreeable about nothing the way you are. Anyhow, they amuse me.

Julien. Don't say that: they can't.

Colombe. Why can't they?

Julien. Because I know you too well.

Colombe [*with a cool look*]. You think so?

Julien. Yes. And in the end you'll go back to being your-self, whether you want to or not.

Colombe [*facing him with the look on an enemy*]. My poor Julien.

Mme. Georges [*tiptoeing in*]. Glad to see one another?

Julien. Tickled to death.

Mme. Georges. It's nice to come back to a wife that everybody raves about, but who's just for you. [*Hands* COLOMBE *her petticoat.*] Look at that little figure, Mr. Julien—you could eat her up. And what a hit she's made. M. Mine-Own thinks it's his play that's packing 'em in, but we know otherwise. Aren't you happy to have such a big success of a wife?

Julien. I could puke from joy.

POET-MINE-OWN *appears in the corridor: knocks discreetly on* COLOMBE's *door.*

Mine-Own. Are you there, my little turtledove?

Julien [*tiptoeing to the door; bellowing*]. Yes, I'm here!

Mine-Own [*jumping at man's voice*]. Forgive me—do please forgive me. I just wanted to tell you to watch your step. [*Stops.*] Forget it, it's nothing—I don't know what I'm saying, I'm so nervous—the King of Spain's out front.

Act your best tonight, dear little lady—and do forgive me. [*Trots away.*]

Julien. Now it's a turtledove. What is this: Aesop's fables? How could you let that slimy old character call you his turtledove: I told you never to speak to him.

Colombe. But he wrote the play I'm in.

Julien. Isn't it enough to have to speak his *lines?* And why do they all want you to watch your step? Count of me—hhm?

Colombe. Can't you ever let up?

Julien. And you smile at them, and purr at them. . . . Wipe off your mouth: I can't stand the way you look.

Mme. Georges [*stopping him*]. Mr. Julien, you'll ruin her make-up. It's her job right now to smile. Look at her —crying. Imagine what'll happen if it drips on her mascara!

Julien. Georgie, get out.

Mme. Georges. Not if you're going to make her cry!

Julien [*taking her arm and putting her out*]. When I say get out—you get out.

JULIEN *comes back.* MME. GEORGES *starts to walk off, then walks back, puts her ear to the door and gradually, during the scene, the* HAIRDRESSER, CHIROPODIST, GOURETTE *in Louis XV costume, and most of the cast silently collect in the corridor behind* COLOMBE's *door.*

Julien [*suddenly*]. Who is he?

Colombe. Who is what?

Julien. Your lover.

Colombe. Please, Julien, stop it. I haven't got a lover.

Julien [*grabs her: wildly*]. You tell me who it is!

Colombe. Darling, how can I tell you something I don't know?

Julien. It's no use, Colombe: I've got proof. Somebody saw you—and wrote and told me.

Colombe [*freeing herself: furious*]. Who dared to write you?

Julien. See—you're scared. No use pretending; I've a letter on me giving the whole story. [*Mimics the others.*] . . . My little snake.

Colombe. I want to know who wrote you.

Julien. I'm sure you do.

Colombe. An anonymous letter no doubt. They all hate you in this business, they're all jealous. Go on, act like a detective, now that you've started all this: ask the janitor, ask the old man who walks the dogs, ask the old woman who mops up the men's room—you'll hear plenty of stories. I won't have one lover, I'll have twenty. They're only happy spreading filth. Anonymous letters while they sit around waiting for parts they'll never get. You'd think you'd know better after being raised in this atmosphere. But you'd rather believe *them* than show a little confidence in your own wife. They don't even have to sign their names. [*Changes her tone: close to tears.*] Those two glorious years when we were broke and I cooked and cleaned and did everything I could to make you happy— *then* you never questioned my fidelity. Do you think this is the first time men have paid attention to me? Do you think if I'd wanted to be unfaithful I had to wait for you to go in the army? It never once entered my head, even when we went without dinner and pretended we'd just come back stuffed from Maxim's. Go on, forget all that, just roll me around in the mud. [*She falls sobbing on a chair.* JULIEN *doesn't move.*]

Julien. I'm sorry.

Colombe. You're sorry—you're sorry! It's done now. You'd believe anyone rather than me.

Julien. I want to believe you.

Colombe [*in a low colorless voice. From beneath her tears*]. The letter was signed?

Julien. Yes.

Colombe. Tell me her name.

Julien. It was a man.

Colombe [*thinks for a minute: exclaims*]. Oh, now I see! It would never occur to you that this . . . pig wrote the letter out of spite, because I wouldn't agree to his charming proposals?

Julien [*leaping up*]. Who wanted you to? Tell me his name!

Colombe. No—you tell me, so I can see whether he's the one. Let me just guess the first letter. It's a P, isn't it?

Julien. No.

Colombe. O—oh! An R! *That's* who it is—that disgusting creature!

Julien. No—it's not a P *or* an R.

Colombe. It's not a W? Low as he is, I don't think, because a woman refused him, he'd do a thing like this!

Julien. No, Colombe, it's not a W.

Colombe. No. But if he's not the one. . . .

Julien. What do you mean—if *he's* not the one?

Colombe. My poor Julien, I can't even guess who it was —there's been one after another. They try to follow you into your dressing room, and you have to slam the door. They grab hold of you in the corridor and you have to slap their face. What do you think happens to a halfway attractive girl when men know she's alone?

Julien [*shouting*]. I want their names—I want every one of their names!

Colombe. My poor darling, you'd need the telephone book. Men are men—don't act so surprised, I'm sure you're no different.

Julien. Since I met you, I've never looked at another girl.

Colombe. Oh, of course not—you wouldn't dream of it. What about the Chenaud twins, when you were teaching them waltzes for four hands.

Julien. They were fifteen years old!

Colombe. Precisely. The dark one wasn't much, I admit —but the other, with her silly childlike manner and firm mature breasts. You were always leaning over to show her the right position for the fourth finger. I dare you to deny it—I've received letters, too, in my day—only I didn't say anything.

Julien. The Chenaud kids—it's insane.

Colombe. And the druggist's wife?

Julien. The druggist's wife?

Colombe. Yes, my pet, the druggist's wife. You'd never go on an errand except when we needed tooth powder or soap—and when we were broke that tightwad, who'd skim milk at both ends if she could, would give *you* credit! I'll give you credit, too—you had quite a way with her. And to . . . to say these things to me—I'm not joking, Julien, I think you're awful.

She starts to cry a second time. JULIEN *stands silent, at a loss for what to do: in the corridor, they feel that things may be straightening out and something had better be done. With pantomime, they persuade the* HAIRDRESSER *to go in. He knocks and half opens the door.*

Hairdresser. They're going to ring up, madame. Shall I run the comb through your hair once or twice?

Colombe [*in tears*]. Oh thanks, Lucien—yes, I need it.

JULIEN *begins getting suspicious again when the* HAIR-
DRESSER *comes in: looks them over suspiciously while*
LUCIEN *works on* COLOMBE.

Colombe [*smiling into the mirror*]. You're a nice man,
Lucien—you try to make women pretty.

Hairdresser [*with an embarrassed smile toward* JULIEN].
You're always pretty to begin with. Doing your hair's not
work, it's a pleasure.

Julien. See here, my friend! [HAIRDRESSER *turns around,
comb in mid-air.*] How long does it take to "run the comb
through her hair once or twice"?

Hairdresser. It depends, Mr. Julien.

Julien. Depends on what? And the comb's not enough;
it also requires your hands, I see.

Hairdresser. You can't comb *curls.*

Julien. Get out of here—or I'll run more than a comb
. . . through more than your hair. [*Pushes him out.
Comes back, shouts.*] He's not the one.

Colombe. He?

Julien. He couldn't be your lover. His hands are like
dough. How can you let him touch you? Answer me, Colombe, before I start a scene: it's not him?

Colombe [*getting up with a cry*]. I know who wrote to
you! It's not true when you say it's a man. All these
hysterics because a drunken old bat saw me having dinner
with the hairdresser.

Julien [*springing up*]. You had dinner with him?

Colombe. I do have to eat, you know. Am I supposed to
fast because you're in the army?

In the corridor the HAIRDRESSER *is very much annoyed:
the others make fun of him.*

Julien. That baboon had the nerve to ask you to dinner
—and you actually went? I'll—beat his brains out.

Runs toward the door: the HAIRDRESSER *pushes through
the crowd away from the door.* COLOMBE *catches hold of*
JULIEN.

Colombe. Darling, you're behaving like a child. He's a
greasy half-wit who never opens his mouth. Do you think if
I wanted a lover I'd pick anything like that? Show a little
sense!

Julien. He's *not* very pretty, is he?

Colombe [*laughs, kisses him*]. My great big dope of a husband! I have him do my hair because he's so good at it: but otherwise—really I prefer you. [*Takes his hands, kisses him again.*] Instead of fighting with me ever since you came, couldn't you once take me in your arms? [*She melts into his arms, locks his hands behind her, offers her lips.*]

Julien [*weakly*]. But who is it then?

Colombe. It's no one, you dope. No, there is somebody —I'd better fess up. It's you. [*She kisses him.*]

Julien [*in her arms*]. I love you, darling, and I'm so miserable. It'd be better to tell me if you've done something wrong. Don't you think I know how tough it is to be all alone? And in this filthy atmosphere. I'll get you out of it and we'll be happy again.

Colombe [*caressing him: genuinely tender*]. My sweet foolish baby, who frightens everybody and is more defenseless than all the others—you're a brave man just the same.

Julien [*groaning, while she caresses him*]. But how could you let them come near you—that fool that calls you his little monkey——

Colombe. Gaulois? [*Guffaws in the corridor.*] Fool is right! He thinks he's irresistible because he was good-looking 30 years ago. So he mumbles and whispers and tries to look passionate——

GAULOIS *hurries into his dressing room.*

Julien. And you let him——

Colombe. Yes, I let him . . . talk. That's all he *can* do. "My little monkey," and "my little mousie," and "I can't sleep for love," and "I can't eat for love"—and I'm sure he can't love for love, either. Pats your hand and then hurries home exhausted and takes off his corset and drinks his cocoa and sinks into bed. And he's in raptures because he has the strength to get up by noon the next day—and strap on, and lace on, and buckle on, and hammer on, all his orthopedic appliances—and come back here and try to hold hands with one of the other girls. You think I need *that*—when I have you?

Julien. But what did he mumble and whisper about?

Colombe. Well—that I should rehearse with him at his apartment—all done up in what he calls Moroccan style.

Julien. And you went?

Colombe [*upset*]. No, darling—— Yes, I did go: but not alone. With Poet-Mine-Own, to run through a scene.

Julien. You see, the letter I got was true. You do go around with them, you do go to their apartments. . . .

Colombe. But I told you: I went with Poet-Mine-Own, in his carriage.

Julien [*wounded once more; shouting*]. But then you were alone with *him!*

Colombe [*trying to be patient*]. But I took him along so I wouldn't be alone with Gaulois. Really, Julien, I couldn't bring someone else along so I wouldn't be alone with Mine-Own.

Julien. Remember how Mine-Own behaved two years ago: I had to teach him manners.

Colombe. You were a very good teacher! Now he's courtly, but very well-behaved.

Julien. Courtly: and you let him be: you let him pay you court. M. Robinet of the Academy—a man like that has juicy little parts to hand out. So we let him kiss the back of our glove—and then stroke the back of our arm—and then . . . it's really very little, considering what you'll get out of it. Too bad he has a tic; but you can stand it, can't you? Well, I can't! I've a little courting to do, too, with that old——[*Starts wildly for the door. Consternation in the corridor.* COLOMBE *grabs him, while breaking into laughter.*]

Colombe. Darling—this is insane. Really it is!

Julien. What's so funny? Because I'm ashamed? Because I'm upset?

Colombe. No, no! What you say—that he has a tic. Can you imagine me in the arms of Poet-Mine-Own? Julien—just think of him in his underdrawers! [*She starts to laugh again: slowly her laughter wins him over.*]

Julien. I must admit that Mine-Own in underdrawers would be quite a sight!

Colombe [*laughing more*]. You don't know the best part of it! He wears baby-pink garters that his wife embroidered. [*For a moment they both roar with laughter; suddenly they both stop.*]

Julien. How would you know?

Colombe [*regaining her laugh*]. Everyone does.

Julien. How do *you* know?

Colombe. Deschamps told me.

Julien. Deschamps? That's the kind of thing you discuss with Deschamps! When was this?

Colombe. If you let me, I'll explain.

Julien. Don't tell me you went to his office—sat on the green divan where he gets reimbursed for handing out parts?

Colombe. No—well yes, once. Please let me explain, Julien: when I signed my contract. [*After a second.*] All right, if you *must* know. He didn't make me any exception to what he does. I stopped him—I slapped his face. I told him what I thought he behaved like—and what I thought he looked like, too. Then I s'pose for fear Poet-Mine-Own might have a little better luck, he told me what *he* looked like—garters, and a few other details. Darling, that's all there was to it!

Julien [*suddenly slapping her face: shouts*]. Just a tramp, like all the rest. God damn you!

COLOMBE *falls down in a faint:* JULIEN *rushes toward the door.* MME. ALEXANDRA, *dressed as a maréchale, who had come out of her dressing room to listen with the others, pushes them all aside; and when* JULIEN *opens the door, she stands directly in front of him:* MME. GEORGES *glides into the dressing room to look after* COLOMBE.

MME. ALEXANDRA [*in her most terrible voice*]. Well, sir?

Julien. Let me through—I want to see——

Mme. Alexandra [*blocking him*]. Must you mess things up wherever you go? Do you always have to scream and start trouble? I felt sorry for you and took in your wife: now you get out of here and leave us alone.

Julien. It's you . . . [*To the crowd.*] . . . it's you who did this to her. [*To his mother.*] And you, looking like a —I can't say what you remind me of. God damn you all!

Mme. Alexandra [*like thunder*]. Stop that! I'm your mother.

Julien. Yes, you're my mother. Who'd know better than I?

Mme. Alexandra. You think I care for it? If it's not money, it's scenes. You let this child alone—she was just beginning to enjoy herself. Is she supposed to lock herself up for life because you had the good taste to fall in love with her? Women will stick—if there's something to stick to! [*To* GOURETTE.] Ring up! And get that child on stage dead or alive! The audience is already making a commotion on account of this fool!

She exits grandly, her cane tapping in rhythm. Having parted to let her pass, the others follow, while GOURETTE *shouts.*

Gourette. On stage for Act One! On stage for Act One!

At this COLOMBE *miraculously revives: looks in the mirror.*

Colombe. Is my hair all right?
Mme. Georges. It's fine, dear. Come along, I'll put your dress on downstairs.

Everyone has gone except JULIEN *who goes, half drugged, into the deserted dressing room. Below, the three taps are heard and the orchestra begins the overture to "The Realm of Passion." After a minute* EDOUARD *appears—walking jauntily in time with the music and carrying a tiny bouquet. He goes into* COLOMBE's *dressing room, stops in surprise on seeing* JULIEN *and doesn't know what to do with the bouquet.*

Julien [*looks at him: suddenly in a stunned tone*]. It's you.
Edouard. It's me all right.
Julien [*this time in a sad voice*]. It's you—I know it's you.
Edouard [*looking quizzical*]. Sorry—I don't guess I know the combination. [*Nervously.*] I'd have thought you'd be glad to see me. You look fine.
Julien. Yes—I look fine.
Edouard. Army life not too hard?
Julien. Damn hard.
Edouard [*still trying to be casual*]. Your feet holding out? When they go, everything goes. [*Tries to laugh, but stops, seeing* JULIEN's *face.*]
Julien. You're feeling chipper?
Edouard [*suddenly very much upset*]. No. [*For a moment they stand silent, face to face.*]
Julien. Why did it have to be you?
Edouard [*quietly, after a moment*]. What can you expect? You know what it's like around here.
Julien [*shouting*]. No, I don't know what it's like—I'll never know what it's like!

Edouard [*lowering his head*]. No, I guess you won't. You're different: you always were; even as a kid, you fought against it. I couldn't, even as a kid—when it only meant chocolates. It's never stopped—I'm scum.

Julien. Yes.

Edouard. What are you going to do? [JULIEN *doesn't move. Loudly.*] Hit me . . . hard—hurt me. I want you to. You ought to have done it oftener when we were kids.

Julien [*choked*]. No, not you—I can't hurt you. I just want to know why. I can't understand.

Edouard. How can you understand our kind of life? We're not for you. All these slimy little male and female games—you'd never understand, if you lived to be a hundred. Sock me, hard as you can: that's so much simpler— we'd be two little boys again. I can't ever say no, but this time I realized I'd have to get what was coming to me— I even want to get it.

Julien. No. I can't.

Edouard [*suddenly*]. The little slut.

Julien [*hollowly*]. Quit that.

Edouard. You think she acted right? I'm not defending myself, I'm damn weak. But she—she knew how you loved her. . . .

Julien [*making a terrible effort*]. God damn you, stop that!

Edouard. She had you, she had something—solid. And the first guy that fussed over her a little—he didn't even have to try hard. You're lucky, to be above all this.

Julien. Yes. Just look at me.

Edouard. I can't—I'm too ashamed.

Julien [*suddenly*]. I said to look at me.

Edouard [*turning away*]. Sock me if you want—but I can't.

Julien [*forcing him*]. I said look at me! [EDOUARD *raises his eyes.*] What's it all about?—a good enough nose, but what the hell? A pretty little girl's weak mouth. The eyes of a drunk—the look of a baby-faced dissipated old man.

Edouard. You think I'm proud of it? But you live off in space somewhere, you don't know what life is.

Julien. I'm beginning to find out.

Edouard [*trying to regain his poise*]. You'd do better to go back to camp and forget about us all. At bottom you really want a hard life—something you can feel resentful about.

Julien. You're not even very clever with those cheap pearls of wisdom you pick up in club bars. I don't think you've ever been really moved in your life.

Edouard. That's not so. I've got just as much heart as you have. Only. . . .

Julien. Only it's still wrapped in tissue paper in the box it came in. If you'd had an air about you—but you even dress like a . . . jockey. [*Loudly.*] Why? In Christ's name, why?

Edouard. Exactly. *You* dope women out!

Julien. I've got to find out. I've got to know what Colombe. . . . Kiss me.

Edouard [*embracing him, tears coming to his eyes*]. You mean it—you mean you'll forgive me?

Julien [*harshly holding on to him*]. Not that kind of kiss—the kind you gave *her!*

Edouard [*trying to break away*]. Have you gone crazy? For God's sake, let me go.

Julien [*struggling with him*]. Kiss me. Exactly the way you did her. I've got to know what she saw in you.

Edouard [*struggling*]. My God, Julien—you're losing your mind. Let me go!

Julien [*catching him by the throat*]. Kiss me, you stinking lousy bastard, the way you did her!

Edouard [*choking*]. You're choking me. Julien, I can't.

Julien. You could, once. Go on, pretend it's her. [*He holds* EDOUARD *against himself.*]

Edouard [*struggling again*]. I can't.

JULIEN *pushes him brutally away.* EDOUARD *gasping, falls into a chair.* JULIEN *doesn't move: looks around with a tormented face.*

Julien [*in a voice of despair*]. Colombe: I don't understand.

Fast Curtain.

SCENE II

Curtain goes up on the final scene of "The Realm of Passion." *Louis XV décor as conceived around 1900. A salon with French windows opening onto a terrace: beyond, a Watteau-like park. On stage at rise:* MME. ALEXANDRA *and* GAULOIS.

Mme. Alexandra.

Too long my lips were sealed, my heart on fire.
Now come, sweet youth, come swooning to my arms.
I am, like you, nineteen; I whisper, "Yes."
Gaulois. High lady, is it you?
Mme. Alexandra.

'Tis I, indeed.

My young love opens to the fragrant night:
Erst I have never dared: tonight is elsewise!
Long in a golden cage my heart has paced
On fire but frustrate: now it melts the bars,
The fire mounts and Love is himself aflame!
Gaulois. My star!
Mme. Alexandra [*with a gesture of receding modesty*].
And now blot out my exalted rank!
Tonight no grande dame, but the maiden clay
Your hand shall mold, the white and quivering flesh
Your flesh shall warm! Yours only, yours to take.
Gaulois [*getting up with much personal difficulty, and pressing himself madly against her*]. Mine, mine forever, forever sweetly mine!

Mme. Alexandra. Moments there are millenniums cannot match!

Gaulois. For your body's rapture, I thank you on my knees.

Mme. Alexandra [*suddenly crying out*]. Quick, off your knees, sweet boy! Quick for he comes!

Gourette *appears, playing the Maréchal de Villardiers.* Colombe *has come in, terrified, through another door, and stations herself humbly near* Mme. Alexandra.

Gourette.

Oh hateful sight! Oh heinous treachery!
Monsieur de Bouglaire kneeling at her feet!
Mme. Alexandra [*like a Racine heroine*]. Monsieur the Marshal of France, I love this boy!
Gourette [*grand and terrible*]. Wrath such as mine could cost your swain his life!
Gaulois. Yours to decree, M. the Marshal of France!
Gourette [*with a smile at once noble, wistful and profligate*].

I envy this boy's youth, I crave his ardor—
My royal master does not wish the sword
A Marshal wears to avenge such injury:

Our swords, monsieur, must serve a nobler cause:
Post have I all night sped here from Versailles:
War is declared!
Gaulois [*drawing himself erect, hand on sword*]. War,
sir?
Gourette.
          Gallantry,
   My gallant, moves from a lady's couch
   To the river Rhine, to save our glorious France!
Gaulois [*drawing his sword; piously*]. Dear France!

          Trumpet calls in the distance.

Gourette.
   Yes—one name we can both adore
   With never a thought of doing each other hurt.
          [*Turns to* MME. ALEXANDRA.]
   Oh chide him not, Marie, if France he choose—
   She is the fiercer mistress—but our Mother!
Mme. Alexandra [*heartbroken but excessively noble*].
   Go, both of you, and leave me to my tears:
   So fair a rival I too must wish should win.
Gourette [*becoming very human*].
   I know how so you suffer: I too have loved.
   Loved *you*, Madame! Alas! Adieu!
[*To* GAULOIS.] Monsieur!
Gaulois [*with a helpless gesture, to* MME. ALEXANDRA].
Adieu!

Amid a blare of trumpets, he follows GOURETTE *out;* MME.
   ALEXANDRA *falls sobbing into* COLOMBE's *arms.*

Mme. Alexandra. My gallant boy!
Colombe [*trying to console her*]. He will return, mad-
ame, still faithful to you!
Mme. Alexandra [*after a brief reverie*]. He—yes! But I?
Colombe. You?
Mme. Alexandra.
   I am young and fair:
Others will come tonight to pay me court—
And madness 'twere, to make Love bide the morrow:
Women will die for love—but not sit waiting!
          [*Sounds of a minuet in the park.*]
Clorinda, let us dance! Come, let's away:
The fiddles sing their love songs by the fountains;
Masked figures haunt the shrubbery. Come, sweet child:

I'm nineteen—I'm a woman—I'm bewitched!
Come, let us blend the violet with the rose,
And swooning in Love's arms, forget Love's woes!

*While music is heard offstage and there is dancing far up-
stage, they exit as fast as* MME. ALEXANDRA's *robes will
permit.*

Curtain.

Frantic applause. Curtain is raised; everyone takes bows.
MME. ALEXANDRA *and* GAULOIS *are recalled several times;
she yielding the stage to him, then coming on alone to be
cheered. She receives flowers; is choked with gratitude, indicates how grateful she is to the rest of the cast; then the
curtain comes down for good. At once everybody's attitude
changes:* MME. ALEXANDRA *tosses her flowers to* MME.
GEORGES, *who has hurried over with* MME. ALEXANDRA's
cane. She exits, worn out. GAULOIS *follows, taking off his
wig while exiting.*

Gaulois. God, they were a tough crowd tonight.

Still in costume, but without his hat and sword, GOURETTE
helps the stagehands start to clear the stage. JULIEN *comes
on and stops* COLOMBE. *During their scene together, the
lights go out and the stagehands clear the stage, till the
two of them are left alone in semidarkness.*

Julien. I've been walking the streets all evening—I've got
to talk to you.
Colombe [*moving a little*]. I have to go up and undress.
Julien [*blocking her*]. Not, not up there. I can't face
them any more: I'm too ashamed.
Colombe. All right, we'll stay here.
Julien. I've seen Edouard.
Colombe [*without expression*]. Yes.
Julien. He told me. You've seen him, too?
Colombe. Yes.
Julien. You realize it was all the harder to take because
it was him.
Colombe [*in a composed little voice*]. Of course I do.
I'm terribly sorry. We'd both have given anything to spare
you this.
Julien. Ever since we were kids, he's taken things from
me; he can't help it. And now—you're *both* young and
pleasure-loving, and I left you here alone. And I realize

that I lectured you too much, I got on your nerves, I guess.

Colombe. Yes.

Julien. The whole time I was walking the streets, I kept talking to you out loud. I explained everything to you. People stared at me, they probably thought I was crazy. I'd bump into them and say "Sorry" and walk on. Funny how you can walk and smile and keep saying "Sorry" when all the time you're dead. [*Silence.*] You know, being dead makes you a lot easier on people. I want to forgive you, I really do: only first I want to understand.

COLOMBE *has listened patiently; suddenly she speaks in a very calm way.*

Colombe. It would take a terribly long time to explain. And I'm petrified I'll be late. Don't you want to come up to my dressing room so we can talk while I get dressed?

Julien [*loudly*]. Late? Late for what?

Colombe [*quietly*]. For the supper date I told you about.

Julien [*not wanting to believe her*]. After what's happened, you don't mean you're going to keep your date? I go back to camp tomorrow.

Colombe. I told you what it can mean to my future.

Julien. Are you out of your mind?

Colombe. It's you who won't understand. Why do we have to stay here—we could talk just as well upstairs. They'll be calling for me any minute.

Julien [*brutally turning her around*]. Look at me! Even now you're acting. You're pretending not to care so you won't have to face up to what you're doing.

Colombe. No, I'm not. I'm willing to answer anything you want to ask. All I want is to dress at the same time because I'm scared I'll be late.

Julien. After all that's happened between us, you're able to leave me and go out and laugh with a bunch of strangers!

Colombe. I'm not going with them to laugh. I told you why I'm going. I'm thinking of my future.

Julien. Your future! It's quite different from your past: if we fought in the old days, you were always very sweet to me afterwards.

Colombe. I want to be sweet now: I understand. But you ought to understand, too.

Julien. It's just not possible. You can't have stopped loving me.

Colombe. Who says I've stopped loving you?

Julien. This thing between us is going to fester. We've got to stop it right away. You've been foolish, but we've still an awful lot to fall back on. [*After a moment, almost with shame.*] We have the baby.

Colombe [*annoyed*]. I was waiting for you to bring that up.

Julien. Wasn't it natural?

Colombe. Sure. It's very easy for you to get sentimental about the baby. But he's my baby too, and I love him very much. And right now someone I'm paying with what I make is looking after him. And tomorrow morning it'll be me who wakes him up and bathes him and dries him off and gets his breakfast. That's what he's interested in, not what goes on between us. When he's older, I'll tell him how unhappy you made me, and that one day I couldn't take it any more.

Julien. I made you unhappy?

Colombe. Yes.

Julien. But I did everything I knew how.

Colombe. Yes, everything you liked. You liked to stay home, so we never went out. I was so young and unsure about everything and you carefully explained what was right and what was wrong, so I used to say yes. But I really wanted to go dancing.

Julien. We *went* dancing.

Colombe. Twice in two years. And if anyone else asked me to dance, you made me refuse.

Julien. But you said you loved me——

Colombe. Couldn't I love you and also want to go dancing?

Julien. I never dreamed you wanted to!

Colombe. Of course you didn't! You thought I'd much rather stay home and hear your lectures on morality and how stupid people can be—or you played Beethoven by the hour, when if even for a minute I listened to a street singer with a guitar, you'd hurry over and slam down the window.

Julien. But I wanted you to like what was . . . beautiful.

Colombe. Who were you to decide what was beautiful? Things are beautiful if you love them, and I loved gypsy

music and dancing and pretty clothes. But you never tried
to find out what I might want, never asked me anything,
never bought me anything.

Julien. We hadn't any money.

Colombe. And you couldn't be bothered to make any.
All that mattered was your becoming a great pianist. And
so that you could become a great pianist, I had to wash
dishes and scrub floors. And if you'd ever become one,
while you stood bowing and drinking in the applause, I'd
have had my beautiful red hands to show the public.

Julien. Please don't—this is awful.

Colombe. It *is* awful. But it's over. I support myself now,
I live the way I like. When something amuses me I laugh
without worrying whether you'll think it's funny, or start
to sulk as soon as we get home.

Julien. If I sulked it was because it hurt me to see you
suddenly do the kind of things that. . . .

Colombe. Well, I won't hurt you after this. We've both
suffered plenty from your always being hurt. It's good to
be sensitive but really, Julien, there are limits. Would you
like me to be honest? I've been very happy since you went
away. When I wake up the sun's shining, I look out the
window and for the first time in years there's no tragedy
in the street. And if the mailman rings and I go to the
door in my nightgown—there's no drama. I'm not a loose
woman—we're just a young girl and the mailman, happy
with each other—he because he gets a kick out of seeing
me in a nightgown, I because I've given him a little pleasure. I like the whole business—being attractive and nibbling breakfast while I do the housework, and washing
myself in the kitchen, naked, with the window open. And
if the old man opposite runs for his opera glasses, I can't
get excited, or feel I'm a loose woman and cry for two
hours trying to calm you down. You'll never know, my
darling, how uncomplicated life can be—without you.

Julien. But if I was jealous and made scenes, it was because I loved you. So would any other man.

Colombe. No. Or if he does, I'll have sense enough now
to laugh.

Julien. Edouard doesn't love you—you know he doesn't.

Colombe. I know he doesn't love me the way one dreams
of being loved. But he makes me happy and that's a lot.
He tells me I'm beautiful and brings me little presents and
takes care of me.

Julien. Me! Me! That's all you know how to say.

Colombe. Yes, I've learned. I heard the word often enough from you.

Julien. I'm hurt.

Colombe. It's very sad. But I was hurt, too.

Julien. But I never meant to hurt you—whatever I did, it was because I loved you.

Colombe. No, Julien—because you loved yourself.

Julien. That's nonsense.

Colombe. The girl you loved was something you dreamed up. I want the next man to love *me* and I want loving me to make him happy. It never made you happy. You'll never understand women—but that's all they know how to do in the world—make men happy. You shouldn't cheat them out of it. Now I'll be late. We've said everything: let me go and get ready.

Julien [*grabbing her by the wrist*]. No.

Colombe. Let me go.

Julien. No.

Colombe. You're hurting me, Julien. Go ahead, you know how. Slap my face. It won't be the first time tonight.

While they've been speaking, the props and furniture have been removed, leaving only the sofa they have fallen onto while struggling. The stagehands come up to them.

Stagehand. Mr. Julien, we've got to move this, too.

JULIEN *gets up without a word; the men take the divan.* JULIEN *has drawn* COLOMBE *to him. They're alone and face to face, on a big empty stage lighted only by a work lamp.*

Julien. We're crazy to yell at each other. I'm going to talk to you very quietly: will you listen?

Colombe. No.

Julien [*grabbing her wrist*]. You're going to have to!

Colombe. You're stronger than I am: you can even kill me if you feel like it. The poor wronged husband—I'm sure they'd acquit you.

Julien. I only want to ask one thing. Will you promise to answer?

Colombe. It all depends. What is it?

Julien. When I came into your dressing room a while ago, why did you throw your arms around me?

Colombe. Because I was so glad to see you. I mean it.

Julien. And then when I questioned you, when I suspected the others, why did you deny it as though you'd
never even kissed another man?

Colombe. Imagine being suspicious of those characters!
But I'd never have admitted it about anybody. It could
only make things worse. I love you; you have to go back
to camp tomorrow. This was no time to upset you.

Julien. Why did you take my hands and kiss them and
put them around your neck?

Colombe. So you'd believe me—I wanted you to be
happy.

Julien. And if I hadn't seen Edouard, and *had* believed
you? You'd have come back from this supper date and got
into bed with me?

Colombe. Yes.

Julien. And given yourself to me?

Colombe [*in a small even voice*]. Of course.

Julien [*after a silence*]. I don't understand.

Colombe. You never understand anything! I love you—
that's all. You're all alone in camp. You've just spent three
months without a woman—I know you haven't been unfaithful. If you hadn't found out, do you think I'd have
invented a headache or something to spoil your leave? I'm
not that mean.

Julien. And you'd have gone through with it like a street-
walker, without any pleasure?

Colombe [*sincerely*]. Why without any pleasure? You
give me a lot of pleasure.

Julien. And Edouard?

Colombe. Yes. But that's something else. You have a
real genius for complicating everything.

Julien. And you'd have told him about it?

Colombe [*indignant*]. Of course not! What business is
it of his? Edouard hasn't any rights over me. Look, I've
never let him say one word against you. What do you
think I am?

Silence. JULIEN, *stunned, dares not answer.*

Colombe [*softly*]. Baby, you'll let me go and get dressed
now? I promise I won't stay at Maxim's long: I'll come
home to you as fast as I can.

Julien [*as though questioning himself*]. We really still
love each other—at any rate, this way?

Colombe. Yes.

Julien. I'm ashamed to ask—you never just pretended with me?

Colombe. No. Never.

Julien. Then why? I just can't understand why. Do you love Edouard more than me?

Colombe. No.

Julien. As much?

Colombe. Do you think I keep score? Could I go out with Edouard all the time, let him look after me, and then give him a kiss on the forehead and say, "Run along now." You've got to make a little effort to understand, too.

Julien [*unhappily*]. I do—I don't do anything else.

Colombe. But *our* way—not just yours.

Julien. Then, if this leave hadn't turned up, you'd have gone on sharing the two of us?

Colombe. If. . . . If. I don't live on *ifs. If* you'd stayed in Paris, this would never have happened. But you didn't: it's partly your fault. Don't always blame other people.

Julien. I had to go into service sometime, like everyone else.

Colombe. If you'd loved me, you could have got deferred. They said they could get you, and you refused. That's precisely when I realized that you think of no one but yourself and that I'd better start thinking of myself, too.

Julien [*suddenly tender*]. My poor baby.

Colombe. Yes, your poor baby. And you're not making her look any prettier when she needs to!

Julien. My poor little baby—all she can think of is her supper date! I loved you the way a little boy loves his mother, or loves another little boy when they prick each other's blood and swear eternal friendship. The way two people do who plan and struggle and worry together till they're old and, sitting side by side, start dreaming back. To love that way seemed all the romance a man could need: he could forget about the things he'd never done; forget about the girls you *don't* forget about.

Colombe [*a little hurt*]. Now you can do them—and take the girls along. Ask them to go away with you, as you did me two years ago.

Julien. Yes, I could.

Colombe. I can see you bewitching them with your sad eyes and your beautiful wounded soul. What a little nitwit I was!

Julien [*grabbing her wrist; loudly*]. Don't run down the old Colombe; at least *she's* still mine.

Colombe. Yours, my poor dodo? What did you know about her? You thought she was a little angel?—in a florist shop where a bunch of old bucks came day after day for their carnations? And the funeral wreaths I'd take to grief-stricken households: but there was always a cousin who'd manage to control his grief and push you in a corner. Keep your little angel if it makes you happy: but there aren't any angels. Even if you want to be. . . .

Julien [*grabbing her*]. Damn you, I won't let you throw mud at that girl!

Colombe [*in an I-will-if-I-feel-like-it tone*]. It's me, after all!

Julien. No—it's not you! [*Looks at her with both pity and hate.*] That's what scares me worst of all—that you could get to be so vile I'd stop loving you.

Colombe [*quietly*]. You're hurting me, Julien—in a minute I'll be all black and blue. I can't see where that'll do us any good.

Julien [*suddenly letting her go*]. All right—this time you can go. Hurry up, keep your date.

She turns and walks off without looking at him as soon as he has released her. He watches her go; suddenly cries.

Julien. Colombe!

Colombe [*turning*]. Now what?

Julien [*tormentedly*]. Nothing. . . . If while you're dressing you decide to break your date, I'll be waiting here.

With a slight shrug, she turns and exits. JULIEN *remains alone, disconsolate, in the middle of the stage. As he stands there,* MME. ALEXANDRA *appears bundled up in scarves and leaning on a cane: after her comes* MME. GEORGES.

Julien. Mother!

Mme. Alexandra. What do you mean—"mother"? Have you gone crazy?

Julien. Mother, I'm so unhappy.

Mme. Alexandra. You made your bed—now you'll have to lie in it alone.

Julien. Mother, I loved her—I'll always love her.

Mme. Alexandra. Your father would have always loved me. That's what made everything so impossible. What *is* this mania to love someone all one's life? Why should we?

Do we always wear the same clothes? Do we always live in the same house? Ask the doctor, he'll tell you that there's not a cell in your body that was there seven years before. Everything else about us changes—why shouldn't our feelings change? These romantic ideas you people pick up in books—they've nothing to do with life. If your sensitive colonel of a father had started in the way I did, in a mangy old road company at fourteen, he'd never have committed suicide. Let's go, Georgie. You haven't forgotten my knee pad?

Julien [*clinging to her*]. But all the same you must have suffered. Nobody can reach your age and not suffer. There must be something we can say to each other: I feel so desperately lonely.

Mme. Alexandra. You'll always feel lonely. Always—because you never think of anyone but yourself. You think *I'm* the selfish one? The really selfish people aren't those who insist on having good times. They're not dangerous, they don't take any more than they give. They know only too well: they pass one another by, they pat one another's hand, you say hello to me, I say hello to you: we both know how little it means, but we can both put up a little better with what's gnawing inside us, what no one gives a damn about except ourselves. The dangerous ones are those who stop you every time you want to turn around, who instead of patting your hand, insist that you feel their guts. And the more they suffer, the more they make you suffer, the happier they are.

Julien [*groaning*]. But I love her!

Mme. Alexandra. Yes, I guess that's true. But now she doesn't love you any more. That's just as true, that counts just as much. What's she supposed to do—be bored to death for the next sixty years because that's the one way to keep you happy?

Julien. I did everything I knew how. . . .

Mme. Alexandra. Yes, but you didn't *know* how—and you never will. Go home and go to bed and tomorrow go back to being a soldier. Spill those guts of yours for France: she may thank you for them; we can't. [*Wincing with pain.*] Let's go, Georgie—my knee's killing me from standing here. [*She hobbles toward the wings. Suddenly calling out.*] Was it money you wanted?

Julien. No, Mother—thank you.

Mme. Alexandra. Have it your own way. Try to get some sense!

She and MME. GEORGES *exit.* JULIEN *is alone on the empty stage. Goes to the piano, opens it, plays a few notes of a song, stops. We hear far off a girl's voice singing the song. "Colombe," says* JULIEN, *"do you remember? I remember." Lights dim till it is dark.*

When the lights slowly come on again for the EPILOGUE, JULIEN *is in civilian clothes, and about to play the same piano. The stage is still empty and only lit by a work lamp, but sunlight streams through the air shafts. Then* CO-LOMBE *stands there in an old dress, carrying a large florist's basket of flowers. She seems to have lost her bearings; suddenly catches sight of* JULIEN.

Colombe. I'm sorry, monsieur: Mme. Alexandra's dressing room?

Julien. It's up a flight. But why don't you wait here? —she'll be down any minute to rehearse. That'll save you a whole flight of steps and a tornado. She's all set to blow down the theatre.

Colombe. Is something wrong?

Julien. In the theatre, something's always wrong.

Colombe. She's such a wonderful actress—and isn't she beautiful?

Julien. Oh, very. Like an old public building. Do you go for the Louvre?

Colombe. That's mean of you. And she's not old: I saw her act once.

Julien. That's different. On the stage she looks twenty.

Colombe. That's not very nice, seeing you work for her. What if she heard you?

Julien [*still at the piano*]. She has. I'm her son.

Colombe. You're her son?

Julien. Uh hum. Not that either one of us boasts about it.

Colombe. Then, you see, she isn't old.

Julien [*smiling, and turning round on the piano stool*]. Why?

Colombe [*stammering a little*]. Because you're . . . so very young.

Julien [*blushing, and stammering, too*]. I don't go in

much for compliments—but you're terribly pretty. [*A sudden pained silence between them.*] Is it fun to be a florist?

Colombe. Not always as much as it is today.

Julien. You must meet a lot of people.

Colombe. Yes, only it's mostly *old men* who buy flowers.

Julien. When I'm rich I'll buy some—and give them to you.

Colombe. Really?

Julien. Do people ever give you flowers?

Colombe. Never!

Julien. What about your boy friend?

Colombe. I don't have one.

Julien [*suddenly getting up and coming to clip a rose from the basket*]. Here—I'll start in right now.

Colombe. Oh, the basket! This'll cause trouble.

Julien. I'll take care of it. There'll be trouble anyhow, just because I'm here.

Colombe [*smelling her rose*]. Funny, when they're given to you, you feel like smelling them. Doesn't your mother like you to come to the theatre?

Julien. No.

Colombe. She's afraid you'll meet the wrong type of people?

Julien [*laughing*]. That's marvelous! No: she's afraid I'll ask her for money. I'm trying to be a concert pianist and I practice eight hours a day: that doesn't leave much time to earn a living. So sometimes I have to come here for . . . supplies. As seldom as possible, because I hate the idea.

Colombe. It's good to have pride.

Julien. It's also tough.

Colombe. If I loved somebody, I'd want him to have pride—to be a real man. [*They smile but don't know what to say next.*]

Julien. Do you make lots of money as a florist?

Colombe. Oh, with tips about 100 francs a month.

Julien. Then you're in my class. If . . . if I pick you up after work some night, would you have dinner with me?— you wouldn't insist on Larue?

Colombe. I wouldn't even know where it was. But I once had dinner at Poccardi's.

Julien. Well, we'll go there again.

Colombe. And eat up all the hors d'oeuvres?

Julien. Sure, and then yell for more.

Colombe. You really *will*?

Julien. I hereby *do*. Tonight. Why wait?

Colombe. You can't call for me tonight; this was my last errand.

Julien [*gets up and takes her hand*]. Wonderful: then we can start off right now.

Colombe. But there's my basket.

Julien. Just leave it here. It's big enough—they're sure to notice it.

Colombe [*suddenly practical*]. Do you think I should wait for my tip?

Julien. I'm crazy: we both gotta wait for our tip. We'd sure do well at Poccardi's on my twenty-one sous.

Colombe. I suppose you think I always say yes—like this. But it's really the first time.

Julien. It's the first time I ever asked anyone. Do you think it's possible?

Colombe. What?

Julien. That people can like each other—no, it's not just *like*—can feel something about each other right away?

Colombe. I don't know.

Julien [*who has sat down next to her on a bench, and puts his arm over her shoulder*]. Do *you* feel that way?

Colombe. Yes.

Julien. Do you, very often?

Colombe. No.

Julien. I *never* have. I'd better tell you before we go out —I'm a dreadful person. I don't like people, I get infuriated at them—and they don't like me.

Colombe. I don't believe it.

Julien. It's true, though.

Colombe. You seem very nice to me.

Julien. You know—I find that I can be! Ever go to the zoo?

Colombe. Um hum.

Julien. D'you ever watch the bears? I'm a bear. Think you'd like to tame me?

Colombe [*leaning against his shoulder*]. They're strong. They protect you—and keep you warm. There's nothing wrong with bears.

Julien. Maybe not, but most girls don't like them.

Colombe. I'm not sure what I like; but right now I know I feel fine. The only thing that scares me is—it's all happening so fast.

Julien. I'm even more scared than you are. I've waited all my life for a girl who likes bears.

Colombe. I'm glad.

Julien. If it were only true—if it could be like in fairy tales: at first sight, and then forevermore. Promise me you'll be faithful till tonight at any rate—till Poccardi's.

Colombe. I promise.

Julien. Cross your heart.

Colombe [*doing so*]. Cross my heart.

Julien [*shyly*]. Is it too soon to kiss you?

Colombe [*whispering*]. No. [*Offers him her lips. He kisses her, then suddenly stands up and cries out.*]

Julien. God, this is wonderful! Can life really be good? Is mother really charming and young, after all? We've got to celebrate this. [*Takes the basket.*] Here, why be stingy— take the rest.

Colombe [*worried*]. But they were sent to your mother, monsieur. [*Suddenly.*] Monsieur what?

Julien. Julien. And you?

Colombe. Colombe.

Julien. Mademoiselle Colombe! But what is happening tonight that makes life suddenly seem so wonderful?

MME. ALEXANDRA *rushes in, followed by her staff:* MINE-OWN, DESCHAMPS, GOURETTE.

Mme. Alexandra. Slime! Those bit-part players are all slime! And we open in three days. [*Sees* JULIEN *and stops.*] What are you doing here? You're all we need!

Julien. Mother darling, as you see, I'm kissing the florist.

Mme. Alexandra [*not understanding*]. What are you talking about? Mademoiselle, put the flowers down; Gourette, give her ten sous. And Deschamps, could you have the kindness to arrange for a few auditions this evening?

Deschamps. But the little brunette who tried out this afternoon——

Mme. Alexandra. The little brunette is chiefly able to wiggle.

Mine-Own [*who has been looking at* COLOMBE]. But we're all crazy—for two hours we've been wrangling . . .

over a girl to play a little florist—and here we have one! And an enchanting one!

Mme. Alexandra [*inspecting her*]. She *is* nice. Turn around, dear—let me see your legs.

Colombe [*flabbergasted*]. My legs?

Mme. Alexandra. You've never heard of legs before?

Mine-Own. Come, little lady, show us your legs: they may make you famous. [*He lifts her skirts.*] They're adorable—see for yourselves.

Colombe [*pulling down her skirt*]. But, monsieur——

Mine-Own. A bit higher, just a tiny bit higher.

Julien [*coming forward and pulling down* COLOMBE's *skirts*]. That will do! You leave this young lady alone!

Mine-Own. But we've got to see her legs—they're part of the plot.

Julien. They're always part of the plot.

Mme. Alexandra. That will do, Julien. [*To the others.*] I agree she has pretty legs. But she still needs to have a voice.

Deschamps. Ever done anything in the theatre?

Colombe. No, monsieur, I work in a flower shop.

Mme. Alexandra. Have you ever done any singing?

Colombe. For my own pleasure.

Mme. Alexandra. Do you know "Love Is Gone"?

Colombe. Sort of.

Mme. Alexandra. We'll see. Julien!—where is that oaf?

Julien [*from his corner*]. I'm here.

Mme. Alexandra. Go to the piano and accompany this girl.

Julien [*without moving*]. No.

Mme. Alexandra. What do you mean, no?

Julien. I've a badly infected finger.

Mme. Alexandra. Where's it infected?

Julien. It's *getting* infected.

Mme. Alexandra. You're a real honest-to-God little stinker. Why won't you play?

Julien. Because I'm not in the mood. Because I think you should leave this girl alone. She's happy where she is.

Mme. Alexandra [*to* COLOMBE]. Sing without any piano. [*To* EDOUARD, *who has just come in.*] Edouard, can you play "Love Is Gone" with one finger?

Edouard. I can play Haydn's *Creation* with one finger.

Mme. Alexandra. Then accompany this child: Your brother has refused to.

Edouard. All right, let her rip. [*Starts to play.*]
Colombe [*singing*].

> A leaf in the spring
> > Will cling to the tree,
> A leaf in the fall
> > Will blow away.
>
> So love like the leaf
> > Will cling to your heart,
> > Will sing at the start
> And then will vanish.
>
> But life must still go on. . . .

MINE-OWN, *in rapture, after hovering over her, puts his arm around her waist. She tries, while singing, to free herself.* JULIEN *suddenly strides over and pulls* MINE-OWN *away from* COLOMBE.

Julien. You stay away from her.
Mine-Own. Who put you in charge?
Julien. This young lady is *with* me.
Mme. Alexandra. You don't even belong here yourself!
Julien. This young lady is with me.
Mme. Alexandra. That will be your exit line! Etienne! Jacques!
Stagehands. Yes, Mme. Alexandra?
Mme. Alexandra. Escort this clown to the street.
Stagehands. Go on, Mr. Julien. Say bye-bye.
Julien. Keep your hands off me.

They try to push him out; he fights them.

Stagehand. Get going, Mr. Julien. Hey!
Colombe [*terrified*]. Stop that. Make them stop, they'll hurt him.

JULIEN *has managed to get out of their clutches and starts running around the stage.*

Julien [*yelling*]. Besides, before I leave, I've a duty to perform. [*Goes up to* MINE-OWN, *turns him around and kicks him in the pants.*] I swing an adorable leg, too!
Deschamps [*yelling at the same time*]. Get him out of here!

The STAGEHANDS *have taken hold of* JULIEN *and are starting to drag him out.*

Mme. Alexandra. I'm leaving myself. The girl's all right,
I'll settle for her. Georgie, try to find her something to
wear—we'll rehearse her after dinner.

Mine-Own [*hurrying over to* COLOMBE]. It means fame,
my child. [*Whispers in her ear.*] I'm wild about you.

Julien [*yelling as he is dragged off*]. Let me go, you
bastards! [*To* COLOMBE.] Poccardi's? You said you would!

Colombe [*pulling away from* MINE-OWN]. You're disgusting—all of you. [*To the* STAGEHANDS.] Let him alone.
[*To* JULIEN.] I meant it! I'll go with you to Poccardi's.

Mme. Alexandra. What's all this crepp about Poccardi's?
You've got a job. You rehearse tonight!

Colombe. Yes. But before I got the job, I accepted an
invitation to dinner.

Mme. Alexandra. Oh? Indeed! [*Turning abruptly to*
DESCHAMPS.] Go fetch your little brunette—if she's free
for the evening. At least she won't act like Joan of Arc.
[*Exits.*]

Deschamps. Thank you, dear lady. You'll see—she's
most unusual. [*Exits.*]

Mine-Own [*starting to exit, then halting as* JULIEN
returns]. Monsieur, two of my friends will wait upon you
tomorrow.

Julien. Splendid. Though I fear they won't find me at
home. [*Puts his arm around* COLOMBE.] We're both . . .
vanishing tonight.

Mine-Own [*in a rage to* COLOMBE]. You ridiculous little
fool.

Exits as fast as dignity permits: JULIEN *wants to go after
him but* COLOMBE *prevents him.*

Colombe [*tenderly*]. No.

Julien. Did you hear what he said?

Colombe. No, I'm too happy. I heard something much
nicer.

Edouard [*who has stayed at the piano: smiling*]. Well,
my lovebirds, that was quite a scene—you sure know how
to bring down the curtain. Have you known each other
long?

Julien. An hour.

Colombe. Don't tell him what happened—he won't
believe it.

Edouard. You'd rather go to dinner at Poccardi's with

this . . . crank than get started in the theatre? [*To* JULIEN.] Where did you find such a marvel?

Julien. That's my secret.

Edouard. No, don't tell. [*To* JULIEN.] I hope you're not planning to make her miserable—you're not going to deliver your famous series of lectures?

Julien. No.

Edouard. Be happy, my children! And say, I had good luck for once last night—we'll go halves like brothers.

Julien [*taking the money*]. You're terribly kind, Edouard.

Edouard [*about to exit*]. Have fun! Have as much fun as you can!

Colombe. Thank you, monsieur.

He goes out. They come back to each other.

Julien. Here we are. I'll always remember what you just did.

Colombe. You mustn't feel that way—I didn't even know I was doing it. I screamed, didn't I, when they started to put you out—and then I found myself in your arms. It's happened too fast, hasn't it—it can't be the real thing.

Julien. Terribly fast, but I think it *is* the real thing— and for the rest of our lives.

They kiss: she leans against him, murmurs.

Colombe. My darling. The rest of our lives.

Julien. That's the very least. . . .

Colombe [*pressing hard against him*]. Always. . . . [*More softly.*] Always, always. . . . [*They kiss.*]

Julien. Now the story begins!

They walk off happily, arms around each other's back.

Curtain.

THE LARK

Adapted by

LILLIAN HELLMAN

CHARACTERS

Warwick
Cauchon
Joan
Joan's Father
Joan's Mother
Joan's Brother
The Promoter
The Inquisitor
Brother Ladvenu
Robert de Beaudricourt
Agnes Sorel
The Little Queen
The Dauphin
Queen Yolande
Monsieur de la Tremouille
Archbishop of Reims
Captain La Hire
Executioner
English Soldier
Scribe
Ladies of the Court
Monks and Soldiers

Act One: The Trial
Act Two: The Trial

ACT ONE

*Before the curtain rises we hear the music of a psalm:
a chorus is singing "Exaudi orationem meam, domine."
When the curtain rises the music changes to a motet on
the words "Qui tollis," from the Mass.*

THE SCENE: *Another day in the trial of* JOAN. *The stage
is a series of platforms, different in size and in height.
The cyclorama is gray in color and projections will be
thrown on it to indicate a change of scene. At this moment we see the bars of a jail as they are projected on
the cyclorama.*

AT RISE: JOAN *is sitting on a stool.* CAUCHON *is standing
downstage near* THE PROMOTER. *The* PRIESTS *are about
to take their places on the* JUDGES' *bench.* THE INQUISITOR
sits quietly on a stool near the JUDGES. JOAN'S *family
stand upstage; the royal family stand in a group.* VILLAGE
WOMEN *cross the stage carrying bundles of faggots and*
ENGLISH SOLDIERS *and* GUARDS *move into place.* BEAUDRI-
COURT *and* LA HIRE *appear and take their places upstage.*

WARWICK *enters and moves through the crowd.*

WARWICK. Everybody here? Good. Let the trial begin at
once. The quicker the judgment and the burning, the
better for all of us.

Cauchon. No, sire. The whole story must be played.
Domremy, the Voices, Chinon——

Warwick. I am not here to watch that children's story
of the warrior virgin, strong and tender, dressed in white
armor, white standard streaming in the wind. If they have
time to waste, they can make the statues that way, in days
to come. Different politics may well require different sym-
bols. We might even have to make her a monument in
London. Don't be shocked at that, sire. The politics of
my government may well require it one day, and what's
required, Englishmen supply. That's our secret, sire, and
a very good one, indeed. [*Moves downstage to address
the audience.*] Well, let's worry about only this minute
of time. I am Beauchamp, Earl of Warwick. I have a

251

dirty virgin witch girl tucked away on a litter of straw in the depths of a prison here in Rouen. The girl has been an expensive nuisance. Your Duke of Burgundy sold her high. You like money in France, Monseigneur, all of you. That's the French secret, sire, and a very good one, indeed. [*He moves toward* JOAN.] And here she is. The Maid. The famous Joan the Maid. Obviously, we paid too much. So put her on trial, and burn her, and be finished.

Cauchon. No, sire. She must play out her whole life first. It's a short life. It won't take very long.

Warwick [*moves to a stool near* CAUCHON]. If you insist. Englishmen are patient, and for the purposes of this trial I am all Englishmen. But certainly you don't intend to amuse yourselves by acting out all the old battles? I would find that very disagreeable. Nobody wishes to remember defeat.

Cauchon. No, sire. We no longer have enough men to act out the old battles. [*Turns toward* JOAN.] Joan? [JOAN *turns to* CAUCHON.] You may begin.

Joan. Can I begin any place I want to?

Cauchon. Yes.

Joan. Then I'll start at the beginning. It's always nicer at the beginning. I'll begin with my father's house when I was very small. [*Her* MOTHER, *her* FATHER *and her* BROTHERS *appear on stage. She runs to join them.*] I live here happy enough with my mother, my brothers, my father. [*We hear the music of a shepherd song and as she leaves the family group she dances her way downstage, clapping her hands to the music.*] I'm in the meadow now, watching my sheep. I am not thinking of anything. It is the first time I hear the Voices. I wasn't thinking of anything. I know only that God is good and that He keeps me pure and safe in this little corner of the earth near Domremy. This one little piece of French earth that has not yet been destroyed by the English invaders. [*She makes childish thrusts with an imaginary sword, and stops suddenly as if someone has pulled her back.*] Then, suddenly, someone behind me touched my shoulder. I know very well that no one is behind me. I turn and there is a great blinding light in the shadow of me. The Voice is grave and sweet and I was frightened. But I didn't tell anybody. I don't know why. Then came the

second time. It was the noon Angelus. A light came over
the sun and was stronger than the sun. There he was.
I saw him. An angel in a beautiful clean robe that must
have been ironed by somebody very careful. He had
two great white wings. He didn't tell me his name that
day, but later I found out he was Monseigneur the Blessed
Saint Michael.

Warwick [*to* CAUCHON]. We know all this. Is it necessary to let her go over that nonsense again?

Cauchon. It is necessary, sire.

Joan. Blessed Saint Michael, excuse me, but you are in
the wrong village. I am Joan, an ignorant girl, my father's
daughter—— [*Pauses, listens.*] I can't save France. I don't
even know how to ride a horse. [*Smiles.*] To you people
the Sire de Beaudricourt is only a country squire, but to
us he is master here. He would never take me to the
Dauphin, I've never even bowed to him—— [*Turns to the
court.*] Then the Blessed Saint Michael said Saint Catherine would come along with me, and if that wasn't
enough Saint Marguerite would go, too. [*She turns back
as if to listen to Saint Michael.*] But when the army
captains lose a battle—and they lose a great many—they
can go to sleep at night. I could never send men to their
death. Forgive me, Blessed Saint Michael, but I must go
home now—— [*But she doesn't move. She is held back by
a command.*] Oh, Blessed Saint Michael, have pity on me.
Have pity, Messire. [*The chorus sings* "Alleluia, Alleluia"
*to the shepherd's tune. She listens, smiles, moves back into
the trial. Simply.*] Well, he didn't. And that was the day
I was saddled with France. *And* my work on the farm.

THE FATHER *who has been moving about near* THE
MOTHER, *suddenly grows angry.*

The Father. What's she up to?

The Mother. She's in the fields.

The Father. So was I, in the fields, but I've come in. It's
six o'clock! I ask you, what's she up to?

The Brother. She's dreaming under the lady tree.

The Father. What's anybody doing under a tree at this
hour?

The Brother. You ask her. She stares straight ahead. She
looks as if she is waiting for something. It isn't the first
time.

The Father [*angrily to* THE BROTHER]. Why didn't you tell me? She is waiting for someone, not something. She has a lover.

The Mother [*softly*]. Joan is as clean as a baby.

The Father. All girls are as clean as babies until that night when they aren't any more. I'll find her and if she is with someone, I'll beat her until——

Joan. I was with someone, but my lover had two great white wings and through the rain he came so close to me that I thought I could touch his wings. He was very worried that day, he told me so. He said the Kingdom of France was in great misery and that God said I could wait no longer. There has been a mistake, I kept saying. The Blessed Saint Michael asked me if God made mistakes. You understand that I couldn't very well say yes?

The Promoter. Why didn't you make the Sign of the Cross?

Joan. That question is not written in your charge against me.

The Promoter. Why didn't you say to the archangel, "Vado retro Satanas?"

Joan. I don't know any Latin, Messire. And *that* question is not written in your charge against me.

The Promoter. Don't act the fool. The devil understands French. You could have said, "Go away, you filthy, stinking devil."

Joan [*angry*]. I don't talk that way to the Blessed Saint Michael, Messire!

The Promoter. The Devil told you he was Saint Michael and you were fool enough to believe him.

Joan. I believed him. He could not have been the Devil. He was so beautiful.

The Promoter. The Devil *is* beautiful!

Joan [*shocked*]. Oh, Messire!

Cauchon [*to* THE PROMOTER]. These theological subtleties are far above the understanding of this poor child. You shock her without reason.

JOAN [*to* THE PROMOTER]. You've lied, Canon! I am not as educated as you are, but I know the Devil *is* ugly and everything that is beautiful is the work of God. I have no doubts. I know.

The Promoter. You know nothing. Evil has a lovely face when a lovely face is needed. In real life the Devil waits for a soft, sweet night of summer. Then he comes on a gentle wind in the form of a beautiful girl with bare breasts——

Cauchon [*sharply*]. Canon, let us not get mixed up in our private devils. Continue, Joan.

Joan [*to* THE PROMOTER]. But if the Devil is beautiful, how can we know he is the Devil?

The Promoter. Go to your priest. He will tell you.

Joan. Can't I recognize him all by myself?

The Promoter. No. Certainly not. No.

Joan. But only the rich have their priests always with them. The poor can't be running back and forth.

The Promoter [*angry*]. I do not like the way you speak in this court. I warn you again——

Cauchon. Enough, enough, Messire. Let her speak peacefully with her Voices. There is nothing to reproach her with so far.

Joan. Then another time it was Saint Marguerite and Saint Catherine who came to me. [*She turns to* THE PROMOTER.] And they, too, were beautiful.

The Promoter. Were they naked?

Joan [*laughs*]. Oh, Messire! Don't you think our Lord can afford to buy clothing for His Saints?

Cauchon [*to* THE PROMOTER]. You make us all smile, Messire, with your questions. You are confusing the girl with the suggestion that good and evil is a question of what clothes are worn by what Angels and what Devils. [*Turns to* JOAN.] But it is not your place to correct the venerable Canon. You forget who you are and who we are. We are your priests, your masters, and your judges. Beware of your pride, Joan.

Joan [*softly*]. I know that I am proud. But I am a daughter of God. If He didn't want me to be proud, why did He send me His shining Archangel and His Saints all dressed in light? Why did He promise me that I should conquer all the men I have conquered? Why did He promise me a suit of beautiful white armor, the gift of my king? And a sword? And that I should lead brave soldiers into battle while riding a fine white horse? If He had left me alone, I would never have become proud.

Cauchon. Take care of your words, Joan. You are accusing our Lord.

Joan [*makes the Sign of the Cross*]. Oh, God forbid. I say only that His Will be done even if it means making me proud and then damning me for it. That, too, is His Right.

The Promoter [very angry]. What are you saying? Could God wish to damn a human soul? How can you listen to her without shuddering, Messires? I see here the germ of a frightful heresy that could tear the Church——

THE INQUISITOR *rises.* THE PROMOTER *stops speaking. The stage is silent.* LADVENU, *a young priest, rises and goes to* THE INQUISITOR. THE INQUISITOR *whispers to him.* LAD-VENU *moves to* CAUCHON, *whispers to him.*

Cauchon [looks toward THE INQUISITOR; *very hesitant].* Messire—— [THE INQUISITOR *stares at* CAUCHON. CAU-CHON *hesitates, then turns toward* JOAN.] Joan, listen well to what I must ask you. At this moment, are you in a State of Grace?

Ladvenu. Messire, this is a fearful question for a simple girl who sincerely believes that God has chosen her. Do not hold her answer against her. She is in great danger and she is confused.

Cauchon. Are you in a State of Grace?

Joan [as if she knew this was a dangerous question]. Which moment is that, Messire? Everything is so mixed up, I no longer know where I am. At the beginning when I heard my Voices, or at the end of the trial when I knew that my king and my friends had abandoned me? When I lost faith, when I recanted, or when, at the very last minute, I gave myself back to myself? When——

Cauchon [softly, worried]. Messire demands an answer. His reasons must be grave. Joan, are you in a State of Grace?

Joan. If I am not, God will help me in Grace. If I am, God will keep me in Grace.

The PRIESTS *murmur among themselves.* THE INQUISITOR, *impassive, sits down.*

Ladvenu [gently, warmly]. Well spoken, Joan.

The Promoter [sharply]. And the Devil would have the same clever answer.

Warwick [to CAUCHON, *pointing to* THE INQUISITOR]. Is that the gentleman about whom I have been told?

Cauchon [softly]. Yes.

Warwick. When did he arrive?

Cauchon. Three days ago. He has wished to be alone.

Warwick. Why was I not told of his arrival?

Cauchon. He is one of us, sire. We do not acknowledge your authority here.

Warwick. Only when you count our money and eat our food. Never mind, the formalities do not matter to me. But time does and I hope his presence will not add to the confusion. I am almost as bewildered as the girl. All these questions must be very interesting to you gentlemen of the Church, but if we continue at this speed we'll never get to the trial and the girl will be dead of old age. Get to the burning and be done with it.

Cauchon [*angry*]. Sire! Who speaks of burning? We will try to save the girl——

Warwick. Monseigneur, I allow you this charade because the object of my government is to tell the whole Christian world that the coronation of the idiot Charles was managed by a sorceress, a heretic, a mad girl, a whore camp follower. However you do that, please move with greater speed.

Cauchon. And I remind you each day that this is a court of the Church. We are here to judge the charge of heresy. Our considerations are not yours.

Warwick. My dear Bishop, I know that. But the fine points of ecclesiastic judgments may be a little too distinguished for my soldiers—and for the rest of the world. Propaganda is a soft weapon: hold it in your hands too long, and it will move about like a snake, and strike the other way. Whatever the girl is or has been, she must now be stripped and degraded. That is why we bought her high, and it is what we will insist upon. [*Smiles.*] I'm coming to like her. I admire the way she stands up to all of you. And she rides beautifully—I've seen her. Rare to find a woman who rides that way. I'd like to have known her in other circumstances, in a pleasanter world. Hard for me to remember that she took France away from us, deprived us of our heritage. We know that God is on the side of the English. He proved himself at Agincourt. "God and my right," you know. But when this girl came along, and we began to lose, there were those who doubted our motto. That, of course, cannot be tolerated. "God and my right" is inscribed on all English armor, and we certainly have no intention of changing the armor. So get on with her story. The world will forget her soon enough. Where were we?

The Father [*comes forward*]. At the moment when I find her under the lady tree. [*He goes to* JOAN.] What are you doing? You were crying out to someone, but the bastard fled before I could catch him. Who was it? Who was it? Answer me. Answer me, or I'll beat you to salt mash.

Joan. I was talking to the Blessed Saint Michael.

The Father [*hits* JOAN]. That will teach you to lie to your father. You want to start whoring like the others. Well, you can tell your Blessed Saint Michael that if I catch you together I'll plunge my pitchfork into his belly and strangle you with my bare hands for the filthy rutting cat you are.

Joan [*softly*]. Father, it was Saint Michael who was talking to me.

The Father. The priest will hear about this, and from me. I'll tell him straight out that not content with running after men, you have also dared to blaspheme!

Joan. I swear to you before God that I am telling the truth. It's been happening for a long time and always at the noon or evening Angelus. The Saints appear to me. They speak to me. They answer me when I question them. And they all say the same thing.

The Father. Why would the Saints speak to you, idiot? I am your father, why don't they speak to me? If they had anything to say they'd talk to me.

Joan. Father, try to understand the trouble I'm in. For three years I've refused what they ask. But I don't think I can say no much longer. I think the moment has come when I must go.

The Father. For forty years I've worked myself to death to raise my children like Christians, and this is my reward. A daughter who thinks she hears Voices.

Joan. They say I can't wait any longer——

The Father. What can't wait any longer?

Joan. They tell me France is at the last moment of danger. My Voices tell me I must save her.

The Father. You? You? You are crazy. Crazy. You are a fool! A fool and a crazy girl.

Joan. I must do what my Voices tell me. I will go to the Sire de Beaudricourt and ask him to give me an armed escort to the Dauphin at Chinon. I'll talk to the Dauphin and make him fight. Then I will take the army to Orléans and we'll push the English into the sea.

The Father. For ten years I have dreamed that you would disgrace us with men. Do you think I raised you, sacrificed everything for you, to have you run off to live

with soldiers? I knew what you would be. But you won't
—I'll kill you first. [*He begins to beat her and to kick her.*]

Joan [*screams*]. Stop! Stop! Oh, Father, stop!

Ladvenu [*rises, horrified*]. Stop him. Stop him. He's
hurting her.

Cauchon. We cannot, Brother Ladvenu. We do not
know Joan. You forget that we first meet her at the trial.
We can only play our roles, good or bad, just as they were,
each in his turn. And we will hurt her far more than he
does. You know that. [*Turns to* WARWICK.] Ugly, isn't
it, this family scene?

Warwick. Why? In England we are in favor of strong
punishment for children. It makes character. I was half
beaten to death as a boy, but I am in excellent health.

The Father [*he looks down at* JOAN *who has fallen at
his feet*]. Crazy little whore. Do you still want to save
France? [*Then, shamefaced, he turns to the* JUDGES.] Well,
messieurs, what would you have done in my place if your
daughter had been like that?

Warwick. If we had known about this girl from the very
beginning, we could have reached an agreement with her
father. We tell people that our intelligence service is remarkable and we say it so often that everybody believes
us. It should be their business not only to tell us what is
happening, but what might happen. When a country virgin talked about saving France, I should have known about
it. I tell myself now I would not have laughed.

THE MOTHER *comes forward. She bends over* JOAN.

The Father [*to* THE MOTHER]. The next time your
daughter talks of running after soldiers, I'll put her in the
river and with my own hands I'll hold her under.

THE MOTHER *takes* JOAN *in her arms.*

The Mother. He hurt you bad.

Joan. Yes.

The Mother [*softly*]. He's your father.

Joan. Yes. He is my father. Oh, Mama, somebody must
understand. I can't do it alone.

The Mother. Lean against me. You're big now. I can
hardly hold you in my arms. Joan, your father is a good
and honest man but—[*She whispers in* JOAN's *ear.*] I've
saved a little from the house money. If you'd like one, I'll
buy you a broidered kerchief at the very next fair.

Joan. I don't need a kerchief. I won't ever be pretty, Mama.

The Mother. We're all a little wild when we're young. Who is it, Joan? Don't have secrets from me. Is he from our village?

Joan. I don't want to marry, Mama. That isn't what I mean.

The Mother. Then what do you mean?

Joan. Blessed Saint Michael says that I must put on man's clothes. He says that I must save France.

The Mother. Joan, I speak to you in kindness, but I forbid you to tell me such nonsense. A man's clothes! I should just like to see you try it.

Joan. But I'll have to, Mama, if I'm to ride horse with my soldiers. Saint Michael makes good sense.

The Mother. Your soldiers? Your soldiers? You bad girl! I'd rather see you dead first. Now I'm talking like your father, and that I never want to do. [*She begins to cry.*] Running after soldiers! What have I done to deserve a daughter like this? You will kill me.

Joan. No, Mama, no. [*She cries out as her* MOTHER *moves off.*] Monseigneur Saint Michael. It cannot be done. Nobody will ever understand. It is better for me to say no right now. [*Pauses, listens.*] Then Saint Michael's voice grew soft, the way it does when he is angry. And he said that I must take the first step. He said that God trusted me and if a mountain of ice did rise ahead of me it was only because God was busy and trusted me to climb the mountain even if I tore my hands and broke my legs, and my face might run with blood—— [*After a second, slowly, carefully.*] Then I said that I would go. I said that I would go that day.

JOAN'S BROTHER *comes forward and stands looking at her.*

The Brother. You haven't got the sense you were born with. If you give me something next time, I won't tell Papa I saw you with your lover.

Joan. So it was you, you pig, you told them? Here's what I'll give you this time—— [*She slaps him.*] And the next time—[*She slaps him again, and begins to chase him. He runs from her.*] and the time after that. [JOAN's *voice changes and she moves slowly about, not concerned with him any longer but speaking into space.*] And so I went to my uncle Durand. And my uncle Durand went to the

seigneur of the manor. And I walked a long way west and
a little way south and there was the night I was shivering
with rain—or with fear—and the day I was shivering with
sun—or with fear—and then I walked to the west again
and east. I was on my way to the first fool I had to deal
with. And I had plenty of them to deal with.

She moves upstage, bumps into two SOLDIERS *as* BEAUDRI-
COURT *comes on stage.*

Beaudricourt. What is it? What's the matter? What
does she want? What's the matter with these crazy fools?
[*He grabs* JOAN *and shakes her.*] What's the matter with
you, young woman? You've been carrying on like a bad
girl. I've heard about you standing outside the doors rag-
ging at the sentries until they fall asleep. [*He holds her
up. She dangles in front of his face.*]

Joan. I want a horse. I want the dress of a man. I want
an armed escort. You will give them orders to take me to
Chinon to see the Dauphin.

Beaudricourt. Of course. And I will also kick you in the
place where it will do the most good.

Joan. Kicks, blows. Whichever you like best. I'm used
to them by now. I want a horse. I want the dress of a
man. I want an armed escort.

Beaudricourt. That's a new idea—a horse. You know
who I am and what I usually want? Did the village girls
tell you? When they come to ask a favor it usually has
to do with a father or a brother who has poached my land.
If the girl is pretty, I have a good heart, and we both pitch
in. If the girl is ugly, well, usually I have a good heart, too,
but not so good as the other way. I am known in this land
for goodheartedness. But a horse is a nasty kind of bargain.

Joan. I have been sent by Blessed Saint Michael.

Beaudricourt [*puts her down hurriedly, makes the Sign
of the Cross*]. Don't mix the Saints up in this kind of
thing. That talk was good enough to get you past the
sentries, but it's not good enough to get you a horse. A
horse costs more than a woman. You're a country girl. You
ought to know that. Are you a virgin?

Joan. Yes, sire.

Beaudricourt. Well, maybe we'll talk about a small horse
You have lovely eyes.

Joan. I want more than a horse, sire.

Beaudricourt [*laughs*]. You're greedy. But I like that

sometimes. There are fools who get angry when the girl wants too much. But I say good things should cost a lot. That pleases me in a girl. You understand what I mean?

Joan. No, sire.

Beaudricourt. That's good. I don't like clear-thinking women in bed. Not in my bed. You understand what I mean?

Joan. No, sire.

Beaudricourt. Well, I don't like idiots, either. What is it you're up to? What else besides a horse?

Joan. Just as I said before, sire. An armed escort as far as Chinon.

Beaudricourt. Stop that crazy talk. I'm the master here. I can send you back where you came from with no better present than the lashes of a whip. I told you I like a girl to come high, but if she costs too much the opposite effect sets in—and I can't—well, I can't. You understand what I mean? [*Suddenly.*] Why do you want to go to Chinon?

Joan. As I said before, sire, I wish to find Monseigneur the Dauphin.

Beaudricourt. Well, you *are* on a high road. Why not the Duke of Burgundy while you're at it? He's more powerful, and he likes the girls. But not our Dauphin. He runs from war and women. An hour with either would kill him. Why do you want to see such a fellow?

Joan. I want an army, Messire. An army to march upon Orléans.

Beaudricourt. If you're crazy, forget about me. [*Shouting.*] Boudousse. Boudousse. [A SOLDIER *comes forward.*] Throw some cold water on this girl and send her back to her father. Don't beat her. It's bad luck to beat a crazy woman.

Joan. You won't beat me. You're a kind man, Messire. Very kind.

Beaudricourt. Sometimes yes, sometimes no. But I don't like virgins whose heads come off at night——

Joan. And you're very intelligent, which is sometimes even better than being kind. But when a man is intelligent *and* kind, then that's the very best combination on God's fine earth.

Beaudricourt [*he waves the* GUARD *away*]. You're a strange girl. Want a little wine? Why do you think I'm intelligent?

Joan. It shows in your face. You're handsome, Messire.

Beaudricourt. Twenty years ago, I wouldn't have said no. I married two rich widows, God bless me. But not now. Of course, I've tried not to get old too fast, and there are men who get better looking with age—— [*Smiles.*] You know, it's very comic to be talking like this with a shepherd girl who drops out of the sky one bright morning. I am bored here. My officers are animals. I have nobody to talk to. I like a little philosophy now and then. I should like to know from your mouth what connection you see between beauty and intelligence? Usually people say that handsome men are stupid.

Joan. Hunchbacks talk that way, and people with long noses, or those who will die of a bitter egg that grows in their head. God has the power to create a perfect man—— [*She smiles at him.*] And sometimes He uses His power.

Beaudricourt. Well, you can look at it that way, of course. But you take me, for example. No, I'm not ugly, but sometimes I wonder if I'm intelligent. No, no, don't protest. I tell you there are times when I have problems that seem too much for me. They ask me to decide something, a tactical or administrative point. Then, all of a sudden, I don't know why, my head acts like it's gone someplace else, and I don't even understand the words people are saying. Isn't that strange? [*After a second.*] But I never show it. I roar out an order, whatever happens. That's the main thing in an army. Make a decision, good or bad, just *make* it. Things will turn out almost the same, anyway. [*Softly, as if to himself.*] Still, I wish I could have done better. This is a small village to die away your life. [*Points outside.*] They think I'm a great man, but they never saw anybody else. Like every other man, I wanted to be brilliant and remarkable, but I end up hanging a few poor bastards who deserted from a broken army. I wanted to shake a nation—— Ah, well. [*Looks at her.*] Why do I tell you all this? You can't help me, and you're crazy.

Joan. They told me you would speak this way.

Beaudricourt. They told you?

Joan. Listen to me, nice, good Robert, and don't shout any more. It's useless. I'm about to say something very important. You will be brilliant and remarkable. You will shake a nation because *I* will do it for you. Your name will go far outside this village——

Beaudricourt [*puts his arms around her*]. What are you talking about?

Joan [*she pulls away from him*]. Robert, don't think any more about my being a girl. That just confuses everything. You'll find plenty of girls who are prettier and will give more pleasure—[*Softly.*] and will not ask as much. You don't want me.

Beaudricourt. Well, I don't know. You're all right.

Joan [*sharply*]. If you want me to help you, then help me. When I say the truth say it with me.

Beaudricourt [*politely*]. But you're a pleasant-looking girl, and it's nice weather, and . . . . [*Laughs.*] No, I don't want you any more than that.

Joan. Good. Now that we have got that out of the way, let's pretend that you've given me the clothes of a boy and we're sitting here like two comrades talking good sense.

Beaudricourt [*fills a glass*]. All right. Have a little wine.

Joan [*drinks her wine*]. Kind, sweet Robert. Great things are about to begin for you. [*As he starts to speak.*] No, no. Listen. The English are everywhere, and everywhere they are our masters. Brittany and Anjou will go next. The English wait only to see which one will pay the higher tribute money. The Duke of Burgundy signs a bitter treaty and the English give him the Order of the Golden Fleece. They invented just such medals for foreign traitors. Our little monkey Dauphin Charles sits with his court in Bourges, shaking and jibbering. He knows nothing, his court knows nothing, and all falls to pieces around him. You know that. You know our army, our good army of brave boys, is tired and sick. They believe the English will always be stronger and that there's no sense to it any more. When an army thinks that way, the end is near. The Bastard Dunois is a good captain and intelligent. So intelligent that nobody will listen to him. So he forgets that he should be leading an army and drowns himself in wine, and tells stories of past battles to his whores. I'll put a stop to that, you can be sure——

Beaudricourt [*softly*]. *You'll* put a stop to——

Joan. Our best soldiers are like angry bulls. They always want to attack, to act fine for the history books. They are great champions of individual bravery. But they don't know how to use their cannon and they get people killed for nothing. That's what they did at Agincourt. Ah, when it comes to dying, they're all ready to volunteer. But what good is it to die? You think just as I do, my dear Robert: war isn't a tournament for fancy gentlemen. You must be smart to win a war. You must think, and be smart. [*Quickly.*] But you who are so intelligent, knew all that when you were born.

Beaudricourt. I've always said it. I've always said that nobody thinks any more. I used to be a thinker, but nobody paid any attention.

Joan. They will, they will. Because you have just had an idea that will probably save all of us.

Beaudricourt. I've had an idea?

Joan. Well, you are about to have it. But don't let anything get in its way. Please sit quiet and don't, well, just—— [*As he is about to move she holds him down.*] You are the only man in France who at this minute can ₃ee the future. Sit still.

Beaudricourt. What is it that I see?

Joan. You know your soldiers. You know they will leave ɣou soon. You know that to keep them you must give them ɼaith. You have nothing else to give them now. A little bread, a little faith—good simple things to fight with.

Beaudricourt. It's too late——

Joan. A girl comes before you. Saint Michael and Saint Catherine and Saint Marguerite have told her to come. You will say it's not true. But I believe it *is* true, and that's what matters. A farm girl who says that God is on her side. You can't prove He isn't. You can't. Try it and see. The girl came a long, hard way, she got so far as you, and she has convinced you. Yes, I have. I have convinced you. And why have I convinced so intelligent a man? Because I tell the truth, and it takes a smart head to know the truth.

Beaudricourt. Where is this idea you said I had?

Joan. Coming, coming just this minute. You are saying to yourself, if she convinced me, why shouldn't she convince the Dauphin and Dunois and the Archbishop? After all they're only men like me, although a good deal less intelligent. [*Very fast.*] All right, that's settled. But now you're saying to yourself, when it comes to dying, soldiers are very intelligent, and so she'll have a harder time with them. No, she won't. She will say English heads are like all others: hit them hard enough, at the right time, and we'll march over them to Orléans. They need faith, ɣour soldiers. They need somebody who believes it to say that

God is on their side. Everybody says things like that. But
I believe it—and that's the difference. Our soldiers will
fight again, you know it, and because you know it you are
the most remarkable man in France.

Beaudricourt. You think so?

Joan. The whole world will think so. But you must move
fast. Like all great political men you are a realist. At this
minute you are saying to yourself, "If the troops will believe this girl has come from God, what difference does it
make whether she has or not? I will send her to Bourges
tomorrow with the courier."

Beaudricourt. The courier does go tomorrow. How did
you know that? He goes with a secret packet——

Joan [*laughs, delighted*]. Give me six good soldiers and
a fine white horse. I want a *white* horse, please. I will do
the rest. But give me a quiet white horse because I don't
know how to ride.

Beaudricourt [*laughs*]. You'll break your neck.

Joan. It's up to Blessed Saint Michael to keep me in the
saddle. [*He laughs. She doesn't like his laughter.*] I will
make you a bet, Robert. I'll bet you a man's dress that if
you will have two horses brought now, and we both ride
at a gallop, I won't fall off. If I stay on, then will you believe in me? All right?

Beaudricourt [*laughs*]. All this thinking makes a man
weary. I had other plans for this afternoon, as I told you,
but any kind of exercise is good for me. Come on.

He exits. JOAN, *smiling, looks toward Heaven. Then she
runs after* BEAUDRICOURT. *But she is stopped by a* SOLDIER
*and suddenly realizes she is back in the trial. She sits
quietly as the lights fade out on the* BEAUDRICOURT *scene.*

Warwick. She made that idiot believe he wasn't an idiot.

Cauchon. It was a man-woman scene, a little coarse for
my taste.

Warwick. Coarse for *your* taste? The trick of making
him believe what she put into his head is exactly what I
do in my trade and what you do in yours. [*Suddenly.*]
Speaking of your trade, sire, forgive a brutal question but,
just between ourselves, do you really have the faith?

Cauchon [*simply*]. As a child has it. And that is why my
judges and I will try to save Joan. To the bitter end we
will try to save her. Our honor demands that—— [WAR-
WICK *turns away.* CAUCHON, *sharply.*] You think of us as

collaborators and therefore without honor. We believed that collaboration with you was the only reasonable solution——

Warwick. And so it was. But when you say reasonable solution it is often more honorable to omit the word honor.

Cauchon [*softly*]. I say honor. Our poor honor, the little that was left us, demanded that we fight for our beliefs.

Warwick. While you lived on English money——

Cauchon. Yes. And while eight hundred of your soldiers were at our gates. It was easy for free men to call us traitors, but we lived in occupied territory, dependent upon the will of your king to kill us or to feed us. We were men, and we wanted to live; we were priests, and we wanted to save Joan. Like most other men, we wanted everything. We played a shameful role.

Warwick. Shameful? I don't know. You might have played a nobler part, perhaps, if you had decided to be martyrs and fight against us. My eight hundred men were quite ready to help.

Cauchon. We had good reason to know about your soldiers. I remember no day without insults and threats. And yet we stood against you. Nine long months before we agreed to hand over a girl who had been deserted by everybody but us. They can call us barbarians, but for all their noble principles I believe they would have surrendered her before we did.

Warwick. You could have given us the girl on the first day. Nine long months of endless what?

Cauchon. It was hard for us. God had been silent since Joan's arrest. He had not spoken to her or to us. Therefore, we had to do without his counsel. We were here to defend the House of God. During our years in the seminaries we learned how to defend it. Joan had no training in our seminaries and yet, abandoned, she defended God's House in her own way. Defended it with that strange conflict of insolence and humility, worldly sense and unworldly grandeur. [*Softly.*] The piety was so simple and sweet—to the last moment of the last flame. We did not understand her in those days. We covered our eyes like old, fighting, childish men, and turned away so that we could not hear the cries of anguish. She was all alone at the end. God had not come to her. That is a terrible time for a religious nature, sire, and brings doubt and despair unknown to others. [CAUCHON *rises and turns away.*] But it is then and there that some men raise their heads, and when they do, it is a noble sight.

Warwick. Yes, it is. But as a man of politics, I cannot afford the doctrine of man's individual magnificence. I might meet another man who felt the same way. And he might express his individual magnificence by cutting off *my* head.

Cauchon [*softly, as if he hadn't heard* WARWICK]. Sometimes, to console myself, I remember how beautiful were all those old priests who tried to protect the child, to save her from what can never now be mended——

Warwick. Oh, you speak in large words, sire. Political language has no such words as "never now be mended." I have told you that the time will come when we will raise her a statue in London.

Cauchon. And the time will come when our names will be known only for what we did to her; when men, forgiving their own sins, but angry with ours, will speak our names in a curse——

The lights dim on WARWICK *and* CAUCHON *and we hear the music of a court song. A throne is brought on stage and as the lights come up slowly on* THE DAUPHIN'S *Court, the cyclorama reflects the royal fleur-de-lis.* THE DAUPHIN, CHARLES, *is lolling about on his throne playing at bilbo-quet.* AGNES SOREL *and* THE LITTLE QUEEN *are practicing a new dance.* YOLANDE *is moving about. Four* COURTIERS *are playing at cards.*

The Little Queen [*she is having a hard time learning the dance steps*]. It's very hard.

Agnes. Everything is very hard for you, dear.

The Little Queen [*as they pass* CHARLES]. It's a new dance. Very fashionable. Influenced by the Orient, they say.

Agnes [*to* CHARLES]. Come. We'll teach you.

Charles. I won't be going to the ball.

Agnes. Well, *we* will be going. And we must dance better than anybody else and look better than anybody else. [*Stops, to* CHARLES, *points to her headdress.*] And I'm not going in this old thing. I'm your mistress. Have a little pride. A mistress must be better dressed than anybody. You know that.

The Little Queen. And so must wives. I mean better

dressed than other wives. The Queen of France in last year's shoddy. What do you think they will say, Charles?

Charles. They will say that poor little Queen married a king who hasn't a sou. They will be wrong. I have a sou. [*He throws a coin in the air. It falls and he begins to scramble on the floor for it.*]

The Little Queen. I can hear them all the way to London. The Duchess of Bedford and the Duchess of Gloucester——

CHARLES, *on the floor, is about to find his sou as the* ARCHBISHOP *and* LA TREMOUILLE *come in.* CHARLES *jumps back in fear.*

La Tremouille [*to* CHARLES]. You grow more like your father each day.

Archbishop. But his father had the decency to take to his bed.

Charles. Which father?

La Tremouille. You act so strangely, sire, that even I, who knew your mother, am convinced you are legitimate. [*Angrily, to* CHARLES *who is still on the floor.*] Move. Move.

The Little Queen. Oh, please don't speak to him that way, Monsieur de la Tremouille.

Archbishop [*who has been glaring at the dancers*]. You believe this is the proper time for dancing?

The Little Queen. But if the English take us prisoner, we have to know a little something. We can't disgrace our country——

LA TREMOUILLE *stares at her, exits.*

Yolande. What harm do they do, sire? They are young —and there isn't much ahead for them.

Archbishop. There isn't much ahead for any of us. [*He moves off.*]

Yolande. Please get up, Charles. It is a sad thing to see you so frightened by so many men.

Charles. And why shouldn't I be frightened of La Tremouille and the Archbishop? I have been all my life. They could order every soldier in the place to cut me up and eat me.

Agnes. They're cheats, every woman in England. We set the styles—and they send spies to steal the latest models. But, fortunately, they're so ugly that nothing looks very well—[*Admires her own feet and hands.*] with cows for feet and pigs for hands. We want new headdresses. Are you the King of France or aren't you?

Charles. I don't know if I am. Nobody knows. I told you all about that the first night you came to bed.

Agnes. The new headdress is two feet tall and has two horns coming from the side——

Charles. Sounds like a man. A very small married man.

The Little Queen. And they have a drape at the back—they will cause a revolution, Charles.

Agnes. The English ladies—the mistresses, I mean, of course—won't be able to sleep when they see us. And if they can't sleep neither will the Dukes. And if the Dukes can't sleep they won't feel well and they won't have time to march on us——

Charles. They won't march on us. Nobody wants this dull town. They're already in Orléans. So there isn't much sense counterattacking with a headdress.

The Little Queen. Oh, Charles, one has to have a little pleasure in life. And Mama—[*Pointing to* YOLANDE.] and the Archbishop and La Tremouille, and all the wise people, tell us that the end is here, anyway, and this will be the last state ball——

Charles. How much do they cost?

Agnes. I flirted with the man—[*Hastily.*] in a nice way —and he's going to let us have them for six thousand francs.

Charles. Where would I get six thousand francs, you little idiot?

The Little Queen. Twelve thousand francs, Charles. I'm here.

Charles. That's enough to pay Dunois' army the six months' wages that I owe them. You are dreaming, my kittens. My dear mother-in-law, please speak to these children.

Yolande. No. I wish to speak to you.

Charles. For two days you've been following me about looking the way good women always look when they're about to give a lecture.

Yolande. Have I ever spoken against your interests? Have I ever shown myself concerned with anything but your welfare? I am the mother of your Queen, but I brought Agnes to you when I realized she would do you good.

The Little Queen. Please, Mama, don't brag about it.

Yolande. My child, Agnes is a charming girl and she knows her place. It was important that Charles make up his mind to become a man, and if he was to become a man he had to have a woman.

The Little Queen. I am a woman and his wife in the bargain.

Yolande. You are my dear little girl and I don't want to hurt you, but you're not very much of a woman. I know because I was just like you. I was honest and sensible, and that was all. Be the Queen to your Charles, keep his house, give him a Dauphin. But leave the rest to others. Love is not a business for honest women. We're no good at it. Charles is more virile since he knows Agnes. [*Worried.*] You are more virile, aren't you, Charles?

Agnes [*too firmly*]. Yes, indeed.

Yolande. I hope so. He doesn't act it with the Archbishop or La Tremouille.

Agnes. Things like that take a while. But he's much more virile. Doesn't read so much any more. [*To* CHARLES.] And since it's all due to me the very least you can do is to give me the headdress. And one for the little Queen. [CHARLES *doesn't answer.*] I feel ill. And if I feel ill it will certainly be for a whole week. And you'll be very bored without me. [*Eagerly, as she sees his face.*] Sign a Treasury Bond and we'll worry afterwards. [*He nods. She turns to* THE LITTLE QUEEN.] Come, my little Majesty. The pink one for you, the green one for me. [*To* CHARLES, *as they exit.*] We'll make fools of those London ladies, you'll see. It'll be a great victory for France.

Charles [*to* YOLANDE]. A great victory for France. She talks like an army captain. I'm sick of such talk. France will be victorious, you'll be a great king—all the people who have wanted to make a king out of me. Even Agnes. She practices in bed. That's very funny. I must tell you about it some day. I am a poor frightened nothing with a lost kingdom and a broken army. When will they understand that?

Yolande. I understand it, Charles.

Charles [*softly, taken aback*]. Do you? You've never said that before.

Yolande. I say it now because I want you to see this girl. For three days I have had her brought here, waiting for you——

Charles. I am ridiculous enough without playing games

with village louts who come to me on clouds carrying a basket of dreams.

Yolande. There is something strange about this girl, something remarkable. Or so everybody thinks, and that's what matters.

Charles. You know La Tremouille would never allow me to see the girl.

Yolande. Why not? It is time they understood that a peasant at their council table might do a little good. A measure of common sense from humble people might bring us all——

Charles [sharply]. To ruin. Men of the people have been at council tables, have become kings, and it was a time of massacre and mistake. At least I'm harmless. The day may come when Frenchmen will regret their little Charles. At least, I have no large ideas about how to organize happiness and death. [*He throws his ball in the air.*]

Yolande. Please stop playing at bilboquet, Charles.

Charles. Let me alone. I like this game. When I miss the cup, the ball only falls on my nose, and that hurts nobody but me. But if I sit straight on the throne with the ball in one hand and the stick in the other, I might start taking myself seriously. Then the ball will fall on the nose of France, and the nose of France won't like it.

The ARCHBISHOP *and* LA TREMOUILLE *enter.*

La Tremouille. We have a new miracle every day. The girl walked to the village church to say her prayers. A drunken soldier yelled an insult at her. "You are wrong to curse," she said. "You will soon appear before our Lord." An hour later the soldier fell into a well and was drowned. The stumbling of a drunkard has turned the town into a roaring holiday. They are marching here now, shouting that God commands you to receive this girl.

Charles. He hasn't said a word to me.

La Tremouille. The day God speaks to you, sire, I will turn infidel.

Archbishop [very angry]. Put up that toy, Your Majesty. You will have the rest of your life to devote to it.

La Tremouille. Get ready to leave here.

Charles. Where will I go? Where will you go? To the English?

Archbishop. Even from you, sire, we will not accept such words.

As La Tremouille *angrily advances on* Charles, Yolande *moves between them.*

Yolande [*to* Archbishop]. Allow him to see the girl.

Archbishop. And throw open the palace to every charlatan, every bonesetter, every faith healer in the land?

La Tremouille. What difference does it make any more? We have come to the end of our rope.

Yolande. If he sees the girl, it will give the people hope for a few days.

Charles. Oh, I am tired of hearing about the girl. Bring her in and have it ended. Maybe she has a little money and can play cards.

Yolande [*to* La Tremouille]. We have nothing to lose, sire——

La Tremouille. When you deal with God you risk losing everything. If He has really sent this girl then He has decided to concern Himself with us. In that case, we are in even worse trouble than we thought. People who govern states should not attract God's attention. They should make themselves very small and pray that they will go unnoticed.

Joan *comes in. She stands small and frightened, staring at* Charles, *bowing respectfully to the* Archbishop. *As she moves toward the throne, one of the* Courtiers *laughs.* Joan *turns to stare, and the* Courtier *draws back as if he is frightened.*

Charles. What do you want? I'm a very busy man. It's time for my milk.

Joan [*bows before him*]. I am Joan the Maid. The King of Heaven has sent me here. I am to take you to Reims and have you anointed and crowned King of France.

Charles. My. Well, that is splendid, mademoiselle, but Reims is in the hands of the English, as far as I know. How shall we get there?

Joan. We will fight our way there, noble Dauphin. First, we will take Orléans and then we will walk to Reims.

La Tremouille. I am commander of the army, madame. We have not been able to take Orléans.

Joan [*carefully*]. I will do it, sire. With the help of our Lord God who is my only commander.

La Tremouille. When did Orléans come to God's attention?

Joan. I do not know the hour, but I know that he wishes us to take the city. After that, we will push the English into the sea.

La Tremouille. Is the Lord in such bad shape that he needs you to do his errands?

Joan. He has said that he needs me.

Archbishop. Young woman—[JOAN *kneels and kisses the hem of his robe.*] if God wishes to save the Kingdom of France he has no need of armies.

Joan. Monseigneur, God doesn't want a lazy Kingdom of France. We must put up a good fight and then He will give us victory.

Archbishop [*to* CHARLES]. The replies of this girl are, indeed, interesting and make a certain amount of good sense. But this is a delicate matter: a commission of learned doctors will now examine her. We will review their findings in council——

La Tremouille [*to* CHARLES]. And will keep you informed of our decision. Go back to your book. She will not disturb you any more today. Come, Madame Henriette——

Joan. My name is Joan.

La Tremouille. Forgive me. The last quack was called Henriette.

Archbishop. Come, my child——

Charles. No! [*He motions to* JOAN.] You. Don't move. [*He turns toward* LA TREMOUILLE, *standing straight and stiff and holding* JOAN'S *hand to give himself courage.*] Leave me alone with her. [*Giggles.*] Your King commands you. [LA TREMOUILLE *and the* ARCHBISHOP *bow and leave.* CHARLES *holds his noble pose for an instant, then bursts into laughter.*] And they went. It's the first time they ever obeyed me. [*Very worried.*] You haven't come here to kill me? [*She smiles.*] No. No, of course not. You have an honest face. I've lived so long with those pirates that I've almost forgotten what an honest face looks like. Are there other people who have honest faces?

Joan [*gravely*]. Many, sire.

Charles. I never see them. Brutes and whores, that's all I ever see. And the little Queen. She's nice, but she's stupid. And Agnes. She's not stupid—and she's not nice. [*He climbs on his throne, hangs his feet over one of the arms and sighs.*] All right. Start boring me. Tell me that I ought to be a great King.

Joan [*softly*]. Yes, Charles.

Charles. Listen. If you want to make an impression on the Archbishop and the council, we'll have to stay in this room for at least an hour. If you talk to me of God and the Kingdom of France, I'll never live through the hour. Let's do something else. Do you know how to play at cards?

Joan. I don't know what it is.

Charles. It is a nice game invented to amuse my papa when he was ill. I'll teach you. [*He begins to hunt for the cards.*] I hope they haven't stolen them. They steal everything from me around here and cards are expensive. Only the wealthiest princes can have them. I got mine from papa. I'll never have the price of another pack. If those pigs have stolen them—— No. Here they are. [*He finds them in his pocket.*] My papa was crazy. Went crazy young—in his thirties. Did you know that? Sometimes I am glad I am a bastard. At least I don't have to be so frightened of going crazy. Then sometimes I wish I were his son and knew that I was meant to be a king. It's confusing.

Joan. Of the two, which would you prefer?

Charles. Well, on the days when I have a little courage, I'd risk going crazy. But on the days when I haven't any courage—that's from Sunday to Saturday—I would rather let everything go to hell and live in peace in some foreign land on whatever little money I have left.

Joan. Today, Charles, is this one of the days when you have courage?

Charles. Today? [*He thinks a minute.*] Yes, it seems to me I have a little bit today. Not much, but a little bit. I was sharp with the Archbishop, and——

Joan. You will have courage every day. Beginning now.

Charles. You have a charm in a bottle or a basket?

Joan. I have a charm.

Charles. You are a witch? You can tell me, you know, because I don't care. I swear to you that I won't repeat it. I have a horror of people being tortured. A long time ago, they made me witness the burning of a heretic at the stake. I vomited all night long.

Joan. I am not a witch. But I have a charm.

Charles. Sell it to me without telling the others.

Joan. I will give it to you, Charles. For nothing.

Charles. Then I don't want it. What you get free costs too much. [*He shuffles the cards.*] I act like a fool so that

people will let me alone. My papa was so crazy they think
I am, too. He was very crazy, did all kinds of strange things,
some of them very funny. One day he thought it would
be nice to have a great funeral, but nobody happened
to die just then so he decided to bury a man who'd been
dead four years. It cost a fortune to dig him out and put
him back, but it was fun. [*He laughs merrily, catches himself, stares at* JOAN.] But don't think you can catch me
too easily. I know a little about the world.

Joan. You know too much. You are too smart.

Charles. Yes. Because I must defend myself against these
cutthroats. They've got large bones, I've got puny sticks.
But my head's harder than theirs and I've clung to my
throne by using it.

Joan [*gently*]. I would like to defend you against them,
Charles. I would give my life to do it.

Charles. Do you mean that?

Joan. Yes. And I'm not afraid of anything.

Charles. You're lucky. Or you're a liar. Sit down and I'll
teach you to play.

Joan. All right. You teach me this game and I'll teach
you another game.

Charles. What game do you know?

Joan. How not to be too smart. [*Softly.*] And how not
to be afraid.

Charles [*laughs*]. You'll be here a lifetime, my girl. Now.
See these cards? They have pictures painted on them.
Kings, queens and knaves, just as in real life. Now which
would you say was the most powerful, which one could
take all the rest?

Joan. The king.

Charles. Well, you're wrong. This large heart can take
the king. It can put him to rout, break his heart, win all
his money. This card is called——

Joan. I know. It is called God. Because God is more
powerful than kings.

Charles. Oh, leave God alone for a minute. It's called
the ace. Are you running this game? God this and God
that. You talk as if you dined with Him last night. Didn't
anybody tell you that the English also say their prayers to
God? Every man thinks God is on his side. The rich and
powerful know He is. But we're not rich and powerful,
you and I—and France.

Joan. That isn't what God cares about. He is angry

with us because we have no courage left. God doesn't like frightened people.

Charles. Then He certainly doesn't like me. And if He doesn't like me, why should I like Him? He could have given me courage. I wanted it.

Joan [*sharply*]. Is God your nurse? Couldn't you have tried to do a little better? Even with those legs.

Charles. I am sorry to know that my legs have already come to your attention. It's because of my legs that Agnes can never really love me. That's sad, isn't it?

Joan. No.

Charles. Why not?

Joan. Because your head is ugly, too, and you can't be sad about everything. But what's inside your head isn't ugly, because God gave you sense. And what do you do with it? Play cards. Bounce a ball in the air. Play baby tricks with the Archbishop and act the fool for all to see. You have a son. But what have you made for him? Nothing. And when he's grown he, too, will have a right to say, "God didn't like me, so why should I like Him?" But when he says God he will mean you because every son thinks his father is God. And when he's old enough to know that, he will hate you for what you didn't give him.

Charles. Give him? What can I give him? I'm glad to be alive. I've told you the truth: I am afraid. I've always been and I always will be.

Joan. And now I'll tell you the truth: I am also afraid. [*With force.*] And why not? Only the stupid are not afraid. What is the matter with you? Don't you understand that it was far more dangerous for me to get here than it is for you to build a kingdom? I've been in danger every minute of the way, and every minute of the way I was frightened. I don't want to be beaten, I don't want pain, I don't want to die. I am scared.

Charles [*softly*]. What do you do when you get scared?

Joan. Act as if I wasn't. It's that simple. Try it. Say to yourself, yes, I am afraid. But it's nobody else's business, so go on, go on. And you do go on.

Charles [*softly*]. Where do you go?

Joan [*slowly, carefully*]. To the English, outside Orléans. And when you get there and see the cannon and the archers, and you know you are outnumbered, you will say to yourself, all right, they are stronger than I am, and that frightens me, as well it should. But I'll march right through because I had sense enough to get frightened first.

Charles. March through a stronger army? That can't be done.

Joan. Yes it can. If you have sense and courage. Do you want to know what happened in my village last year? They tell the story as a miracle now but it wasn't. The Bouchon boy went hunting. He's the best poacher in our village, and this day he was poaching on the master's grounds. The master kept a famous dog, trained to kill, and the dog found the Bouchon boy. The boy was caught and death faced him. So he threw a stone and the dog turned his head. That was sense. And while the dog turned his head the boy decided the only way was to stand and fight. That was courage. He strangled the dog. That was victory. See?

Charles. Didn't the dog bite him?

Joan [*as if to a stupid child*]. You're like the old people in the village—you really believe in miracles. Of course the dog bit him. But I told you the boy had sense, and sense saved his life. God gave man an inside to his head, and He naturally doesn't want to see it wasted. [*Smiles.*] See? That's my secret. The witches' secret. What will you pay me for it now?

Charles. What do you want?

Joan. The army of France. Believe in God and give me the army.

Charles [*moves away from her*]. Tomorrow. I'll have time to get ready——

Joan [*moves after him*]. No, right now. You are ready. Come on, Charlie.

Charles. Perhaps I am. Perhaps I've been waiting for you and didn't know—— [*Laughs nervously.*] Shall we send for the Archbishop and La Tremouille and tell them that I have decided to give the army to you? It would be fun to see their faces.

Joan. Call them.

Charles [*in a panic*]. No. I am frightened.

Joan. Are you as afraid as you ever can be, ever were or will be, then, now and in the future? Are you sick?

Charles [*holding his stomach*]. I think so.

Joan. Good. Good. Then the worst is over. By the time they get scared, you'll be all over yours. Now, if you're as sick as you can get, I'll call them. [*She runs upstage and calls out.*] Monseigneur the Archbishop. Monseigneur de La Tremouille. Please come to the Dauphin.

Charles [*almost happy*]. I am very sick.

Joan [*moves him gently to the throne and arranges his hands and feet*]. God is smiling. He is saying to Himself, "Look at that little Charles. He is sicker than he's ever been in his life. But he has called in his enemies and will face them. My, such a thing is wonderful." [*With great force.*] Hang on, Charles. We'll be in Orléans. We'll march right up.

The ARCHBISHOP *and* LA TREMOUILLE *enter, followed by* YOLANDE *and the* COURTIERS.

Archbishop. You sent for us, Your Highness?

Charles [*very sharply*]. I have made a decision. The Royal Army is now under the command of Joan the Virgin Maid, here present. [*Roars out.*] I wish to hear no word from you. None.

They stare at CHARLES.

Joan [*clapping her hands*]. Good. Good, my Charles. You see how simple it is? You're getting better looking, Charles. [CHARLES *giggles. Then he suddenly stops the giggle and stares at* JOAN. *She stares at him. She drops to her knees.*] Oh, my God, I thank you.

Charles. There is not time to lose. We will need your blessing, sire. Give it to us. [*To* LA TREMOUILLE.] Kneel down, sire.

LA TREMOUILLE, YOLANDE *and the* COURTIERS *drop to their knees. As the* ARCHBISHOP *pronounces the blessing, we hear the chorus sing the* Benedictus. *A* COURT PAGE *gives a sword to* THE DAUPHIN. THE DAUPHIN *gives the sword to* JOAN. WARWICK *comes into the scene and moves downstage to address the audience.*

Warwick. In real life, it didn't work out exactly that way. As before, now, and forever, there were long discussions in the French fashion. The council met. Desperate, frightened, with nothing to lose, they decided to dress the girl in battle flags and let her go forth as a symbol of something or other. It worked well. A simple girl inspired simple people to get themselves killed for simple ideals.

JOAN *rises and moves away from* THE DAUPHIN. *She puts her hand on the sword, and lowers her head in prayer.*

Curtain.

ACT TWO

Before the curtain rises we hear the music of a soldier's song. The SOLDIERS *sing of* JOAN *and her victories. As the curtain rises we see* JOAN, *in full armor, move across the stage to the music. She carries her sword high above her head in a kind of hero's salute to a group of admiring* VILLAGE WOMEN. *She marches off as* CAUCHON, THE INQUISITOR, *and the* JUDGES *take their places.* WARWICK *moves down to address the audience.*

WARWICK. She was in the field. from that day laws of strategy no longer made any difference. We began to lose. They say that Joan worked no miracles at Orléans. They say that our plan of isolated fortresses was absurd, that they could have been taken by anyone who had courage enough to attack. But that is not true. Sir John Talbot was not a fool. He's a good soldier, as he proved long before that miserable business, and after it. By all military laws his fortified positions could not have been broken. And they could not have been broken except by—— Well, by what? What shall we call it even now? The unknown, the unguessed—God, if that's the way you believe. The girl was a lark in the skies of France, high over the heads of her soldiers, singing a joyous, crazy song of courage. There she was, outlined against the sun, a target for everybody to shoot at, flying straight and happy into battle. To Frenchmen, she was the soul of France. She was to me, too. [*Smiles, to* CAUCHON.] Monseigneur, I like France. Of course, you have your fair share of fools and blackguards. [*Somebody coughs nervously.* WARWICK *laughs.*] But every once in a while a lark does appear in your sky and then everything stupid and evil is wiped out by the shadow of the lark. I like France very much.

Cauchon. Your guns prove your affection.

Warwick. They prove nothing. I love animals but I hunt with guns. [*Sharply.*] Too difficult to explain to a

man of your simple piety, Monseigneur. So let's get on
with the trial. The lark has been captured. The King she
crowned, the royal court she saved—for a minute, at least
—are about to abandon their little girl. Their loyalty
lasted through victory. When we took her prisoner, their
luck ran out. They are returning as fast as they can to
the old, stale political games.

CHARLES *and the* ARCHBISHOP *appear.*

Joan [*as she goes back to the trial*]. Charles. [*No answer.*]
Charles.

Charles [*he turns toward her, then turns away again. He
speaks to the* ARCHBISHOP]. I didn't want to send the
letter. I tell you I have a feeling that——

Archbishop. The letter was necessary, sire. We must be
rid of the girl now. She is dangerous to us.

Charles. I didn't like the letter——

Cauchon [*gently, to* JOAN]. Yesterday Charles disavowed
you in a letter sent to all his cities.

Joan. Charles. [*No answer. To* CAUCHON.] Well. He is
still my King. And he is your King.

Cauchon. No, he is not my King. We are loyal subjects
of Henry of Lancaster, King of England, King of France.
Joan, we love France as much as you do, but we believe
that English Henry will put an end to this terrible war.
That is why we have taken him as king. The man you
call king is, for us, a rebel, claiming a throne that does
not belong to him, refusing a good peace because it does
not suit his ambitions. He is a puppet man, and we do
not wish him as master. [*Sharply.*] But I only confuse
you. This is not a political trial in which you state your
beliefs and we state ours. We are here only to return a lost
girl to the bosom of the Sainted Mother Church.

Joan [*pointing to* CHARLES]. That puppet man is the
king God gave you. He is a poor, skinny, miserable thing,
but given a little time——

Charles [*to the* ARCHBISHOP]. I object as much to being
defended in this fashion as I do to being attacked.

Archbishop [*maliciously*]. Let them speak, sire. Turn
away. It will be over soon. They will speed up the trial
now. They will burn her at the stake.

Charles [*softly, as if he were sick*]. I hate violence. It
makes me sick——

Archbishop [*sharply*]. Count yourself a lucky man. If

the English do not condemn her to death, we will have to do it.

Charles. I will never do that, Monseigneur. After all, the girl loved me. I will never do that.

Archbishop. No, sire, certainly not. We will do it for you.

They move off.

Cauchon [to JOAN]. You are not stupid, Joan. You can understand what we think. You swear that you heard voices and you swear to the messages they sent you. But because we believe in another king, we cannot believe that it was God Who sent you to fight against us. We are priests but we are men. And man cannot believe that God has turned against him.

Joan. You'll have to believe it when we've beaten you.

Cauchon. Ah, you answer like a foolish child.

Joan. My Voices told me——

Cauchon. How often have we heard those words? Do you think you are the only girl who has ever heard voices?

Joan. No, I don't think that.

Cauchon. Not the first and not the last. Every village priest has had his share of young girls in crisis. If the Church believed every sick child—— [*Wearily.*] You have good sense. You were commander in chief of the army.

Joan [*with pride and sudden energy*]. I commanded brave men. *They* believed in me, and *they* followed me.

Cauchon. Yes. And if on the morning of an attack one of your brave men had suddenly heard Voices that ordered him *not* to follow you, what would you have done with him?

JOAN *laughs and there is sudden, loud laughter from off-stage* SOLDIERS.

Joan [*calls out toward the laughter*]. The Seigneur Bishop is a priest. He has never been close to you, my soldiers. [*The laughter dies off. Amused, she turns back to* CAUCHON.] A good army fights, drinks, rapes—but they don't hear voices.

Cauchon. A jest is not an answer. You know that a disobedient soldier in your army, in any army in this world, would be silenced. The Church Militant is also an army of this earth and we, its priests, do not believe in the Divine origin of *your* disobedience. Nobody believes in you now, Joan.

Joan. The common people believe in me——

Cauchon. They believe in anything. They will follow another leader tomorrow. You are alone, all alone.

Joan. I think as I think. You have the right to punish me for it.

Cauchon. You are strong and you are stubborn, but that is not a sign that God is on your side.

Joan. When something is black I cannot say that it is white.

The Promoter [*rises and speaks angrily to* JOAN]. What spell did you cast upon the man you call your king? By what means did you force him to give his armies to you?

Joan. I have told you. I cast no spell upon him.

The Promoter. It is said that you gave him a piece of mandrake.

Joan. I don't know what mandrake is.

The Promoter. Your secret has a name. We want to know what it is.

Joan [*sharply*]. I gave him courage. That is the only word I know for what was between us. When a girl says one word of good sense and people listen to her, that's proof that God is present and no strange spells or miracles are needed.

Ladvenu [*softly*]. Now there is a good and humble answer, Monseigneur. An answer that cannot be held against her.

The Promoter. I do not agree. She is saying that she does not believe in the miracles as they are taught in our Holy Book. [*To* JOAN.] You declare that you deny the act of Jesus at the Marriage of Cana? You declare that you deny the miracle raising of Lazarus from the dead?

Joan. No, Messire. Our Seigneur changed the water into wine and retied the thread of Lazarus' life. But for Him Who is Master of life and death, that is no more miracle than if I were to make thread for my loom.

The Promoter [*with great anger, to the* JUDGES]. Mark her words. Write them down. She says that Jesus made no miracles.

Joan [*runs toward the* JUDGES *with great force*]. I say that true miracles are not tricks performed by gypsies in a village square. True miracles are created by men when they use the courage and intelligence that God gave them.

Cauchon. You are saying to us, *to us*, that the real miracle of God on this earth is man. Man, who is naught but sin and error, impotent against his own wickedness——

Joan. And man is also strength and courage and splendor in his most desperate minutes. I know man because I have seen him. He is a miracle.

Ladvenu [*quickly, nervously*]. Monseigneur, Joan speaks an awkward language. But she speaks from the heart, and without guile. Perhaps when we press down upon her, we risk making her say here what she does not mean.

The Promoter [*to* JOAN]. Do you believe that man is the greatest miracle of God?

Joan. Yes, Messire.

The Promoter [*shouts*]. You blaspheme. Man is impurity and lust. The dark acts of his nights are the acts of a beast——

Joan. Yes, Messire. And the same man who acts the beast will rise from a brothel bed and throw himself before a blade to save the soldier who walks beside him. Nobody knows why he does. He doesn't know. But he does it, and he dies, cleansed and shining. He has done both good and evil, and thus twice acted like a man. That makes God happy because God made him for just this contradiction. We are good and we are evil, and that is what was meant.

There is indignant movement among the JUDGES. THE INQUISITOR *rises, holds up his hand. Immediately there is silence. They have been waiting for him to speak.*

The Inquisitor. I have at no time spoken. [*To* JOAN.] I speak to you now. I represent here the Holy Inquisition of which I am the Vicar for France. I have arrived from the south of Spain, and have little knowledge of the French and English war. It does not concern me whether Charles or the Lancaster Henry rules over France. It does not concern me that the French Duke of Burgundy has joined the English, and thus Frenchman fights French brother. They are all children of the Church. Nor have I interest in defending the temporal integrity of the Church in these quarrels. [*Turns toward* CAUCHON.] We leave such matters to our bishops and our priests. [*Bows to* CAUCHON.] Nor time to be curious about the kindness and humanity which seem to move the judgment. [*Sharply, toward* THE PROMOTER.] Nor do we find interest in these endless dreams of the Devil that haunt the nights of the Promoter. The Holy Inquisition fights in the dark world of night, against an enemy it alone can recognize. [*Stops, moves toward* WARWICK.] We do not care that the princes of the earth have sometimes laughed at the vigilance with which we hunt the enemy, the time and thought that we give to the judgment of the enemy. The princes of the earth are sometimes hurrying and shallow men. They remove their enemies with a length of rope and, in the crudeness of their thinking, they believe the danger ended there. We hear the mocking laughter of such men and we forgive it. The Holy Inquisition concerns itself in matters unknown to temporal kings. Our enemy is a great enemy and has a great name. [*To* JOAN.] You know his name?

Joan. No, Messire. I do not understand you.

The Inquisitor. You will understand me. Stand up. You will answer now to me. Are you a Christian?

Joan. Yes, Messire.

The Inquisitor. The trees that shaded the village church threw shadows on the house of your father. The bells of the Church brought you to prayer and sent you to work. The men we sent to your village all bring the same word: you were a pious girl.

Joan. Yes, Messire.

The Inquisitor. You were a tender little girl. And you were a tender woman. You cried for the wounded in every battle——

Joan. Yes. I cried for the wounded. They were French.

The Inquisitor. And you cried for the English. You stayed with a wounded English soldier who screamed through a night of pain. You held him until he died, calling him your child and giving him a hope of Heaven.

Joan. You know that, Messire?

The Inquisitor. Yes. The Holy Inquisition knows much of you, Joan. Grave considerate talk was given to you. And they sent me here to judge you.

Ladvenu. Messire Inquisitor, Joan has always acted with kindness and Christian charity, but this court has buried it in silence. I am happy to hear you remind them that——

The Inquisitor [*sternly*]. Silence, Brother Ladvenu. I ask you not to forget that the Holy Inquisition alone is qualified to distinguish between theological virtues and that troubled brew that man so boastfully calls the milk of human kindness. [*Turns to the* JUDGES.] Ah, my masters. What strange matters concern you all. Your business is to defend the Faith. But you see the kind eyes of a young girl and you are overwhelmed.

Ladvenu. Our Lord loved with charity and kindness, Messire. He said to a sinner, "Go in peace." He said——

The Inquisitor. Silence, I said to you, Brother Ladvenu. [*Softly, carefully.*] You are young. I am told your learning is very great and that is why you were admitted to this trial. Therefore I am hopeful that experience will teach you not to translate the great words into the vulgar tongue, nor embroider the meaning to suit your heart. Be seated and be silent. [*He turns back to* JOAN.] You were very young when you first heard your Voices.

Joan. Yes, Messire.

The Inquisitor. I am going to shock you: there is nothing very exceptional about the Voices you heard in those days. Our archives are full of such cases. There are many young visionaries. Girls frequently experience a crisis of mysticism. It passes. But with you—and your priest should have recognized it—the crisis was prolonged. The messages became precise and the Celestial Voices began to use most unusual words.

Joan. Yes. My Voices told me to go and save the Kingdom of France.

The Inquisitor. A strange order to an ignorant peasant girl.

Joan. Not so strange, Messire, because it turned out to be the truth.

The Inquisitor. I say a strange order to a girl who had seen nothing of war. The troubles of France could have been no more to you than tales told at twilight. And yet suddenly you went out into the great world of kings and battles, convinced that it was your mission to aid your brothers in their struggle to keep the land on which they were born, and which they imagine belongs to them.

Joan. Our Lord could not want the English to kill us and to conquer us. He could not want us to live by their laws and wishes. When they have gone back across the sea, to their own land, I will not go and pick a quarrel with them. They can rest easy in their own house. I've always said that.

The Inquisitor [*sternly*]. And I say your presumption is not suited to my taste.

Ladvenu. She did not mean, Messire—she speaks in a youthful fashion.

Cauchon [*softly*]. Be still, Brother Ladvenu.

The Inquisitor [*to* JOAN]. It would have been more fitting for a pious girl to have spent her life in prayers and penitence and, in such manner, obtained from Heaven the promise that the English would be defeated.

Joan. I did all that. But I think you must first strike and then pray. That's the way God wants it. I had to explain to Charles how to attack. And he believed me and Dunois believed me and La Hire—good men, wild bulls they were, and warriors. Ah, we had some fine battles together. It was good, in the dawn, riding boot to boot with friends——

The Promoter. To the kill. Did your Voices instruct you to kill?

Joan [*angrily*]. I have never killed a man. But war is war.

Cauchon. You love war, Joan.

Joan [*softly*]. Yes. And that is one of the sins from which God will have to absolve me. But I did not like pain or death. At night, on the battlefield, I would weep for the dead——

The Promoter. You would weep at night for the dead but by morning you were shouting for a new battle.

Joan [*moves to him, with great force*]. I say God did not wish one Englishman to remain in France. That's not so hard to understand, is it? We had to do our work, that's all. You are wise men, you think too much. Your heads are filled with too much celestial science. You don't understand even the simplest things any more—things that my dullest soldier would understand without talk. Isn't that true, La Hire?

She stumbles, moves away from the JUDGES, *and falls to the ground. The lights dim on the trial and we hear again the whistling of the soldier's song.* LA HIRE, *in full armor, appears upstage and moves toward* JOAN.

La Hire. The morning has come, Madame Joan.

She sits up, shivers, stares at LA HIRE.

Joan. The night was cold, La Hire. [*He sits beside her, warms her hands in his own.* JOAN *looks toward the trial, then up, then back to* LA HIRE, *as if she were confused by the place and the time.*] Good La Hire. Great La Hire. You've really come to help me as I knew you would.

La Hire [*he takes out an onion and begins to peel it*].
Come to help you? I was sleeping fifty feet from you,
Madame Joan, watching over you as I always do. [*She
laughs and moves closer to him.*] Don't come too close. I
stink of wine and onions.

Joan. No, no. You smell fine.

La Hire. Usually you tell me I stink too much to be a
Christian. You say I am a danger to the army because if
the wind is behind me the English will know where we
are.

Joan. Oh, La Hire, I was so stupid in those days. You
know how girls are. Nothing ever happens to them, they
know nothing, but they pretend they know everything. But
I am not so stupid any more. You smell good because you
smell like a man.

La Hire. I can't stand a man who washes in the field
because to me a man like that isn't a man. I was brought
up on an onion in the morning. The rest can have their
sausage. The smell is more distinguished, you tell me. I
know you think a breakfast onion is a sin.

Joan [*laughs*]. A breakfast onion is not a sin. Nothing
that is true is a sin, La Hire. I was a fool. I tormented
you. But I didn't know anything then. I didn't. [*Softly.*]
Ah, you smell so good. Sweat, onions, wine. You have all
the smells a man should have. And you curse, you kill, and
you think of nothing but women.

La Hire. Me?

Joan. You. But I tell you that with all your sins you
are like a bright new coin in the hand of God.

La Hire. Well, I have had a bastard life and when I go
into battle, I say my prayers. I say, "God, I hope You'll help
me as I would help You if You faced those God
damned——"

Joan [*shocked*]. La Hire!

La Hire [*softly*]. To tell you the truth, I'm frightened
of what will happen to me if I get killed.

Joan. Paradise will happen to you. They are looking
forward to having you with them.

La Hire. That gives me heart, Madame Joan. I've
always wanted to go to Paradise. But if it's all full of
saints and bishops, I might not be too happy——

Joan. It's full of men like you. It's the others who are
kept waiting at the gates—— [*Suddenly.*] The gates. The
gates of Orléans. They're ahead of us—the day has come,

La Hire. To horse, my boy, to horse. [*She climbs on her stool.* La Hire *stands next to her. They hold imaginary reins in their hands as they ride imaginary horses.*] It's dawn, La Hire. The woods are still wet from the night, the trees are still dark and strange. It's fine to ride into battle with a good soldier by your side.

La Hire. Some people don't like it. Some people like to make a little garden out of life and walk down a path.

Joan. But they never know what we know. [*As if she were puzzled and ashamed.*] Death has to be waiting at the end of the ride before you truly see the earth, and feel your heart, and love the world. [*Suddenly, in a whisper.*] There are three English soldiers. [*She looks back.*] We've outridden the others. We are alone.

La Hire. Get off your horse, Madame Joan. Lead him back. You have never used your sword.

Joan. No. Don't meet them alone, La Hire——

La Hire [*he draws his sword*]. I'll kill them . . . God damned English bastards. [*Sword in hand, he disappears.*]

Joan [*kneels in prayer*]. Dear God, he is as good as bread. I answer for him. He's my friend. [*She turns toward the* Judges, *angry, defiant.*] The last word will not be spoken at this trial. La Hire will come to deliver me. He will bring three hundred lancers, I know them all, and they will take me from my prison——

Cauchon. Yes. They came to deliver you, Joan.

Joan [*running to him*]. Where are they? I knew they would come——

Cauchon. They came to the gates of the city. When they saw how many English soldiers were here, they turned and went away.

Joan [*shaken*]. Ah. They turned and went away. Without fighting? [Cauchon *turns away.*] Yes. Of course. It was *I* who taught them to do just that. I would say to them, "Have a little sense. It doesn't cost a sou. Learn not to be brave when you are outnumbered, unless—— [*Violently.*] That's what they did. They went to get reinforcements for me——

Cauchon. No. Your friends will not return, Joan.

Joan. That's not true. "Learn not to be brave when you are outnumbered," I said, "*unless* you can't retreat. Then you must fight because there is no other way——" [*Proudly.*] La Hire will return. Because there is no other way to save me now.

Cauchon. La Hire sells himself to whichever prince has need. When he discovered that your Charles was tired of war and would sign any peace, he marched his men toward Germany. He looks for a new land on which to try his sword. [*Comes to her.*] You have been abandoned. It will sound strange to you, but the priests of this court are the only men who care for your soul and for your life. Humble yourself, Joan, and the Church will take your hand. In your heart, you are a child of the Church.

Joan [*softly*]. Yes.

Cauchon. Trust yourself to the Church. She will weigh your deeds and take from you the agony of self-judgment.

Joan [*after a long silence*]. For that which is of the Faith, I turn to the Church, as I have always done. But what I am, I will not denounce. What I have done, I will not deny.

There is a shocked silence. Then there is great movement in the courtroom, as if this were the answer that would bring the judgment. THE INQUISITOR *rises. The* PRIESTS *are suddenly silent.* THE INQUISITOR *slowly moves before the* PRIESTS, *peering into their faces. The* PRIESTS *draw back, frightened.*

The Inquisitor [*to one* PRIEST]. Not you. [*To another* PRIEST.] Not you. [*To a third* PRIEST.] Not you. [*Pauses before* CAUCHON, *stares at him.*] And not you, Bishop of Beauvais. I have spoken of the great enemy, but not even now do you know his name. You do not understand on whom you sit in judgment, nor the issues of the judgment. I have told you that the Holy Inquisition is not concerned with royal rank or merchant gold or peasant birth. To us, a scholar in his room is equal in importance to an emperor in his palace. Because *we* know the name of our enemy. His name is natural man. [*There is silence.* LADVENU *moves forward.*] Can you not see that this girl is the symbol of that which is most to be feared? She is the enemy. She is man as he stands against us. Look at her. Frightened, hungry, dirty, abandoned by all, and no longer even sure that those Voices in the air ever spoke to her at all. Does her misery make her a suppliant begging God for mercy and for light? No. She turns away from God. She dares to stand under torture, thrashing about like a proud beast in the stable of her dungeon. She raises her eyes, not to God, but to man's image of himself.

I have need to remind you, Masters, that he who loves Man does not love God.

Ladvenu [*with great force*]. It cannot be. Jesus Himself became a man.

The Inquisitor [*turns to* CAUCHON]. Seigneur Bishop, I must ask you to send your young assessor from this courtroom. I will consider after this session whether he may return or whether I will bring charges against him. [*Shouts.*] Against him, or against any other. *Any* other. I would bring charges against myself if God should let me lose my way.

Cauchon [*softly*]. Leave us, Brother Ladvenu.

Ladvenu. Messire Inquisitor, I owe you obedience. I will not speak again. But I will pray to our Lord Jesus that you remember the weakness of your small, sad, lonely —enemy. [LADVENU *exits.*]

The Inquisitor. Do you have need to question her further? To ask all the heavy words that are listed in your legal papers? What need to ask her why she still persists in wearing man's dress when it is contrary to the commandments? Why she dared the sin of living among men as a man? The deeds no longer matter. What she has done is of less importance than why she did it, the answers less important than the one answer. It is a fearful answer, "What I am, I will not. . . ." You wish to say it again? Say it.

Joan [*slowly, softly*]. What I am, I will not denounce. What I have done, I will not deny.

The Inquisitor [*carefully, as if he has taken the measure of an enemy*]. You have heard it. Down through the ages, from dungeon, from torture chamber, from the fire of the stake. Ask her and she will say with those others, "Take my life. I will give it because I will not deny what I have done." This is what they say, all of them, the insolent breed. The men who dare our God. Those who say no to us. [*He moves toward* JOAN. CAUCHON *rises.*] Well, you and all like you shall be made to say yes. You put the Idea in peril, and that you will not be allowed to do. [*Turns to the* JUDGES.] The girl is only a monstrous symbol of the faith decayed. Therefore I now demand her immediate punishment. I demand that she be excommunicated from the Church. I demand that she be returned to secular authority there to receive her punishment. I ask the secular arm to limit her sentence to this side of death and the mutilation of her members. [CAUCHON *moves to* THE INQUISITOR *as if to stop the judgment.*]

Warwick [*to* CAUCHON]. A passionate man and so sincere. I think he means simply to throw the dirty work to me. I am the secular authority here. Why didn't your French Charles have her burned? It was his job.

Charles [*very disturbed*]. I don't want to do it. I don't like killing.

A large, masked figure appears.

Cauchon [*calls to the masked man*]. Master Executioner, is the wood for the stake dry and ready to burn?

Executioner. All is ready. Things will go according to custom. But I will not be able to help the girl this time.

Cauchon. What do you mean help her, Master?

Executioner. We let the first flames rise high. Then I climb up behind the victims and strangle them the rest of the way. It's easier and quicker for everybody. But I have had special instructions this time to make the fire very high. And so it will take longer and I will not be able to reach her for the act of mercy.

Cauchon [*moves to* JOAN]. Did you hear that?

Joan. I've remembered a dream from years ago. I woke screaming and ran to my mother—— [*Screams as if in pain.*] Ah.

Cauchon [*desperately*]. Joan, for the last time I offer you the saving hand of your Mother Church. We wish to save you, but we can delay no longer. The crowd has been waiting since dawn. They eat their food, scold their children, make jokes, and grow impatient. You are famous and they have nothing better to do with their lives than bring garlands to the famous—or watch them burn.

Joan [*as if she is still in the dream*]. I forgive them, Messire. I forgive you, too.

The Promoter [*furiously*]. Monseigneur speaks to you like a father in order to save your miserable soul and you answer by forgiving him.

Joan. Monseigneur speaks to me gently, he takes great pains to seduce me, but I do not know whether he means to save me or conquer me. In any case, he will be obliged to have me burned.

Cauchon [*comes to her*]. For the last time I say: Confess your sins and return to us. We will save you.

Joan [*she clings to his robe*]. I wish to return to the

Church. I want the Holy Communion. I have asked for it over and over again. But they have refused to give it to me.

Cauchon. After your confession, when you have begun your penance, we will give it to you. [*There is no answer. Very softly.*] Are you not afraid to die?

Joan. Yes. I am afraid. What difference does that make? I've always been so afraid of fire. [*Gasps.*] I've remembered a dream——

Cauchon [*pulls her to him*]. Joan, we cannot believe in the Divinity of your Voices. But if we are wrong—and certainly that thought has crossed our minds——

The Promoter [*furious*]. No, I say no. Even to you, my Bishop of Beauvais——

Cauchon [*to* JOAN]. But if we are wrong then we will have committed a monstrous sin of ignorance and we will pay for it the rest of our eternal lives. But we are the priests of your Church. Trust our belief that we are right, as you trusted your good village priest. Place yourself in our hands. You will be at peace.

Joan. I cannot follow what you say. I am tired. Oh, sire, I do not sleep at night. I come here and all is said so fast that I cannot understand. You torture me with such gentle words, and your voice is so kind. I would rather have you beat me——

Cauchon. I talk to you thus because my pride is less than yours.

Joan [*she moves away from him, as if she were sick and wanted to be alone*]. Pride? I have been a prisoner so long —I think my head is sick and old, and the bottom of me does not hold any more. Sometimes I don't know where I am and my dungeon seems a great beech tree. I am hungry, or I was, and I want a taste of country milk——

Cauchon [*desperately, as if he were at the end*]. Look at me, Joan, keep your mind here. I am an old man. I have killed people in the defense of my beliefs. I am so close to death myself that I do not wish to kill again. I do not wish to kill a little girl. Be kind. [*Cries out.*] Help me to save you.

Joan [*very softly; broken now*]. What do you want me to say? Please tell me in simple words.

Cauchon. I am going to ask you three questions. Answer yes three times. That is all. [*With passion.*] Help me, Joan.

Joan. But could I sleep a few hours, sire?

Cauchon. No! We cannot wait. Do you entrust yourself with humility to the Holy Roman and Apostolic Church, to our Holy Father, the Pope, and to his bishops? Will you rely upon them, and upon no one else, to be your judges? Do you make the complete and total act of submission? Do you ask to be returned to the bosom of the Church?

Joan. Yes, but—[THE INQUISITOR *rises.* CAUCHON *becomes nervous.*] I don't want to say the opposite of what my Voices told me. I don't ever want to bear false witness against Charlie. I fought so hard for the glory of his consecration. Oh, that was a day when he was crowned. The sun was out——

Charles [*to* JOAN]. It was a nice day and I'll always remember it. But I'd rather not think it was a divine miracle. I'd rather people didn't think that God sent you to me. Because now that you're a prisoner, and thought to be a heretic and a sorceress, they think that God has abandoned me. I'm in bad enough trouble without that kind of gossip. Just forget about me and go your way.

JOAN *bows her head.*

Cauchon. Do you wish me to repeat the question? [JOAN *does not answer.* CAUCHON *is angry.*] Are you mad? You understand now that we are your only protectors, that this is the last thing I can do for you? You cannot bargain and quibble like a peasant at a village fair. You are an impudent girl, and I now become angry with you. You should be on your knees to the Church.

Joan [*falls to her knees*]. Messire, deep in your heart do you believe that our Lord wishes me to submit to the judgment?

Cauchon. I so believe.

Joan [*softly*]. Then I submit.

There is great movement in the court. THE INQUISITOR *rises;* THE PROMOTER *moves to him.*

Cauchon [*very tired now*]. You promise to renounce forever the bearing of arms?

Joan. But, Messire, there is still so much to do——

Cauchon [*angrily*]. Nothing more will ever be done by you.

Warwick. That is true, Joan.

Charles. And if you're thinking of helping me again,

please don't. I won't ever use you any more. It would be very dangerous for me.

Joan [*broken now, almost as if she were asleep*]. I renounce forever the bearing of arms.

Cauchon [*in great haste*]. Do you renounce forever the wearing of that brazen uniform?

Joan. You have asked me that over and over again. The uniform doesn't matter. My Voices told me to put it on.

The Promoter. It was the Devil who told you to put it on.

Joan. Oh, Messire, put away the Devil for today. My Voices chose the uniform because my Voices have good sense. [*With great effort.*] I had to ride with soldiers. It was necessary they not think of me as a girl. It was necessary they see in me nothing but a soldier like themselves. That is all the sense there was to it.

Cauchon. But why have you persisted in wearing it in prison? You have been asked this question in many examinations and your refusal to answer has become of great significance to your judges.

Joan. And I have asked over and over to be taken to a Church prison. Then I would take off my man's uniform.

The Promoter [*to* CAUCHON]. Monseigneur, the girl is playing with us, as from the first. I do not understand what she says or why you——

Joan [*angry*]. One doesn't have to be an educated man to understand what I am saying.

The Promoter [*turns to* JUDGES]. She says that she submits to the Church. But I tell you that as long as she refuses to put aside that Devil dress, I will exercise my rights as master judge of heretics and witchcraft. [*To* CAUCHON.] Strange pressures have been put upon all of us. I know not from where they come, but I tell even you——

Joan. I have said that if you put me in a Church prison I will take off this uniform.

The Promoter. You will not bargain. Put aside that dress or, no matter who feels otherwise, you will be declared a sorceress.

Joan [*softly, to* CAUCHON]. I am not alone in prison. Two English soldier guards are in the cell with me night and day. The nights are long. I am in chains. I try hard not to sleep, but sometimes I am too tired—— [*She stops, embarrassed.*] In this uniform it is easier for me to defend myself.

Cauchon [*in great anger*]. Have you had so to defend yourself since the beginning of this trial?

WARWICK *moves to* JOAN.

Joan. Every night since I've been captured. I don't have much sleep. In the mornings, when I am brought before you, I am confused, and I don't understand your questions. I told you that. Sometimes I try to sleep here in the trial so that I will stay awake in the night——

Cauchon. Why haven't you told us this before?

Joan. Because the soldiers told me they would be hanged if I said anything——

Warwick [*very angry*]. They were right. [*To* CAUCHON.] Detestable bastards. It's disgusting. They've learned such things since they came to France. It may be all right in the French Army, but not in mine. [*Bows to* JOAN.] I am sorry, Madame. It will not happen again.

Cauchon [*to* JOAN]. The Church will protect you from now on. I promise you.

Joan. Then I agree to put on woman's dress.

Cauchon. Thank you, my child. That is all. [*He moves to* THE INQUISITOR.] Messire Inquisitor, Brother Ladvenu drew up the Act of Renunciation. Will you permit me to recall him here? [*With bitterness.*] The girl has said yes, this man has said yes.

The Promoter [*to* THE INQUISITOR]. Messire Inquisitor, you are going to allow this to happen?

The Inquisitor. If she said yes, she has fulfilled the only condition that concerns me.

The Promoter [*turns to* CAUCHON]. This trial has been conducted with an indulgence that is beyond my understanding. [*To* THE INQUISITOR.] I am told that there are those here who eat from the English manger. I ask myself now if they have arranged to eat better from the French manger.

The Inquisitor [*rises, moves toward* JOAN]. It is not a question of mangers, Messire Promoter. *I* ask myself how did it happen that this girl said yes when so many lesser ones did not bow the head. I had not believed it to be possible. [*Points to* CAUCHON.] And why was tenderness born in the heart of that old man who was her judge? He is at the end of a life worn out with compromise and debasement. Why now, here, for this girl, this dangerous girl, did his heart—— [*He kneels, ignoring the others. As he prays, we hear only the words. . . .*] Why, Oh Lord Why, Oh Lord . . . ? Consecrate it in peace to Your Glory. . . . Your Glory——

Cauchon [as LADVENU *enters].* Please read the act.

Ladvenu [comes to JOAN. *With great tenderness].* I have prayed for you, Joan. [*Reading.*] "I, Joan, commonly called The Maid, confess having sinned through pride and malice in pretending to have received revelations from our Lord God. I confess I have blasphemed by wearing an immodest costume. I have incited men to kill through witchcraft and I here confess to it. I swear on the Holy Gospels I will not again wear this heretic's dress and I swear never to bear arms again. I declare that I place myself humbly at the mercy of our Holy Mother Church and our Holy Father, the Pope of Rome and His Bishops, so that they may judge my sins and my errors. I beseech Her to receive me in Her Bosom and I declare myself ready to submit to the sentence which She may inflict upon me. In faith of which, I have signed my name upon this Act of Renunciation of which I have full knowledge. [LADVENU *hands the pen to* JOAN. *She moves it in the air, as if she had not heard and did not understand.* LADVENU *takes her hand and puts it on the paper.*] I will help you.

Cauchon [as if he were a very old man]. You have been saved. We, your judges, in mercy and mitigation, now condemn you to spend the remainder of your days in prison. There you will do penance for your sins. You will eat the bread of sorrow and drink the water of anguish until, through solitary contemplation, you repent. Under these conditions of penance, we declare you delivered of the danger of excommunication. You may go in peace. [*He makes the Sign of the Cross.*] Take her away.

CAUCHON *stumbles and is helped by* LADVENU. *A* SOLDIER *pushes* JOAN *away from the trial. The* JUDGES *rise and slowly move off.* CAUCHON *moves past* WARWICK.

Warwick. There were several times, sire, when I thought I would have to interfere. My King must have what he paid for. But you were right and I was wrong. The making of a martyr is dangerous business. The pile of faggots, the invincible girl in the flames, might have been a triumph for the French spirit. But the apologies of a hero are sad and degrading. You did well, sire; you are a wise man.

Cauchon [with great bitterness]. I did not mean to earn your praise.

He moves off. The lights dim on the trial as WARWICK *moves off. Four* SOLDIERS *appear with spears, and their spears become the bars of* JOAN'S *jail cell.* CHARLES *appears and stands looking at* JOAN *through the bars.*

Charles. I didn't want you to sacrifice yourself for me, Joan. I know you loved me, but I don't want people to love me. It makes for obligations. This filthy prison air is wet and stinks. Don't they ever clean these places? [*He peers into her cell, sees the water pail that sits beside her, and draws back.*] Tell them to give you fresh water. My God, what goes on in this world. [*She does not answer him.*] Don't you want to speak to me, Joan?

Joan. Good-by, Charlie.

Charles. You must stop calling me Charlie. Ever since my coronation I am careful to make everyone say sire.

Joan. Sire.

Charles. I'll come and see you again. Good-by.

He moves off. JOAN *lies in silence. Then she tries to drink from the water pail, retches, and puts her hand over her mouth as if she were very sick.*

Joan. Blessed Saint Michael. [*She makes a strange sound, shivers.*] I am in prison. Come to me. Find me. [*Cries out.*] I need you now. [*Very loudly.*] I told you that I was afraid of fire, long before I ever knew—or did I always know? You want me to live? [*When there is no answer.*] Why do I call for help? You must have good reason for not coming to me. [*She motions toward courtroom.*] They think I dreamed it all. Maybe I did. But it's over now. . . .

WARWICK *comes slowly into the cell.*

Warwick [hesitantly]. You are weeping?

Joan. No, Monseigneur.

Warwick. I am sorry to disturb you. I only came to say that I am glad you are saved. You behaved damned well. I, er, well, it's rather difficult to say in my language, but the plain fact is that I like you. And it amused me to watch you with the Inquisitor. Sinister man, isn't he? I detest these intellectual idealists more than anything in the world. What disgusting animals they are. He wanted only to see you humiliate yourself, no matter your state or your misery. And when you did, he was satisfied.

Joan [*softly*]. He had reason to be satisfied.

Warwick. Well, don't worry about him. It all worked out well. Martyrs are likely to stir the blood of simple people and set up too grand a monument to themselves. It's all very complex and dangerous. Tell me, are you a virgin?

Joan. Yes.

Warwick. I knew you were. A woman would not talk as you do. My fiancée in England is a very pure girl and she also talks like a boy. You are the greatest horsewoman I have ever seen. [*When there is no answer.*] Ah, well. I am intruding on you. Don't hesitate to let me know if I can ever do anything for you. Good-by, madame.

Joan. Nobody else came to see me here. You are a kind man, Monseigneur.

Warwick. Not at all. [*Motions toward courtroom.*] It's that I don't like all those fellows who use words to make war. You and I killed because that was the way things turned out for us.

Joan. Monseigneur, I have done wrong. And I don't know how or why I did it. [*Slowly, bitterly.*] I swore against myself. That is a great sin, past all others——-[*Desperately.*] I still believe in all that I did, and yet I swore against it. God can't want that. What can be left for me?

Warwick. Certainly they are not going to make you a gay life, not at first. But things work out and in time your nasty little Charles might even show you a speck of loyalty——

Joan. Yes, when I am no longer dangerous, he might even give me a small pension and a servant's room at court.

Warwick [*sharply*]. Madame, there will be no court.

Joan. And I will wear castoff brocade and put jewels in my hair and grow old. I will be happy that few people remember my warrior days and I will grovel before those who speak of my past and pray them to be silent. And when I die, in a big fat bed, I will be remembered as a crazy girl who rode into battle for what she said she believed, and ate the dirt of lies when she was faced with punishment. That will be the best that I can have—if my little Charles remembers me at all. If he doesn't there

will be a prison dungeon, and filth and darkness——
[*Cries out.*] What good is life either way?

Warwick. It is good any way you can have it. We all
try to save a little honor, of course, but the main thing is
to be here——

Joan [*rises, calls out, speaking to the Voices*]. I was
only born the day you first spoke to me. My life only
began on the day you told me what I must do, my sword
in hand. You are silent, dear my God, because you are
sad to see me frightened and craven. And for what? A
few years of unworthy life. [*She kneels. Softly, as if she
is answering a message.*] I know. Yes, I know. I took the
good days from You and refused the bad. I know. Dear
my God forgive me, and keep me now to be myself. Forgive me and take me back for what I am. [*She rises. She
is happy and cheerful.*] Call your soldiers, Warwick. I deny
my confession.

Warwick. Joan. No nonsense, please. Things are all right
as they are. I——

Joan. Come. [*She holds out her hand to him.*]

Warwick. I don't want anything to do with your death.

Joan [*smiles*]. You have a funny gentleman's face. But
you are kind. Come now. [*She calls out.*] Soldiers! Englishmen! Give me back my warrior clothes. And when I have
put them on, call back all the priests. [*Stops, puts her
hands in prayer and speaks simply.*] Please God, help me
now.

The music of the "Sanctus" *begins as the* JUDGES, CAU-
CHON, THE INQUISITOR, THE PROMOTER, CHARLES, *the*
PEOPLE OF THE COURT, *return to the stage. Two* SOLDIERS
bring a crude stake. JOAN *herself moves to the stake and
the* SOLDIERS *lash her to it. Other* SOLDIERS *and* VILLAGE
WOMEN *pick up the bundles of faggots and carry them
off stage. The* EXECUTIONER *appears with lighted torch and
moves through the crowd.*

Joan [*as they are about to carry her off*]. Please. Please.
Give me a Cross.

The Promoter. No Cross will be given to a witch.

An English Soldier [*he has taken two sticks of wood
and made a Cross. Now he hands his Cross to* JOAN]. Here,
my daughter. Here's your Cross. [*Very angry, to* THE
PROMOTER.] She has a right to a Cross like anybody else.

JOAN *is carried off stage. The lights dim and we see flames*
—or the shadows of flames—as they are projected on the
cyclorama. LADVENU *runs on stage with a Cross from the*
  church and stands holding it high for JOAN *to see.*

  The Inquisitor [calling to EXECUTIONER]. Be quick. Be
quick. Let the smoke hide her. [*To* WARWICK.] In five
minutes, Monseigneur, the world will be crying.
  Warwick. Yes.
  The Inquisitor [shouting to EXECUTIONER]. Be quick,
master, be quick.
  Executioner [calling in to him]. All is ready, messire.
The flames reach her now.
  Ladvenu [calling out]. Courage, Joan. We pray for you.
  Cauchon. May God forgive us all.

CAUCHON *falls to his knees and begins the prayer for the*
dead. The prayers are murmured as the chorus chants a
Requiem. The SOLDIERS *and the* VILLAGE PEOPLE *return*
to the stage: a WOMAN *falls to the ground; a* SOLDIER
cries out; a GIRL *bends over as if in pain and a* SOLDIER
helps her to move on; the COURT LADIES *back away, hiding*
their faces from the burning; the PRIESTS *kneel in prayer.*

  Charles [in a whisper as he leaves]. What does she do?
What does she say? Is it over?
  The Inquisitor [to LADVENU]. What does she do?
  Ladvenu. She is quiet.
  The Inquisitor [moves away]. Is her head lowered?
  Ladvenu. No, messire. Her head is high.
  The Inquisitor [as if he were in pain]. Ah. [*To* LAD-
VENU.] She falters now?
  Ladvenu. No. It is a terrible and noble sight, messire.
You should turn and see.
  The Inquisitor [moves off]. I have seen it all before.

The lights dim. CAUCHON *rises from his prayers. He stum-*
bles and falls. LADVENU *and* WARWICK *move to help him.*
He takes LADVENU's *arm, but moves away from* WARWICK,
refusing his help. As the stage becomes dark, CAUCHON,
THE PROMOTER, LADVENU *and* WARWICK *move downstage*
and the light comes up on LA HIRE *who stands above*
them. LA HIRE *is in full armor, holding helmet and sword.*

  La Hire. You were fools to burn Joan of Arc.
  Cauchon. We committed a sin, a monstrous sin.

Warwick. Yes, it was a grave mistake. We made a lark into a giant bird who will travel the skies of the world long after our names are forgotten, or confused, or cursed down.

La Hire. I knew the girl and I loved her. You can't let it end this way. If you do, it will not be the true story of Joan.

Ladvenu. That is right. The true story of Joan is not the hideous agony of a girl tied to a burning stake. She will stand forever for the glory that can be. Praise God.

La Hire. The true story of Joan is the story of her happiest day. Anybody with any sense knows that. Go back and act it out.

The lights dim on the four men and come up on the Coronation of Charles in Reims Cathedral. The altar cloth is in place, the lighted candles are behind the altar, stained glass windows are projected on the cyclorama. The ARCH-BISHOP appears, and the people of the royal court. JOAN stands clothed in a fine white robe, ornamented with a fleur-de-lis.

Warwick [*moves into the coronation scene, stares bewildered as* CHARLES, *in coronation robes, carrying his crown, crosses to the altar*]. This could not have been her happiest day. To watch Holy Oil being poured on that mean, sly little head!

Charles [*turns to* WARWICK, *amused*]. Oh, I didn't turn out so bad. I drove you out of the country. And I got myself some money before I died. I was as good as most.

Warwick. So you were. But certainly the girl would never have ridden into battle, never have been willing to die because you were as good as most.

Joan [*comes forward, smiling, happy*]. Oh, Warwick, I wasn't paying any attention to Charlie. I knew what Charlie was like. I wanted him crowned because I wanted my country back. And God gave it to us on this Coronation Day. Let's end with it, please, if nobody would mind.

As the curtain falls the chorus sings the "Gloria" of the Mass.

DRAMABOOKS
(Plays)

WHEN ORDERING, please use the Standard Book Number consisting of the publisher's prefix, 8090-, plus the five digits following each title. (Note that the numbers given in this list are for paperback editions only. Many of the books are also available in cloth.)

Elmer Rice: Three Plays (Adding Machine, Street Scene, Dream Girl) (0735–5)
The Day the Whores Came Out to Play Tennis . . . by Arthur Kopit (0736–3)
Platonov by Anton Chekhov (0737–1)
Ugo Betti: Three Plays (The Inquiry, Goat Island, The Gambler) (0738–X)
Jean Anouilh Vol. 3 (Thieves' Carnival, Medea, Cécile, Traveler Without Luggage, Orchestra, Episode in the Life of an Author, Catch As Catch Can) (0739–8)
Max Frisch: Three Plays (Don Juan, The Great Rage of Philip Hotz, When the War Was Over) (0740–1)
New American Plays Vol. 2 ed. by William M. Hoffman (0741–X)
Plays from Black Africa ed. by Fredric M. Litto (0742–8)
Anton Chekhov: Four Plays (The Seagull, Uncle Vanya, The Cherry Orchard, The Three Sisters) (0743–6)
The Silver Foxes Are Dead and Other Plays by Jakov Lind (The Silver Foxes Are Dead, Anna Laub, Hunger, Fear) (0744–4)
New American Plays Vol. 3 ed. by William M. Hoffman (0745–2)

THE NEW MERMAIDS
Bussy D'Ambois by George Chapman (1101–8)
The Broken Heart by John Ford (1102–6)
The Duchess of Malfi by John Webster (1103–4)
Doctor Faustus by Christopher Marlowe (1104–2)
The Alchemist by Ben Jonson (1105–0)
The Jew of Malta by Christopher Marlowe (1106–9)
The Revenger's Tragedy by Cyril Tourneur (1107–7)
A Game at Chess by Thomas Middleton (1108–5)
Every Man in His Humour by Ben Jonson (1109–3)
The White Devil by John Webster (1110–7)
Edward the Second by Christopher Marlowe (1111–5)
The Malcontent by John Marston (1112–3)
'Tis Pity She's a Whore by John Ford (1113–1)
Sejanus His Fall by Ben Jonson (1114–X)
Volpone by Ben Jonson (1115–8)
Women Beware Women by Thomas Middleton (1116–6)

SPOTLIGHT DRAMABOOKS
The Last Days of Lincoln by Mark Van Doren (1201–4)
Oh Dad, Poor Dad . . . by Arthur Kopit (1202–2)
The Chinese Wall by Max Frisch (1203–0)
Billy Budd by Louis O. Coxe and Robert Chapman (1204–9)
The Devils by John Whiting (1205–7)
The Firebugs by Max Frisch (1206–5)
Andorra by Max Frisch (1207–3)
Balm in Gilead and Other Plays by Lanford Wilson (1208–1)
Matty and the Moron and Madonna by Herbert Lieberman (1209–X)
The Brig by Kenneth H. Brown (1210–3)
The Cavern by Jean Anouilh (1211–1)
Saved by Edward Bond (1212–X)
Eh? by Henry Livings (1213–8)
The Rimers of Eldritch and Other Plays by Lanford Wilson (1214–6)
In the Matter of J. Robert Oppenheimer by Heinar Kipphardt (1215–4)
Ergo by Jakov Lind (1216–2)
Biography: A Game by Max Frisch (1217–0)
Indians by Arthur Kopit (1218–9)
Narrow Road to the Deep North by Edward Bond (1219–7)

For a complete list of books of criticism and history of the drama, please write to Hill and Wang, 72 Fifth Avenue, New York, New York 10011.